This book is dedicated to the One who is its SUBJECT,
Who became the companion to Enoch and Noah
And who walks the Emmaus Road,
With the sad, to make them glad.

CW01501111

Typing :   Ruth Kelling, Glasgow, Scotland
           Jocelyn Anderson, Edinburgh, Scotland
           Helen Macrae, Edinburgh, Scotland
Computer assistance: Charles Jardine, Lesmahagow, Scotland
Proof reading: William Hanlon, Bristol, England
               Jim Jardine, Uberlândia, Brazil
Cover Design: Andrew McNeish, Glasgow, Scotland
Cover introduction: George Hanlon, Bothwell , Scotland

Published by Nathan Publications
A division of Nathan Software
352 New Trows Road
Lesmahagow
Scotland
ML110JS

ISBN -   978-0-9557494-1-4

Walk with Jesus

Fred Kelling

FOREWORD

It was a privilege and an honor to be asked by our late brother Fred Kelling to write the foreword to this volume of daily readings.

Fred was a lecturer in aerodynamics at Glasgow University, but although the "job" (as he called it) helped to pay the expenses, his interest was in the work of the Lord, particularly in Eastern Europe and Scandinavia. As a young man, teaching at Burnbank Technical College, he lodged with Mr and Mrs William Lees. William's brother James, was a missionary, first to Sweden and then, based in Austria. to many of the countries of Eastern Europe, especially Poland and Yugoslavia. Fred and his wife Ruth (whose two brothers, George and Sam Hanlon were also missionaries), during the long vacations, visited many of the Eastern European countries as well as Scandinavia, the Faeroe Islands and other lands. Fred's interest in the Faroese assemblies was to give fruit many years later in his biography of William Sloan "Fisherman of Faeroes", the pioneer of the work there.

From 1974 onwards, Fred and Ruth gave themselves full time to the work, first of all associated with Gospel Literature Outreach and then as fully autonomous missionaries.

Fred was a delightful person to know, although, at times, you never were quite sure if he was being serious, when he made some poker faced comment! As a young single man, I always felt very welcome at the Kellings home in Motherwell, and remember the nights spent in enveloping for later dispatch, Spearhead, the G.L.O. magazine. I thank God for the spiritual help and warm friendship I received from Fred and Ruth.

They later moved to Largs then Glasgow where they were in happy fellowship in Anniesland Hall. The Kellings continued their ministry in Eastern Europe right up to the day that Fred was called home to glory.

These readings are Christ exalting, challenging, evangelistic, thoroughly biblical, and will, I am sure, be a blessing to all who read them day by day.

"Remember your leaders, those who spoke the Word of God to you; consider the outcome of their way of life, and imitate their faith." (Heb 13:7)

Jim Jardine,
Uberlândia, Brazil.

PREFACE

Some years ago, the editor of the Polish magazine "Laska i Pokój" ("Grace and Peace") asked me to write several pages featuring the Person of the Lord Jesus. I did this gladly. Unfortunately, the brother had to relinquish his post when he moved to Germany and the project was left unfinished. However, my own interest in the subject had been kindled and I continued with the work.

Eventually I completed the writing of 366 pages, the content being centered on our Lord Jesus Christ, His names, titles, descriptions and types. Obviously, the topics of these pages have been culled from the Bible and are presented in an orderly fashion as follows:

The first page of each group of seven pages contains the topic found in the doctrinal section of the Old Testament from the book of Job to the Song of Songs.

The second page contains topics found in the Gospel according to Matthew.

The third page contains subjects from the historical part of the Old Testament, from Genesis to Esther.

The fourth page contains subjects found in the New Testament from Acts to Hebrews chapter 5.

The fifth page contains subjects from the prophetical part of the Old Testament from Isaiah to Malachi.

The sixth page centers on Gospel subjects again, from Matthew chapter 28 to John chapter 7.

The seventh page of each week concludes the Gospel studies from John chapter 7 to chapter 21, and then topics from Hebrews chapter 6 to Revelation chapter 22 are dealt with, to complete the studies.

Fred Kelling.

January 1

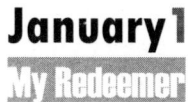

'For I know that my Redeemer liveth and that He shall stand at the latter day upon the earth.' *(Job 19. 25.)*

As we begin a new year, it is good to remind ourselves that we need a Redeemer. But who could pay the price to buy us out of the slave-market of sin? Only Jesus could do that through His death and the out-pouring of His precious blood.

But the important thing is to be able to say, like Job, that He is my Redeemer. Job had lost his possessions, his health, his family (except his wife, who advised him to curse God and die!) but he never lost his trust in God. He believed in a living Redeemer, God Himself, Who would one day 'stand up above the dust' in resurrected Manhood after completing His redemptive work on the Cross.

Job also knew that he, in his flesh and with his own eyes, would see God, despite the fact that his body would see corruption. He knew that the day would come when he would be re-united with his body in resurrected glory and see his Redeemer, face-to-face. We, as believers in the Lord Jesus, our Redeemer, have this same assurance of hope that our bodies of humiliation will be transformed into conformity with His body of glory at His return. We know that when He shall appear we shall be like Him, for we shall see Him as He is. What a purifying effect this should have on our lives day-by-day.

'My Redeemer, oh what beauties in that lovely name appear!
None but Jesus in His glory shall the honoured title wear.
My Redeemer, Thou hast my salvation wrought.'

Can we, like Job, say that 'root of the matter is in us' (Job 19.28.); that by faith in Christ our Redeemer, we have received a perfect righteousness which is not of our own making ?

Is the Redeemer your Redeemer? If not, why not?

January 2

'Book of the generation of Jesus Christ' --- *'We have found the Messias (which is, being interpreted, the Christ)'* --- *'Thou art the Christ.'* --- *'Jesus is the Christ.'* *(Mat. 1.1: Jn. 1.41: Mk. 8.29: 1 Jn. 5.1: 2.22:).*

Matthew Levi, the son of Alphaeus, was aware that Jesus of Nazareth was no ordinary man. The evidence was very clear, in the works of healing performed and the words of wisdom uttered by the Man of Galilee. So when the call came, "Follow Me", he obeyed without hesitation. He left his customs house on the shore of the lake and followed Jesus. We do well to follow Levi's example. Later, when he put pen to paper to record the history of this amazing Man, it was very easy for him to call Him the Christ, the Anointed of God, the true King of Israel.

Andrew never forgot that day when he and John Bar-Zebedee were standing with John the Baptiser on the east bank of the river Jordan. Looking at Jesus as He walked, John said, "Look! the Lamb of God!" Andrew and his companions followed Jesus. The place was called Beth-Oniyah and the time was four in the afternoon. After that encounter, Andrew quickly found his brother, Simon Peter, and said to him "We have found the Christ." He led him to Jesus. May this be an encouragement to us to lead a relative, friend or colleague to the Lord Christ.

It was in the region of Caesarea Philippi, when Jesus asked His disciples the question, "Whom do ye say that I am?" Peter said, "Thou art the Christ." This spiritual insight was given to him by God, the Father in Heaven.

Later on in his life, John wrote, 'Everyone who believes that Jesus is the Christ is born of God.' Earlier in the same letter he wrote; 'Who is the liar but he who denies that Jesus is the Christ.'

The Father sent the Son to be the Saviour of the world. Have you believed on Him as the Christ, your Saviour, and been born again?

January 3
The Divine Executer

'In the beginning God created the heavens and the earth.' *'For by Him, (i.e. God, the Son) were all things created, that are in the heavens and that are upon the earth, visible and invisible, whether thrones, or lordships, or principalities, or authorities; all things were created by Him and for Him'* *(Gen. 1.1: Col. 1.16.).*

The Bible begins with God creating all things. The Hebrew word for God used here in the creation narrative is the word 'Elohim' which implies plurality of Persons. We know from other Scriptures that God is One, yet three Persons, Father, Son and Holy Spirit, in the high order of the Trinity.

So, in eternity, the Son was there, co-equal with the Father and the Holy Spirit. He is portrayed in Colossians 1.16 as the Divine Executor of the universe. Nothing escaped His attention - all things were created by His intrinsic power. The couplets and quadruplets are all embracing -

> the heavens and the earth;
> the visible and the invisible;
> thrones, lordships, principalities and authorities;
> created by and for Him.

Included in the creation of the invisible heavens were the angelic beings with their various orders and ranks. The cherubim, were created by Him then set to guard the way to the tree of life after Adam and Eve were banished from the Garden of Eden, (Gen. 3. 24.). Michael, the archangel, and Gabriel were His handiwork, as was the anointed covering cherub who became Satan when he rebelled against God.

The tiniest particle of the atom and the far-flung galaxies in the great reaches of space were all made by Him - 'He made the stars also'!

The Son of the Father's love also made us. Therefore we are responsible to Him as our Creator.

Have you bowed your heart and bent your will to Jesus, the Son of God, and worshipped Him as your Creator? Why not do it now?

January 4

'Therefore let all the house of Israel know assuredly, that God hath made that same Jesus, Whom ye have crucified, both Lord and Christ.'   (Acts 2. 36.)

Peter's Proclamation: The day of Pentecost had come: It was seven weeks since our Lord Jesus had risen from the dead and ten days since His disciples had seen Him taken up into Heaven from the Mount of Olives.   That very morning, the promise of the Father and the Son had been fulfilled in the sending of the Holy Spirit.   All in the room were filled with the Holy Spirit and began to speak in languages understood by the many Jewish pilgrims who were in Jerusalem at that feast time.

Peter seized the opportunity to witness to the great crowd that had gathered. With holy boldness, he proclaimed,   "Let all the house of Israel know assuredly ----." He had already said,   "Him   (Jesus of Nazareth)   being delivered up by the determinate counsel and foreknowledge of God, ye have taken and by wicked hands have crucified and slain: Whom God raised up ---." (vs. 23. 24)

The People's Action: The blame of Jesus' crucifixion was laid fairly and squarely at the feet of the nation.   Undoubtedly, all the Jewish leaders were implicated - chief priests, Sadducees and Pharisees   -   in the death of the Nazarene.   Pilate, the Roman governor, was only used as a means of accomplishing their purpose.   This Galilean blasphemer must die.

God's Reaction: Of course, it was in the plan of God that His Son should die, as an Offering for sin, including   the sin of the Jewish nation.   So God reversed the judgment of the nation and made Jesus both Lord and Christ.   He said to His ascended Son, "Sit at My right hand until I make Thine enemies Thy footstool."

What God has done in exalting His Son, we too must do in our individual lives.

Have you invited Jesus as Lord and Christ into the throne-room of your heart?

January 5

'For out of Zion shall go forth the law, and the word of the Lord from Jerusalem, and He shall judge among the nations, and shall rebuke many people; and they shall beat their swords into ploughshares and their spears into pruning hooks: Nation shall not lift up sword against nation, neither shall they learn war any more.' (Isa. 2. 3,4.)

The Time: Isaiah is writing about the last days, or the end of days, meaning the time when Messiah would come; and Messiah did come and God spoke in the Person of the Son (Heb. 1.2.) to the nation of Israel, but the Word was despised and rejected, crucified and slain.

Then began the 'acceptable year of the Lord' which has been extended for almost two thousand years during which God is taking out of all the nations a people for His Name which He calls His Church. On the completion of the Church and its removal to the air, to meet the Lord there, God's plan for Israel will re-commence. After a period of seven years of tribulation, Isaiah's prophecy will be fulfilled.

The Place: The word that Isaiah saw was concerning Judah and Jerusalem. It will become the central attraction of the world, when 'the mountain of Jehovah's house shall be established on the top of the mountains, and shall be lifted up above the hills.' Thus great topographical changes must take place during the tribulation.

The Judge: Jehovah-Jesus will sit on His throne and judge the nations with equity for a millennium. His ways, His paths, His law and His word will be paramount. The Father has given all judgment to the Son, because He is Son of Man, so that all may know the Son. (Jn. 5. 23, 27.).

The People: All nations shall flow unto Zion and many peoples shall go up to the mountain of Jehovah in those days, for judgment and reproof. An era of peace and plenty will be maintained. (Micah 4. 4-7.).

> "Jesus shall reign where-ere the Sun,
>   doth his successive journeys run;
>   His Kingdom stretch from shore to shore,
>   'til Moon shall wax and wane no more".

Is Jesus judge of your life now ?

January 6

'And Jesus coming up spoke to them saying; "All authority has been given to Me in heaven and upon earth. Go therefore and make disciples of all the nations, baptising them into the Name of the Father and of the Son and of the Holy Spirit; teaching them to observe all that I have commanded you: And behold, I am with you all the days, until the completion of the age." ' (Mat. 28. 18-20.)

The Risen Christ had already appeared to His disciples, as a group, on three occasions. (Jn. 21.14.).   On this fourth appearing, in the Galilean hills, it seems that others were there apart from the eleven.   When they, the eleven, saw Him, they worshipped Him but some (others) doubted.   It was a suitable venue for a pre-arranged rendezvous with 500 brethren. (1 Cor. 15.6.).   So the word of the Lord to the women on that first resurrection morning was fulfilled. (Mat. 28.10.).   He would meet with His brethren in Galilee.   It was also understandable that Matthew refrains from mentioning the number of those present, for their sake, to avoid a clash with political authority.

The Divine Commander reminds His followers of His absolute authority, and then He gives His orders:-

Firstly, they must go to all the nations.   It is evident that the apostles were reluctant to do. that (Acts 8.1.) but eventually, in spite of persecution, Peter and John obeyed (vs. 14.15.).   We too must accept this as a principle.

Secondly, they must make disciples.   The process begins with winning others for Christ; then encouraging the converts by personal example to follow Christ.

Thirdly, the disciples must be baptised as a witness to their faith and new life in Christ. They have died (spiritually) and their life is hid with Christ in God.   The authority for baptism is of the highest order - the Name (singular) of the Triune God.

Lastly, the disciples must be taught to obey the word of the Lord.   So they will be edified in the fundamentals of the faith and equipped with the tools of evangelism.

This mammoth task can only be accomplished because of our Lord's abiding Presence with us by the Holy Spirit.

Am I obeying the orders of the Commander ?

January 7

The dispenser of living water

'In the last day, that great day of the feast, Jesus stood and cried, saying, "If any one thirst, let him come to Me and drink. He who believes on Me, as the Scripture has said, out from within him shall flow rivers of living water." ' (Jn. 7. 37, 38.).

It was the last and great day of the Feast of Tabernacles. A great multitude of pilgrims had gathered in the court of the Temple at Jerusalem. They watched as the priest poured water, from a vessel filled at the pool of Siloam, into a silver funnel which would take it to the base of the altar. The people finished chanting the Hallel, ending with the words, "Give thanks unto the Lord, for He is good, for His loving-kindness endures for ever." Then there was silence.

The silence was shattered by a strong clear voice - that of Jesus, Jehovah. That same One, Who had satisfied the thirst of His people in the wilderness with water from the Rock, was there in Person. But on this occasion, He was offering spiritual drink. To whom is this offer made? To the thirsty. How does one receive this living water? By coming to the Source, the Lord Jesus. By believing on Jesus as Jehovah Messiah, the Scripture would be fulfilled; 'And thou shall be like a watered garden, and like a water-spring, whose waters deceive not.' (Isa. 58. 11.).

"But this He said of the Spirit, Whom they who believed on Him were about to receive; for the Spirit was not yet given, because Jesus was not yet glorified."
(Jn. 7. 39.). In Spring of the following year, our Lord was crucified, then glorified, and on the Day of Pentecost of that same year, the Holy Spirit arrived. The promise was fulfilled and ever since then, the desert of this world has been refreshed by the 'rivers of living water'.

> 'I heard the voice of Jesus say, Behold, I freely give
> The living water, thirsty one, stoop down and drink and live.
> I came to Jesus and I drank of that life-giving stream:
> My thirst was quenched, my soul revived
> And now I live in Him.'

How can we share in the dispensing of living water?

January8

'If there is a messenger with him, an interpreter, one among a thousand, to show unto man his duty; then He is gracious unto him and saith, "Deliver him from going down to the pit: I have found a ransom." ' *(Job 33. 23,24.)*

Elihu, the younger man, has waited until Job and his three 'comforters' had finished speaking. But now he cannot contain himself, as he brings to Job's attention the true remedy.

Firstly, he outlines man's desperate condition, both physically and spiritually. Sheol, with its terrors, is not far away from him; every day he draws nearer to it and them. Our Lord Jesus described the plight of a rich man in hell as being in torment.
(Lk. 16. 23.).
Secondly, he speaks of the possibility of timely help; and that help has arrived for us in the Person of God's Son, the Bringer of Life, the One in a thousand speaking to us the language of love.
Thirdly, Elihu declares the purpose of this Interpreter. He wishes to point out to man his duty, in judging himself as unfit for God's presence because of his sinful state.
Fourthly, it is only then, when a man confesses his sin, that God can show him grace and speak to him deliverance from going down to the pit. But a righteous basis has been laid for God to pardon sinners. A Ransom has been found by God in the work of His Son on the Cross. The precious Blood of Christ was the ransom price demanded by God and that alone could provide God with a righteous foundation for forgiveness.
But lastly, what are the remarkable consequences when a sinner confesses his sin and is delivered? He will be physically renewed with his flesh fresher than in childhood and a return to the days of his youth. God hears his cry for mercy and accepts him in the Beloved One, the Lord Jesus. He sees the Face of his Saviour and will be clothed in His righteousness. He has a song now, as he makes full confession before men - his past state as a sinner and what God has done for him. In his song, he says, "God has delivered my soul from going down to the pit, and my life shall see the light." (Job. 33.28.).

God has found a Ransom. Have you?

January 9
Jesus

'And she shall bring forth a Son, and thou shalt call His name JESUS; for He shall save His people from their sins.'   (Mat. 1. 21.).

The meaning of this personal name of the Son of God is very significant; "the 'I AM' (is our) Saviour", and is from the Greek equivalent of the Old Testament name 'Joshua'. The Name of Jesus occurs more than 900 times in the New Testament.

The angel Gabriel was sent to the Virgin Mary to tell her that she would conceive and bear a son, and to name Him 'Jesus'. (Lk. 1. 31.)   No reason was given to Mary for the choice of such a Name by God.   By faith, she accepted all that the angel said - a wonderful example for us to follow.

Subsequent to Mary's return to Nazareth, after visiting Elizabeth, the mother of John Baptist, in the Judean hills, the new life within her was evident.   Joseph, to whom she was betrothed, thought to divorce her quietly.   But God intervened - Joseph had a dream in which an angel of the Lord spoke to him: "Joseph, son of David," he said, "don't be afraid to take Mary home as your wife, for that which is conceived in her is of the Holy Spirit."   Then Joseph was instructed to name the Child 'Jesus' "for He shall save His people from their sins."   No doubt, Joseph was reminded of Psalm 130. 8, that the Lord Himself would redeem Israel from all their sins - the redemption price was the precious blood of Jesus.

The redemption of Israel still awaits fulfilment but Jesus is presently saving another people, His church, composed of both Jews and Gentiles, from their sins.

Joseph obediently named the Babe 'Jesus' at His circumcision, eight days after His birth, in accordance with the Law.   (Lk. 2. 21.).   This was the first wounding of the Saviour, pre-figuring His putting an end to the flesh by His death on the Cross and bringing in new life by His resurrection on the 'eighth' day.   The number of the Greek equivalent of the name 'Jesus' is 888.

'What a wonderful Saviour is Jesus, my Jesus! '

Are you trusting Jesus for full salvation?

January 10

'So the Lord God caused a deep sleep to fall upon the man, and he slept; then He took one of his ribs, and closed up the flesh at that place. And the Lord God fashioned into a woman the rib which He had taken from the man, and brought her to the man.' (Gen. 2. 21, 22.).

God was very busy on the sixth day of creation. He created all the land animals, then the first man, Adam. He planted the Garden of Eden and there he placed the man whom He had formed. He gave instruction to Adam and encouraged him to name certain animals. But there was no suitable helper found for Adam. It was then that God, the Son, became a surgeon. (Jn. 1. 3; Col. 1. 16.).

It seems evident, from what Adam said subsequently, that the Lord shared with him His plan for making his counterpart. Then, as the Divine Anaesthetist, He caused the man to fall into a deep sleep. The operation was performed to remove one his ribs, and the wound healed perfectly and instantly.

Jahweh Elohim used the rib to make the woman. 'She wasn't made out of Adam's head to lord it over him, nor out of his feet to be trampled upon by him, but out of his side to be equal to him, under his arm to be protected by him and near his heart to be beloved.' (Matthew Henry.)

The first wedding ceremony ensued, with God as the Divine Officiator.

But in this history of Adam, there is a pattern of the coming One. (Rom. 5. 14.). From the 'deep sleep' of Golgotha and the wounded side of the Saviour, God is forming a bride for His Son. One day soon, the second Man, the Lord out of Heaven, will return and present to Himself a radiant church, His counterpart. (Eph. 5.27.). His love will not rest until He has us by His side in Paradise.

Are we allowing God to fashion us into the likeness of His Son ?

January 11
The prince of life

'But you disowned the Holy and Righteous One, and asked for a murderer to be granted to you, but put to death the Prince of Life, Whom God raised from the dead , a fact to which we are witnesses.' (Acts 3. 14, 15.)

A remarkable healing had taken place at the Beautiful Gate of the Temple in Jerusalem. The evidence was incontrovertible - there was the man, who had been a lame beggar, now walking and leaping and praising God. The power which had brought new life to his legs was through faith in the Name of Jesus.

Peter used the event to witness fearlessly to the crowd that had gathered. He reminded them that they had chosen Barabbas, a taker of life, to be released rather than Jesus, the Giver of life. They had put to death the Author of life but God had raised Him from the dead.

The Deity of our Lord Jesus is implicit in this description of Him as the Originator of life. He is the Living One Who became dead but is alive for evermore. He is the Source of all life, whether physical, spiritual or eternal. In Him, we live and move and exist. He breathed into Man the breath of life and Man became a living soul.

The D.N.A. molecule, the blue-print of life, did not and could not happen by chance. Our Lord Jesus is the Author of it. He was the Planner and Perfector of all life, whether it was vegetable, animal, human or angelic.

But He freely creates new and eternal life in the hearts of all those who put their trust in Him. For He is the true God and Eternal Life. 'He who has the Son of God has the Life. He who does not have the Son of God does not have the Life.' (1 Jn. 5.12.).

Are you enjoying this abundant life that is in our Lord Jesus, the Prince of life?

January 12

' "Woe is me!" I cried, "I am ruined! For I am a man of unclean lips, and I live among a people of unclean lips, and my eyes have seen the King, Jehovah of Hosts" '
(Isa. 6. 5.)

Isaiah was given a vision of the pre-incarnate glory of the Son of God. (Jn. 12. 41.). He saw Him as King seated on a throne in the Temple, a Priest after the order of Melchisedek. King Uzziah, who had just died that year, had been judged by Jehovah because he sought to take the office of priest, and was smitten with leprosy.

Isaiah saw the Lord, high and lifted up, that same One Who would, in the fullness of time, be lifted up on a cross of shame to die, so that Isaiah's and our sins could be covered by the shedding of His precious blood.

He saw the King upon His throne of glory to be worshipped by those who surround it. It is also a throne of government before which His subjects serve Him. But it is now a throne of grace, to which we can approach at all times as suppliants to obtain mercy and find grace to help in time of need.

The prophet saw the King, Jehovah of Hosts, Who commands all the armies of heaven and earth. Nothing and no-one can withstand His power and authority. Our Lord is Sovereign of the universe.

As a consequence of seeing the Sovereign Ruler, Isaiah became aware of his own sin and ruin. A seraph ('burning one') applied a burning coal from the altar to his lips; his guilt was removed and his sin expiated.

Now he is ready to serve the King. The question is asked by the Tri-une God, "Whom shall I send and who will go for Us?" He was willing to reply, "Here am I. Send me!" God sent him to his own people with a sad message. That same Lord sends us to all the world with a glad message.

Are we ready to reply "Here am I.   Send me!"

January 13

'And He said unto them, "The sabbath was made for man, and not man for the sabbath; therefore the Son of Man is Lord also of the sabbath." ' *(Mk. 2. 27, 28.)*

In this section of his gospel, Mark describes five incidents in which the Pharisees, the self-appointed interpreters and custodians of the Mosaic law, are in conflict with the Lord Jesus. The final two instances are concerned with the sabbath.

The first case had to do with Jesus' disciples. As they walked through the grain fields, they began to pluck some heads of grain. According to Rabbinical law, this act was equivalent to reaping. Thus the disciples were 'doing work' on the sabbath, which was unlawful, according to the Pharisees.

Our Lord replied by referring them to the account in 1 Samuel 21, when David and his men were hungry and ate the consecrated bread. So the principle is established that danger to life and well-being supersedes the levitical and sabbatical law. The man is more important than the sabbath.

The second case illustrates this admirably. Our Lord heals a man's withered hand by commanding him to stretch it out. By doing so, the man did 'work', again on a sabbath day. Thus the Son of Man demonstrates His Lordship of the sabbath.

As creator, our Lord instituted the sabbath when the work of creation was done. But the Creator became our Redeemer to bring every believer in Him into a new sabbath rest. (Mat. 11. 28-30. Heb. 4. 9.).

The Son of Man will also be Lord of the millennial sabbath, when all creation will find rest at His coming to reign.

Do we use the sabbath rest that we have found in Him to worship Him?

January 14
The light of the world

'Again, therefore, Jesus spoke to them, saying. "I am the Light of the world; whoever follows Me will never walk in darkness, but shall have the light of life." "As long as I am in the world, I am the light of the world." '   (Jn. 8. 12;   9. 5.).

The Apostle John reminds us that 'God is Light' (1 Jn. 1. 5.), which portrays His holy and righteous character.

Our Lord Jesus, God with us (Emmanuel), describes Himself as this dark world's Light and daubs His disciples 'the light of the world'. (Mat. 5. 14.). But He is the Sun and we are the planets;   He is the Source of light and we are merely its reflectors. He is the true Light, which, coming into the world, sheds its light upon every man. (Jn. 1. 9.). Sad to say, not every man wants to receive this Light.

We need the living, loving Light of the Lord because of the darkness around and within us, caused by sin.   Thus we are plunged into a double darkness which can only be dispelled by the Presence of the Light of the world in our lives

The Lord exhorts us to follow Him Who is the Light. Later, Jesus said, "While you have the Light, believe in the Light, that you may become sons of Light." (Jn. 12. 36.) ----- "I have come as Light into the world, that everyone who believes in Me may not remain in darkness." (v.46.). We must 'walk in the light as He Himself is in the light; (then) we have fellowship with one another, and the Blood of Jesus His Son cleanses us from all sin.' (1 Jn. 1. 7.).

How long will this Light shine? As long as the Lord Jesus is in the world. He entered the darkness of death for a season but emerged victoriously on the third day. Now He is in the world again dispensing light through His servants. We should be like a city on a hill and a lamp in the house. (Mat. 5. 14-16.).

But this Light will shine eternally.   In the holy city, the heavenly Jerusalem, the Lamb is its Lamp and there shall be no night there. (Rev. 21. 23,25.).

Are we shining for Jesus now, day by day?

January 15

'For Jehovah knoweth the way of the righteous ones, but the way of the wicked ones shall perish.' (Ps. 1. 6.)

There has only ever been one truly Righteous One Who lived here on planet Earth, the Son of God incarnate. Both the apostle Peter and the martyr Stephen speak of Him as such. (Acts 3. 14;   7. 52.).   The way of this Righteous One was, firstly, characterised by purity. John Baptist looked on Jesus as He walked and said, "Behold, the Lamb of God!"   He never walked in the counsel of the wicked, neither would He stand in the way of sinners. When our Lord stood before Pilate, the governor, He witnessed to him the good confession.   Nor did He sit in the company of mockers until He elected to do so as he hung on the Cross.   But now, he sits at the right hand of God.

The way of this Righteous One was also characterised by piety. It was His constant delight to listen to the Father's word and to do His Father's will. (Ps. 40. 7.).   The Lord God awakening Him morning by morning.   He listened and was not disobedient, nor did he turn back. (Isa. 50. 4,5.).

Thirdly, the way of this Righteous One is characterised by prosperity. 'He is like a Tree planted by streams of water, yielding its fruit in season and whose leaf does not wither. Whatever He does prospers.'   He is the Anti-type of the tree of life in the Heavenly City,   the new Jerusalem. (Rev. 22. 2.).

But God, in His grace, has other Righteous Ones, who, through faith in Christ, the Righteous One, are reckoned righteous by a holy and righteous God.   So what characterises our Lord should be seen in them, as they walk with Him day by day, stand for Him when confronted by sinners and sit with Him in sweet communion, as Lazarus did. (Jn. 12. 2.).

'The Lord watches over the way of the righteous ones.'

Does our daily practice conform with our eternal position as righteous ones ?

January 16

'Then Joseph being raised from sleep did as the angel of the Lord had bidden him, and took unto him his wife; and knew her not till she had brought forth her first-born son, and he called His name Jesus.' (Mat. 1. 24, 25.).

'And she brought forth her first-born son, and wrapped Him in swaddling clothes and laid Him in a manger; because there was no room for them in the inn.'   (Lk. 2.7.).

Mary was of the tribe of Judah and of the lineage of David, which must be so, to fulfil the prophetic Word. (Gen. 49. 8-10;   Jer. 23. 5.).   She was also a virgin, as predicted in Isa. 7.14.   The birth of the Child took place in Bethlehem Ephrata, again fulfilling prophecy. (Mic. 5. 2.). He was her first-born son.

That the Lord should choose such a humble person as the mother of Messiah is an evidence of His grace; not a princess in a palace but a peasant girl with the birth-place in a stable.   'There was no room for them in the inn'.

But Mary, although an exemplary mother, was no different from all others in her need for salvation.   In her hymn of praise, her spirit rejoiced in God, her Saviour.
(Lk. 1. 47.).

She watched and wondered as her Son grew up into boyhood and manhood.   She noted His words when they had lost him and found Him in the Temple;   "Did you not know that I must be in the things of My Father?" (Lk. 2. 49.).   This from a twelve year-old boy!

Mary had other children in the normal course of events (Mat. 13. 55,56;   Mk. 3. 32.) but her first-born was unique in His sinlessness and suffering.   She was there at the Cross, watched His agony and heard His words, as He committed her to the care of John.   A sword pierced her soul as the spear pierced His side. (Luke 2. 35.)

Now Mary's first-born sits enthroned in heaven - a real man of flesh and bone, and He is returning soon to reign.

Does He reign supreme in your heart ?

January17

The seed of the woman

' "And I will put enmity between thee and the woman, and between thy seed and her Seed; He shall crush thy head and thou shall crush His heel" ' (Gen. 3. 15.).

Here is the first truly prophetic statement in the Bible. It was made by God to Satan, that old serpent; he had done this deadly work and enticed not only the woman, but also her husband, to disobey God's command not to eat of the tree of the knowledge of good and evil.

Here we find the beginnings of 'new age' beliefs. The serpent said to the woman, "You shall not surely die?" which gives rise to the error of re-incarnation. "You will be as gods," he said, introducing pantheism. "Knowing good and evil," makes way for relativism, and absolutes are lost. Their eyes were opened, to introduce them to 'the deep things of Satan.' (Rev. 2. 24.).

Now God judges the serpent: He has already spoken to the man, who has blamed the woman and also God Who gave her to him! When God challenges the woman, she blames the serpent. Then God curses the serpent and declares war on him through the woman. Her communication with the serpent resulted in mortal combat with him, particularly through her Seed, the Christ.

So we have here a prophecy of the Incarnation, through which, at the Cross, the power of Satan would be annulled. (Heb. 2. 14; Col. 2. 15.). The serpent's head would be crushed, but, in the process, the Seed's heel would suffer. There is reason to believe that the nail was hammered into that part of Jesus' feet on the Cross.

But God graciously allows us to have a part in the humbling of the Serpent. 'And the God of peace will soon crush Satan under your feet.' (Rom. 16. 20.).

Is the promise contained in Psalm 91. 13. being fulfilled through us now?

January 18

' "Neither is there salvation in any other; for there is none other name under heaven given among men, whereby we must be saved." ' (Acts 4.12.).

The act of kindness by Peter and John in healing a helpless man in the Temple precinct had been 'rewarded'. The authorities, in the persons of the priests, the captain of the temple guard and the Sadducees arrested and imprisoned them!

The following day, Peter and John were brought before a hastily-convened ecclesiastical court and cross-examined. Peter, filled with the Holy Spirit, told the court that the cripple had been completely cured by the power of the Name of Jesus Christ, the Nazarene, "Whom you crucified, but Whom God raised from the dead." (v.10.). There is still power in the Name of Jesus to make spiritual cripples walk straight and tall for God.

Peter then reminded them that God had reversed their decision. They, the builders, had rejected Christ, the Stone, but God, the Architect, had given Him the pre-eminent place. (Mat. 21. 42; Ps.118. 22.). This was obviously in harmony with the foretelling of the ancient Scriptures.

Now Peter broached the vital subject of salvation. Only a crucified, risen and glorified Son of God could be our Saviour. Parade the names of all this world's great philosophers and pundits, and they all pale into insignificance before the mighty and majestic Name of Jesus, the Saviour. Peter stated, by the power of the Holy Spirit, that ' "Salvation is found in no-one else." '

God has appointed this Name under heaven and among men to provide them with salvation, should they accept it; and we have nothing to pay, since salvation is free and for the asking. (Eph. 2. 8,9.). If we are going to enjoy an eternity with Christ, then we must be saved by Him, and Him alone.

Can you list some of the various facets of salvation in Christ?

January 19

'Therefore the Lord Himself shall give you a sign: Behold, the virgin shall conceive and bear a Son and shall call His Name Immanuel.'   (Isa. 7.14.).

'Now all this was done, that it might be fulfilled which was spoken of the Lord by the prophet, saying, "Behold, the virgin shall be with child and shall bring forth a Son and they shall call His Name Immanuel," which being interpreted is, God with us.' (Mat. 1. 22, 23.).

The southern kingdom of Judah under king Ahaz was being threatened by the northern kingdoms of Israel and Syria.   But the Lord instructed the prophet Isaiah to take his son and meet Ahaz.   The prophet had a message from the Lord which was calculated to allay the king's fears, if he believed it.   Then God graciously gave Ahaz the promise of the advent of Immanuel, fulfilled at the birth of Jesus in Bethlehem.   God was found in human flesh, coming to redeem His people - God with us, Immanuel!

In the following chapter of Isaiah's prophecy, Immanuel is mentioned twice.   (Isa. 8. 5-10.).   In the first instance, it is in connection with the invasion of Israel by the king of Assyria.   Like a mighty river, Assyria sweeps over the land - Immanuel's   land!   So today the throne of Earth is occupied by the usurper, Satan, but not for long;   Immanuel is returning.

The nations will be utterly broken in pieces despite all their plans and proposals at the return of   Immanuel.   Here is the battle-cry of the saints - Immanuel,   God with us!

He is with us as we seek to work for Him.   (Mat. 28. 20.).
He is with us as we witness for Him.   (Acts 18. 9.).
He is with us as we walk through the valley of the shadow of death - then we can say that we fear no evil, 'For Thou are with me.'   (Ps. 23. 4.)

What does the Presence of Immanuel   mean to you?

January 20

'And unclean spirits, when they saw Him, fell down before Him, and cried, saying, "Thou art the Son of God," ' (Mk. 3. 11.).

Here is one of the first confessions of the Sonship of our Lord Jesus. It came from unclean spirits indwelling human beings. They were quick to recognise His identity and announce it, and receive His rebuke. At the outset of our Lord's public ministry, His half-cousin, John the baptiser, said this of Him: "I have seen and borne witness that this is the Son of God." (Jn. 1. 34.).

The following day, Philip brought Nathanael to Jesus. The Lord described him as a true Israelite without guile, and said that He had seen him under the fig tree. Nathanael answered "Rabbi, Thou art the Son of God -----." (Jn. 1. 49.).

When the Lord Jesus was speaking with Martha after her brother had died and was buried at Bethany, she made her great confession of faith that He was the Christ, the Son of God, Who should come into the world. (Jn. 11. 27.). The raising of Lazarus and others from the dead, but pre-eminently His own glorious resurrection, marked Him out as Son of God with power. (Rom. 1. 4.).

Consider the contrast of Christ on the Cross, bearing the taunts of the passers-by as they wagged their heads and said; "If you are the Son of God, come down from the cross." But when Jesus expired, the centurion, who was standing in front of Him, said, "Truly this man was Son of God."

So we have heard this testimony, not only from spirits but also from humans, acquaintances and strangers, male and female, Jew and Gentiles. But the greatest witness of all came from God, Who, again and again, said "This is My Beloved Son ----- ."

'But these are written that you may believe that Jesus is the Christ, the Son of God, and believing you may have life in His Name.' (Jn. 20.31.).

Do you believe in the Name of the Son of God? Then what is the outcome? Read 1 John. 5. 12, 13.

January 21

'Jesus said to them, "Amen, Amen, I say to you, before Abraham was, I am." '
(Jn. 8. 58.).

When God appeared to Moses in the burning bush at Horeb, He instructed him to tell the sons of Israel that 'I am' had sent him. Thus God revealed His special Name to Moses. (Ex. 3. 14.). Now God incarnate uses the same Name of Himself, thus declaring His deity.

In the Gospel according to John, this Name is used by our Lord on at least four different occasions. In the first instance, the disciples were crossing the Sea of Galilee by boat and Jesus came to them, walking on the stormy sea. He said to them, "It is I (literally 'I am'); be not afraid." (Jn. 6. 20.). Our Lord is superior to the turbulent seas of life, and is willing and able to calm all our fears by His presence.

In the second instance, our Lord Jesus was addressing the Jews in the treasury of the Temple at Jerusalem. He said, "Unless you believe that 'I am', you shall die in your sins." (Jn. 8. 24.). Acceptance, by faith, of the deity of Jesus is essential for salvation. Again, He said, "When you shall have lifted up the Son of Man, then you shall know that 'I am ----'" (v.28.). Our Lord was speaking of His death on the Cross and His subsequent resurrection. Then He made the astounding claim of being the 'I am' before Abraham was born (v. 58.), thus asserting His deity. The Jews understood this and sought in vain to stone Him for apparent blasphemy.

The third instance was during the 'last supper', when our Lord spoke of His betrayal by Judas, in fulfilment of Ps. 41. 9. "I tell you ----- that when it happens, you may believe that 'I am' ". (Jn. 13. 19.).

The final instance occurred when Judas brought the band of armed men to arrest Jesus in Gethsemane. "When therefore He said to them, 'I am', they drew back and fell to the ground." (Jn. 18. 6.). Here is not the victim of circumstances, but the controller of them.

Are you conscious of the constant Presence of the 'I am', re-assuring you that all is under His control?

January 22

'Yet have I set My King upon My holy hill of Zion. I will declare the decree; the Lord hath said unto Me, "Thou art My Son; this day have I begotten Thee." '
(Ps. 2. 6, 7.).

There is high drama in this Psalm. David, the author (Acts 4. 25.) is the observer and reporter of it. The drama reaches cosmic proportions as David draws attention to the battle lines of the enemy; nations and peoples, the kings of the earth and the rulers take their stand and take counsel against Jehovah and His Anointed. "Let us break their chains and throw away their fetters," they cry. Sinful man, as a rebel against God, is seen clearly at the Cross, the persecution of the church and at Armageddon. None of us, except Christ, is exempt from this rebellious nature.

The One enthroned in heaven laughs, scoffs at, rebukes and terrifies them in His anger and wrath. Then He replies to their rebellion: "But, as for Me, I have anointed My King upon Zion, the hill of My holiness." Men anointed Jesus with all their venom and even God poured upon Him all his fury against sin at that sacred spot. But now, in resurrection, God has anointed Him with the oil of gladness. (Ps. 45. 7.). Jehovah's King is seated on the throne of the universe.

Now the King proclaims Jehovah's decree, "Thou art My Son; today I have begotten Thee." The eternal Son became a perfect Man to die as a Sacrifice and to be raised up from among the dead by the glory of the Father. (Rom. 6. 4.). We therefore assume that our Lord appeared before His Father in Heaven on that first resurrection morning, after His encounter with Mary Magdalene (Jn. 20. 17.) and before His meetings with the other women (Mat. 28. 9.) and His disciples (Lk. 24. 39.).

What should be our reaction to Jehovah's Son? Give Him our love and loyalty by taking refuge in Him. Then we shall be truly blessed. (Psalm 2. 12.).

January 23

The little child

'And having come into the house, they saw the little Child with Mary His mother and falling down they worshipped Him; and having opened their treasures, they presented to Him gifts; gold and frankincense and myrrh.' (Mat. 2. 11.)

The unimaginable-imaginable had happened - the Ancient of Days had become the Infant of days. Shepherds, angel-directed, had seen the Babe in the manger, and had spread the word concerning this little Child to others. (Lk. 2. 17.).

When the forty days (prescribed by the law of the Lord) of the mother's ceremonial uncleanness were completed (Lev. 12. 1-4.) His parents brought Him to the Temple in Jerusalem, to present Him to the Lord. (Ex. 13. 2, 12.). The law demanded an appropriate sacrifice; they offered the humblest, a pair of pigeons, because of their meagre means. (Lev. 12. 8.). It was then that a man called Simeon, Spirit-led, received the little Child into his arms and said, "Sovereign Lord, now let Thy bond-slave depart in peace according to Thy Word for mine eyes have seen Thy Salvation, which Thou hast prepared in the presence of all peoples. A light of revelation to the Gentiles and the glory of Thy people Israel." (Lk. 2. 29-32.). For almost two millennia, that Light of Salvation has shone on the Gentiles, but soon, at our Lord's return to earth, He will become Israel's glory.

Subsequently, The Magi, guided supernaturally, came to the house and saw the little Child. They fell down and did Him homage. Then they presented to Him their gifts; these were costly - they were treasures, fitting for a royal Personage, and necessary to help the little family in their journey to and from Egypt, and their sojourn there.

What treasures can we offer the King? We can present to Him our bodies as a living sacrifice. We can offer to Him the sacrifice of praise, the fruit of our lips. We can give Him, Who was the little Child, the homage and love of our hearts.

January 24

'Unto Adam also and to his wife did the LORD God make coats of skins and clothed them' (Gen. 3. 21.).

The shame of their sin had smitten the conscience of our first parents, there in the garden; they knew that they were naked. So they fashioned for themselves futile fig-leaf garments, which could never cover their sin and guilt. They heard the sound of the LORD God walking in the garden, and hid from Him, but 'nothing in all creation is hidden from God's sight. Everything is uncovered and laid bare before the eyes of Him to Whom we must give account.' (Heb. 4. 13.). All our righteous acts are like a filthy garment in God's sight.

But the Lord Himself provided suitable covering for Adam and his wife. Appropriate animals had to be sacrificed, their blood shed and coats of skin prepared. It was the work of a Master-Craftsman, reminding us of an infinitely greater work accomplished millennia later at Golgotha.

Jesus was stripped and put to an open shame on the Cross and, as the Lamb of God, was slain, so that we might be given the opportunity of putting on the garment of His righteousness.

When Jehovah Elohim clothed Adam and Eve, it was a gracious act. By His grace, He has made available, for us, the 'best robe'. the garment of salvation, the robe of righteousness. (Isa. 61. 10.). It costs us nothing, since God freely provides it, but it cost God everything. We must receive this perfect righteousness by faith and thank God for it.

Jesus, the Lord, our Righteousness!
Our beauty, Thou - our glorious dress;
'Midst flaming worlds whilst thus arrayed,
With joy shall we lift up our head.

Could anyone refuse such an offer? From rags to riches and righteously so, in a moment, and for eternity.

January 25

' "For truly in this city, there were gathered together against Thy Holy Servant Jesus, Whom Thou didst anoint, both Herod and Pontius Pilate, with the nations and peoples of Israel, to do whatever Thy hand and Thy purpose predestined to occur." '
(Acts 4. 27, 28.).

The Greek word, translated 'servant' in the above text, had a variety of meanings. It is similarly translated in the story of the healing of the centurion's servant. (Mat. 8. 6, 8, 13.). It is rendered as 'boy' or 'young man' in the story of the reviving of Eutychus at Troas. (Acts 20. 12.). It is translated 'children', referring to those who were crying "Hosanna" to Jesus in the Temple. (Mat. 21. 15.). In each case, the context helps in determining the meaning. There is no doubt that, in the context of the prayer meeting in Jerusalem (Acts 4. 23 - 31.), the most appropriate translation is 'servant'.

Mark, the re-instated servant, describes in his Gospel, God's Holy Servant, Jesus. No genealogy is given, since a servant does not need that. But a servant must have a good testimony and God's Servant receives such from men, God and even demons. The Lord's Servant is stamped with alacrity and constant activity; for example, the word translated 'immediately' is found eleven times in Mark's Gospel, chapter one.

God's Holy Servant is noted for His purity (Mk. 1. 24.); in His work, He demonstrates His supremacy over demons, disease and death. In His true humanity, He shows complete dependency upon His Father in prayer. (1. 36.). His utter humility is seen in His willingness to give His life a ransom for many (10. 45.). Yet He always maintained His dignity, even before Pontius Pilate (15. 5.) and Golgotha (15. 23.).

How many of these qualities (apart from those associated with our Lord's deity) are observed in us, as the Lord's servants?

January 26
A sanctuary and a stumbling stone

'Sanctify the LORD of Hosts Himself; and let Him be your fear and let Him be your dread; and He will be for a Sanctuary; but for a Stone of stumbling and for a Rock of offence to both the houses of Israel, for a trap and for a snare to the inhabitants of Jerusalem.' (Isa. 8. 13, 14.).

The apostle Peter, writing of God's elect but aliens in the world, says, "Do not fear their fear and do not be troubled, but set apart Christ as Lord in your hearts, -----." (1 Pe. 3. 14, 15.).   This quote by Peter from Isaiah is most illuminating.   Firstly, he equates Jehovah Tsebaoth (the LORD of Hosts) with the Lord Jesus, thus witnessing to His deity.   Secondly, he reminds us that we have enemies too, whom we are not to fear but to bless.   We are reminded of Stephen's attitude, so like that of his Lord - when he was being stoned to death. (Acts 7. 60.).

The negative injunction - do not fear - is followed by the positive - sanctify the LORD of Hosts.   Give the Lord Jesus prior place in your heart, and fear and reverence Him. Then He will be our Sanctuary and our life will be hidden with Christ in God.

Here is the difference between faith and unbelief.   Faith finds in Christ a shelter and sanctuary.   Unbelief, like that of Israel, stumbles over the Stone in the darkness of this world's night: With what awful results - to stumble and fall, to be broken and snared and caught, like an animal in a trap.   In 70 A.D. the Roman army under Titus besieged Jerusalem and destroyed its walls and the Temple.   Five hundred or more Jews were crucified daily, according to the historian Josephus.   The words of the Saviour were fulfilled, "Behold, your house is left unto you desolate" (Mat. 23. 38.).

Christ is either a Sanctuary or a Stumbling Stone, depending on whether we respond to Him in faith or in unbelief.

What is your choice?

January27

The stronger man

'No one can enter a strong man's house and plunder his property unless he first binds the strong man and then he will plunder his house.'   (Mk. 3. 27.).

Satan (the Adversary) is a mighty angelic being with many names which describe his evil character and deeds.   He is the Devil (Accuser);   the Evil One;   Apollyon or Abaddon (Destroyer).   He was the Anointed Cherub before he lifted himself up in pride. He is Helel (Shining One);   the god of this age,   the prince of this world,   the ruler of the authority of the air,   the king of the abyss,   controlling myriads of demons.   He is Beliar, the worthless, a liar and a murderer.   He is the old Serpent, the Dragon and Satan;   Ba'al Zebul (Lord of the Dwelling).   He can be like a roaring lion or an angel of light.   In our text, the Lord Jesus likens him to a strong man.   The same thought is in Isaiah 49. 24 - 26:   'Can the prey be taken from the mighty man, or the captives of the tyrant be rescued?   Thus says the LORD, even the captives of the mighty man will be taken away and the prey of the tyrant will be rescued.'

Who would accomplish this?   The Stronger Man, Jehovah, Jesus, our Saviour and Redeemer, the Mighty One of Jacob did this by His entry into the strong man's house. He partook of our humanity, sin apart, 'so that by His death he might render powerless him who holds the might of death, that is, the devil.'   (Heb. 2. 14.).

So the Stronger Man is now ransacking the strong man's household goods right and left, and seizing them as plunder.   What a great deliverance is being wrought in the lives of many throughout the world, as the Stronger Man sets free those who were bound by the strong man's chain.   Satan is a defeated foe and we need not fear him;   the Stronger Man broke free from death's domain and He gives us the victory in Him.

Whose property am I?   The strong man's or the Stronger Man's?

January 28

'He answered and said, "A Man that is called Jesus made clay, and anointed my eyes and said to me, "Go to the pool of Siloam and wash:" and I went and washed and I received sight." ' (John. 9. 11.).

It all began with the healing of a blind man. He had been blind from birth but Jesus saw him, anointed his eyes with clay made with His spittle and told him to go, wash in the pool of Siloam. The blind man went and washed and came home seeing.

But, according to the regulations of the Pharisees, work had been done on the Sabbath. Clay had been made and a man's eyes had been opened! So they interrogate him carefully and he answers them courageously. As he does so his spiritual insight concerning Jesus deepens.

When asked how his eyes had been opened, he said that the Man called Jesus was responsible. There was only One out of many who bore that name who could do that work, either then or now, spiritually. "Where is this Man?" they asked; "I don't know," he replied. But we know that the Man called Jesus is seated now at God's right hand.

The Pharisees then asked him his opinion of Jesus. "He is a Prophet," he said, as he recalled the words of Jesus at the outset of his encounter with Him. The pharisees were adamant that Jesus was a sinner because He had broken their rules on the Sabbath day. The man wasn't sure of this, but he concluded that Jesus was a God-fearing and God-sent Man.

Later, when Jesus found the man, He revealed Himself as the Son of God, become Son of Man. The man responded in faith, owning the Lordship of Christ and worshipped Him as God. The spiritual journey of a man who once was blind had led him upwards to the heights of accepting the deity of the One Who had given him sight.

Do you accept that the Man called Jesus is God ?

January 29

'Thou has made him a little lower than the angels,   and hast crowned him with glory and honour.' (Ps. 8. 5.).

The author of the Epistle to the Hebrews quotes this verse, then uses it as follows;
'But we see Jesus, Who was made for a little while lower than the angels for the suffering of death, crowned with glory and honour; that He, by the grace of God should taste death for everything.' (Heb. 2. 9.).

We see two men in this Psalm, the first man, Adam, and the second Man, Jesus, the Lord from heaven.

As the Psalmist, David, considers the immensity of God's universe, he sees the apparent insignificance of man.   Yet God made Adam and gave him a place below angelic beings, but above all other creatures on the planet earth.   He was given dignity and authority which were marred as a result of his sin and disobedience.

Then we see another Man of heavenly origin, Who demonstrated His authority over creation during His public ministry among men.   He, the Creator, became like one of His creatures in His true and perfect humanity.   Why did He humble Himself to be made lower than angels?   In order to taste death as a sacrifice for sins not His own, and eventually redeem the whole creation.

By faith, we see Jesus crowned, no more with thorns, but now with glory and splendour seated on the throne of God in Heaven.   He is the Head of a new race of humanity composed of all who have trusted in Him for salvation and now possess a new, eternal life.   We shall judge the 'cosmos' and even judge angels.

Jehovah, Jesus our Lord, how excellent is Thy Name in all the earth!

How has His Name been enhanced by His humiliation?

January 30
Nazarene

'And he (Joseph) came and dwelt in a city called Nazareth; that it might be fulfilled which was spoken by the prophets, He (Jesus) shall be called a Nazarene.'
(Mat. 2. 23.).

Joseph had to make a decision, as to where he should settle with Mary and her young child. Again, he received guidance in a dream to go back to Galilee and set up home in Nazareth. It is important for us, also, to seek guidance from the Lord regarding our residence, should we be forced to make such a choice.

We see the over-ruling hand of God in Joseph's decision, since it led to the fulfilment of what was spoken by the prophets, "He shall be called a Nazarene". Although there is specific reference here by Matthew to an oral tradition, yet there is also a record in the writings of the prophets. The Hebrew word for branch or shoot is 'Netser', and is akin to the word 'Notsri', meaning Nazarene. Isaiah uses this word in his prophecy of the Messiah (Isa. 11. 1.); a word with a similar meaning ('Tsemach') is used of the Messiah in the prophecies of Jeremiah and Zechariah.

The name 'Nazarene' carried with it a sense of reproach and contempt. "Can any good thing come out of Nazareth?" (Jn. 1. 46.). Our Saviour was described as such by Pilate in the superscription above the Cross. (Jn. 19. 19.). He was spoken of as such to the faithful women by the angel sitting in the empty tomb, where the body of Jesus had lain. (Mk. 16. 6.). The Lord identified himself as such to Saul of Tarsus, thus bringing about his conversion. (Acts 22. 8.).

The apostle Paul was described as a ringleader of the sect of the Nazarenes (Ac. 24. 5.). In his defence before King Agrippa, Paul spoke of 'doing much against the Name of Jesus, the Nazarene.' (Acts 26. 9.).

Are you willing to suffer reproach as followers of the despised Nazarene?

January 31

'And Enoch walked with God; and he was not, for God took him.' (Gen. 5. 24.).

Enoch was a notable saint in sad days, before the great flood of Noah. He is the second hero of faith in the short-list given by the writer to the Hebrews. (Heb. 11. 5.). He walked with God through a filthy world and kept clean.

His walk began after his son was born. His name was Methuselah, meaning 'when he is dead, it will be sent'. The great flood came the same year that Methuselah died, so his name was a prophecy. His father also foretold the Lord's coming to execute judgment upon all the ungodly. (Jude 14. 15.).

Enoch was in agreement with God and therefore could walk with Him. (Amos. 3. 3.). It became a regular habit to meet and to walk with the Lord. The walks became longer and longer, until one day the Lord took him to Paradise without dying. A search was made for him in vain - he was not found, because God had translated him. He had this testimony, that he pleased God: Faith always pleases God.

In our day, we are exhorted to walk honestly (Rom. 13. 13.), in the Spirit (Gal. 5. 16.), in love (Eph. 5. 2.) and in the light (1 Jn. 1. 7.).

Enoch's translation before the Flood judgment is a picture of our translation into the Lord's immediate Presence before the Tribulation judgment. The Lord Jesus is our Deliverer from the coming wrath. (1. Thes. 1. 10.).

'Oh joy, oh delight, should we go without dying:
 No sickness, no sadness, no dread and no crying.
Caught up, through the cloud, with our Lord into Glory,
When Jesus receives "His own" '.

Is Jesus your walking Companion ?

February 1
Some other man

'And the eunuch answered Philip and said, "I pray thee, of whom speaketh the prophet this? Of himself, or of some other man?" Then Philip opened his mouth, and began at the same scripture, and preached unto him, Jesus.' (Acts 8. 34, 35.).

The history containing the above two verses is woven around four men. The first to appear in the narrative is Philip, the evangelist, a sent man. The angel of the Lord sent him from a scene of blessing in Samaria to a scene of barrenness on the highway to Gaza. There the Spirit sent him to rendezvous with a man in a chariot.

This man of Ethiopia was a seeking man. He was seeking the one true God; his search had brought him to Jerusalem, the city of God. He had come to worship God there in the Temple, in the court of the Gentiles. Being a man of substance, indeed the queen's treasurer, he was able to buy a scroll containing the writings of the prophet Isaiah.

Isaiah was a seeing man. God gave him visions of the destiny of his own and many other nations. He was privileged to see God's glory. But above all, he saw Jehovah's Servant, the Messiah.

The eunuch, reading aloud in his chariot, had just reached Isaiah chapter 53. Who was this suffering Servant, the prophet or some other man? Philip preached to him Jesus, God's Lamb, slain for our sins, yet alive from the dead. The eunuch believed, was baptised and went on his way rejoicing.

There is no other man like this 'some other man', the God-Man, Christ Jesus.

Does your response to Him match that of the Ethiopian ?

February 2

'For unto us a Child is born, unto us a Son is given; and the government shall be upon His shoulder; and His Name shall be called wonderful Counsellor, the mighty God, the everlasting Father, The Prince of peace.' (Isa. 9. 6.).

Here, the nation Israel recognises at last that Mary's child is God's Son, their Messiah. Note that the Child is born, but the Son is given: God gave His unique Son to die for our sins on the Tree. Note, also, that the reference to the first advent of God's Son is followed immediately by one concerned with His second advent when 'the government shall be upon His shoulder'. Our present era, the 'Church age', which has run its course for well nigh 2,000 years, is not mentioned.

The four-fold Name of this Child-Son proclaims His deity and His deeds. Later in Isaiah's prophecy, we read 'this also comes from the Lord of Hosts, Who has made His counsel wonderful and His wisdom great.' (Isa. 28. 29.). In the Gospels, our Lord's wonderful counsel is enshrined in the Sermon on the Mount, His many parables, the Olivet discourse, the Upper Room Ministry, as well as His words to a variety of individuals. The great power of His miracles displayed our Lord's Name as the mighty God, especially His resurrection.

Our Lord will be the eternal Father of His people during His millennial reign and on into eternity. He will also be 'Sar-Shalohm', Prince of Peace, as the only One who can produce and promote peace for His people, Israel, and for the nations. He who spoke peace to the troubled sea, in the days of His sojourn, can speak peace to the troubled heart now. He who made peace through the blood of His cross wants to give us that peace, Himself. But we must receive it and Him as God's great gift and let that peace of God guard our hearts and minds in Christ Jesus.

Which facets of the Name of the Child-Son have a special importance to you ?

February3

'But when he saw Jesus afar off, he ran and worshipped Him, and cried with a loud voice and said, "What have I to do with Thee, Jesus, Son of the most high God. I adjure Thee by God that Thou torment me not." ' (Mk. 5. 6, 7.).

The boat carrying the Lord Jesus and His disciples had reached the eastern shore of the lake. They had gone to the other side, fulfilling the expressed wish of our Lord. One of the reasons for their journey was about to be revealed. No sooner had Jesus stepped out of the boat, but a wild, naked man ran towards Him.

Then a strange thing happened; the man bowed down before Jesus and acknowledged Him as the Son of the most high God. The demonic occupants of the man recognised Jesus as God, while human, even His own disciples, were not able to do so. (Mk. 4. 41.)

In reply to our Lord's question, the man revealed that his name was 'Legion'; "For we are many," he said. A Roman legion consisted of around 6,000 soldiers. At the command of exorcism from the Lord, the man, motivated by the demons, prayed that they may not be sent from the country. "Send us into the swine," they begged Him. When Jesus allowed them to do so, they entered the herd of 2,000 swine, which rushed headlong into the sea and were choked.

The inhabitants then asked the Lord to leave, preferring the demons to the Deliverer. Their request was granted and Jesus left them. But when the ex-demoniac, now seated clothed and sensible, requested that he might accompany the Lord, his wish was not granted. He was sent by the Lord to proclaim to his own people in the Decapolis (10 cities) how great things the Lord (Jesus) had done for him.

The Son of the most high God showed His supremacy over the storm, the sea, the spirits and the swine. Also, the ex-demoniac bowed to His authority. Do we ?

February 4

' "I am the Door; by Me, if any one enter in, he shall be saved, and shall go in and shall go out, and shall find pasture." ' (Jn. 10. 9.).

Our Lord Jesus solemnly asserts His claim to be the Door of the sheep by prefixing it with a double 'Amen' (v. 7.). Those who came before Him, the legalistic Pharisees, the rationalistic Sadducees and the nationalistic Zealots, were thieves and robbers.

The Lord is painting the picture of the Eastern shepherd who, when night approaches, leads his flock into the security of a stone-built circular-shaped hill fold. When all are safely gathered in, the shepherd positions himself in the only access to the enclosure, and literally becomes the 'door'.

So the Saviour is making a three-fold pledge to those who believe on Him. Firstly, He offers perfect safety - "if any one enter by Me, he shall be saved.". No 'if' nor 'but' nor 'maybe'! He shall be saved.

Secondly, He gives total liberty - 'shall go in and shall go out'. Liberty to go in to God's presence to worship and out into the world to witness. Thirdly, He guarantees an ample supply - 'shall find pasture'. He has given us the sweet pasture of His Word to feed on and satisfy our soul's hunger; and this, in the barren wilderness of the world.

But we must make the move; we must respond to His call and enter by faith into the security of the fold by Him. Then we become part of the flock of God, the true church, and are saved eternally. The Lord says, "I give to My sheep eternal life and they shall never perish and no one shall seize them out of My hand ----- no one shall seize them out of My Father's hand." We are in the double grip of Deity, eternally secure.

There is something else we must do - we must find pasture. It is there to be found.

What portion of pasture have you found today ?

February 5

'And He shall judge the world in righteousness; He shall minister judgment to the people in uprightness. The Lord also will be a Refuge for the oppressed, a refuge in the times of trouble.' (Ps. 9. 8, 9.).

Psalms 9 to 15 describe the 'Man of the Earth' (10. 18.), the Antichrist. The first two Psalms in this series (9 and 10) are linked together by an acrostic alphabet which is broken, like the 'times of trouble' mentioned in these Psalms (9. 9; 10. 1.), referring particularly to the 'time of Jacob's trouble' (Jer. 30. 7.), the 'Great Tribulation'. (Mat. 24. 21.).

The first letter missed out is 'Daleth', the fourth letter in the Hebrew alphabet, denoting the number '4' (the symbol of world order) between vs. 5 and 6 of Psalm 9, which speak of great disorder and destruction. Then, in Psalm 10, there is a gap of 6 letters from 'Mem' to 'Tzaddi', between vs. 2 to 12, when the series recommences and is completed. This section of Psalm 10 portrays the 'Wicked One', the 'Man of Lawlessness' (2 Thes. 2. 3, 8.) the number of whose name is 666 (Rev. 13. 18.) 'the number of a man'.

But Jehovah-Jesus will intervene in judgment and destroy the 'Man of Lawlessness'. The apostle Paul pointed this out to his hearers on Mars hill, Athens. The crucified, risen Christ will return to judge the world in righteousness.

Yet even in that terrible time, the Lord will be a 'high fortress' for the oppressed one. The saints will be secure in their high tower, while sinners sink in their own pit (v. 15.). The promise is also given to us who have come to trust the Saviour after getting to know His Name (v.10.). He will never, never leave us, nor will He ever, ever forsake us, so that we may boldly say: "The Lord is my Helper, and I will not fear what man shall do unto me." (Heb. 13. 6.).

Have you sought refuge in Christ and found it ?

February6

'And Jesus, when He was baptised, went up straightway out of the water; and, lo, the heavens were opened unto Him and He saw the Spirit of God descending like a dove and coming (lighting) upon Him; and, lo, a voice from heaven, saying, "This is My beloved Son, in Whom I am well pleased." ' (Mat. 3. 16, 17.).

From the carpenter's shop in Nazareth to the river Jordan, where John was baptising, was not far: But the Son of God's love had stepped down from heaven to earth, from eternity into time to keep that appointment.

John protested vehemently when Jesus presented Himself for baptism, saying, "I need to be baptised by Thee and comest Thou to me ?" Our Lord overcame these protestations by pointing out to John that it was proper for them to do this, in order to fulfil all righteous obligations. So John baptised Jesus; it was but a picture of our Lord's experience when He would be immersed in the deep dark waters of death, on the Cross.

As Jesus came up out of the water, the heavens were torn open and the Spirit like a dove descended upon Him, anointing Him for service. At that moment, the Father said to Him, "Thou are My Beloved Son in Whom I am well pleased." Then, as the Spirit came upon our Lord, the public announcement was made; "This is My Beloved Son, in Whom I am well pleased." Thus the Father's word to John was fulfilled; "Upon Whom thou shalt see the Spirit descending and remaining on Him, the same is He who baptises with the Holy Spirit."

So the three Persons of the Trinity, Father, Son and Holy Spirit, were involved in this act of commissioning and identification. The Father set His seal of approval upon His Son, as He appraised and approved 30 years of perfect humanity.

How could God be well-pleased with us ?

The ark of Noah

'And God said to Noah, "The end of all flesh is come before Me; for the earth is filled with violence through them; and, behold, I will destroy them with the earth. Make thee an ark of gopher wood; rooms shall thou make in the ark and shalt pitch it within and without with pitch." ' (Gen. 6. 13, 14.).

The ark is a beautiful picture of Christ and the salvation that He offers.

It found its origin in the heart and mind of God, as evil enveloped the minds of men of that day. Similarly, Christ was the Lamb slain from before the foundation of the world. God planned salvation in eternity past.

The details of the ark were revealed to a chosen human vessel, Noah, who was responsible for building it. In like manner, God's plan was revealed to and effected through the virgin Mary.

The ark was made to meet the need. There was ample accommodation for all its occupants, just as the redeemed find in Christ One who meets all their needs. But there was only one door in the side of the ark. It is through the riven side of the Saviour that we find security and salvation.

The ark was capable of withstanding all the waters of God's judgment. Its dimensions and materials made it so. But Christ endured the floods of God's judgment against sin. He said prophetically, "I am come into deep waters, where the floods overflow Me." (Ps. 69. 2.).

The ark was the only way to a new environment. All, including the eight souls, were safe and secure inside it for more than a year; they emerged to enjoy the cleansed earth. Jesus is the only Way to the Father's house. He said, "No-one comes to the Father, but by Me."

Are you in the Ark, or are you outside ?

February 8

'The word which God sent unto the sons of Israel, preaching peace through Jesus Christ (He is Lord of all).' *(Acts 10. 36.).*

The apostle Peter had been directed by God to the city of Caesarea. There, he entered the home of Cornelius, a Roman centurion and a Gentile. At the very outset of his address to the assembled company, Peter stressed the Lordship of Jesus Christ, that He is Lord of all.

Firstly, He is Lord of the cosmos, since He is its Creator. So, whether we look through a telescope or a microscope, all that we see was made by Him. He is also the Controller of the cosmos; otherwise it would become chaos. For in Him, all things are held together. (Col. 1. 17.).

Then Jesus is Lord of the Church, His body; He is the Head. Her power comes from the Lord Who added (and still adds) daily those who were being saved. Her preaching is centred on the Lord. (2 Cor. 4. 5.). Her practice is governed by the Lord. (Acts 19. 5; 1 Cor. 11. 23; 14. 37). Her praise is focused on the Lord and her prospect is founded on Him. (1 Thes. 4. 16.).

Jesus Christ is Lord of the individual Christian; of our bodies, our physical afflictions (2 Cor. 12. 8.) and our associations (Col. 3. 18 - 24.). We must acknowledge His Lordship in all our human relationships.

Jesus proved Himself to be Lord of all circumstances of life. Disease, demons and death were subject to Him, during His public ministry. Even creation obeyed His command. He controls all our circumstances, too.

But, pre-eminently, He is Lord of the Cross. He has vanquished death, hades and the tomb: God has made Him both Lord and Christ.

Have I made Jesus Lord of all the departments of my life ?

February 9
Jesse's fruitful branch

'A Shoot will come up from the stump of Jesse; A Branch out of his roots shall be fruitful.' (Isa. 11. 1.).

Isaiah has just described how the Lord, Jehovah of Hosts would cut down the pride of Assyria, as the branches of a great tree are lopped off violently. Then, in stark contrast, he speaks of the stump of Jesse, the father of King David, who would have remained in obscurity but for his famous son.

But David is completely eclipsed by the Fruitful Branch from the forgotten stump of Jesse. For He is none other than our Lord Jesus Christ, upon Whom the Spirit of Jehovah rested as a Dove after His baptism in Jordan.

Firstly, His inner qualities are noted: He has the Spirit of wisdom and discernment. (Ps. 139. 1 - 4.). Solomon with all his wisdom pales into insignificance before Him. He is the Discerner of the thoughts and intents of the heart. (Heb. 4. 12.). He is the personification of wisdom.

Secondly, in the next couplet, the outward manifestations of the Spirit are described. He has the Spirit of counsel and of might. No matter what problem arises, He has the solution and the power to implement it. He will be the Divine Autocrat in that day to come.

Thirdly, there rests on Him the Spirit of knowledge and fear of Jehovah, describing His upward or Godward relationship. As perfect Man, our Lord Jesus knew and knows the perfect will of God and accomplished it on the Cross, and will accomplish it on the Throne at His return.

Then, He will judge with justice and equity to save His poor people, the remnant of Israel and destroy that 'Wicked One', with the breath of His mouth. (2 Thes. 2. 8.).

Are we, who are Christ's and therefore possess the Holy Spirit now, allowing Him to produce His fruit in our lives ?

February 10

The carpenter

'And many, hearing Him, were astonished, saying: "From whence hath this (man) these things, and what wisdom is this which is given unto Him, that even such mighty works are wrought by His hands? Is not this the carpenter ----- ?" ' (Mk. 6. 2, 3.).

After a considerable interval, Our Lord Jesus had returned to Nazareth, where He was brought up. His disciples were with Him. On the Sabbath, He taught in the synagogue where He had already announced His anointing and calling to preach the Gospel. (Lk. 4. 17 - 21.). On this second occasion the reaction of the local people was not so violent but just as potent. They took offence at Him and He marvelled because of their unbelief.

But they had to acknowledge His words of wisdom and His works of power, but could not bring themselves to confess the source of them. Instead they said, "Is not this the Carpenter ?"

No doubt evidence of His handiwork could be seen in and around Nazareth. The strongest and most serviceable of ploughs, and the easiest and gentlest of yokes, not to mention the many household articles which He had made during His years of toil at the carpenter's bench.

But now His hands were being used to do other mightier work; to heal the sick, give sight to the blind and even raise the dead.

Then the mightiest work of all was done when His hands were pinned to a cross made by another carpenter. His was a perfect work of salvation, done to the entire satisfaction of a holy and a righteous God.

At present, the pierced hands of the Carpenter are being used to remake the lives of many throughout the world.

Has the Carpenter of Nazareth begun to mould your life according to His perfect will?

February 11
The good shepherd

' "I am the Good Shepherd; the Good Shepherd lays down His life for the sheep." '
(Jn. 10. 11.).

Here is the fourth of seven great claims made by our Lord Jesus in the Gospel of John. Contained in the claim is a self-description. Our Lord's claim to Deity is evident in the 'I am'; also in the word 'good', which conveys all the characteristics of what is ideal. Literally, our Lord said, "I am the Shepherd, the good One."

There can be no mistake in identifying the genuine Shepherd: He lays down His life for the sheep. (vs. 15, 17, 18.). The hired hand saves himself by sacrificing the sheep and leaving them to the wolf. The good Shepherd sacrifices Himself to save His sheep from the wolf, who is Satan's emissary. Such tender-hearted shepherds are needed today, when there are so many savage wolves entering in and not sparing the flock. (Acts 20. 29.).

Our Lord repeats His claim in verse 14; but now, as the true Shepherd, He knows and recognises His own sheep as they do Him. Just as an eastern shepherd would do, He calls His own sheep by name and they follow Him. They receive the gift of eternal life from Him and they shall never perish. The mutual recognition and understanding between the Father and the Son eternally is now shared between the Shepherd and His sheep. The righteous basis for this new relationship is in the death of the Shepherd. Hence, the Saviour says again, "I lay down My life for the sheep."

The Father's authority was behind both the laying down and the taking up again of the Shepherd's life. The good Shepherd who died is alive from the dead and leads His flock onward and upward.

Do we take time daily to listen to the voice of the good Shepherd so that we can follow Him more closely ?

February 12

' "For Thou wilt not leave My Soul in Sheol, neither wilt Thou allow Thine Holy One to see corruption." ' (Ps. 16. 10.).

This Psalm is undoubtedly Messianic: Who else but Messiah - Jesus could say, "I have set Jehovah before Me continually" (v. 8.).

Then our Lord Jesus refers to His heart (or soul) rejoicing. His glory (or spirit) exulting and His flesh (or body) resting in hope, even at the onset of death. In common with all other humans, our Lord became and is a tri-partite being, having a body, soul and spirit. This is seen very clearly at the Cross. At the precise moment of His choice, He yielded up His spirit: His soul descended into Sheol or Hades and His body was laid in the new tomb of Joseph of Arimathea.

The apostle Peter took up the theme in his preaching on the day of Pentecost.
(Acts 2. 25 - 32.). His audience consisted of Jews gathered from many parts of the Roman Empire. He quoted Psalm 16. 8 - 11, and showed that the prophecy was fulfilled in Jesus, the Nazarene and not in David, the King. Jehovah's Holy One (as to His body) never saw corruption during that period of three complete days in the tomb. It was completely contrary to nature, and it was proof of the sinless and sanctified character of the Christ of God. Sin always produces corruption, both spiritual and physical.

The apostle Paul used the same text in his address to the people in the synagogue in Antioch of Pisidia. (Acts. 13. 35.). Then he said, "But he whom God raised up did not see decay." (v. 37.). That same Holy and Gracious One is now exalted in Heaven, a glorified Saviour, through Whom is proclaimed the forgiveness of sins.

Have you received forgiveness by believing on God's Holy One?

February 13
Maker of men-fishers

'And Jesus, walking by the sea of Galilee, saw two brethren, Simon called Peter, and Andrew his brother, casting a net into the sea, for they were fishers, and He said unto them, "Follow Me and I will make you fishers of men." ' (Mat. 4. 18, 19.).

Our Lord had launched into His public ministry (v. 17.) and, graciously, He wishes others to share with Him in it.   He already knows them, because He knew all men and did not need man's testimony about man, for He knew what was in a man.   He certainly knew His men   when He called Peter and Andrew.

They had already met Him as the Lamb of God by Jordan's banks.   Now they knew Him as the Fisher of men by Gennesaret's shores.   The command was clear, "Come here after Me -----!"   If they wished to be   men-fishers, they must leave their nets and follow Jesus;   and this they did.

They learned their new trade as they watched the Master at work.   With hook and line, He drew the woman of Samaria to the celestial shore, and with net flung wide He then encompassed the men. (Jn. 4. 41. 42.).

Andrew was a 'hook and line' man.   His first 'catch' was a big 'fish', his own brother Simon whom be brought to Jesus.   It is good to begin in home waters.   Then he introduced a little boy to Jesus whose five barley loaves and two small fishes were used by the Lord to feed a great multitude.   Later on, in Jerusalem, he and Philip told Jesus of certain Greeks who wanted to see Him. (Jn. 12. 22.).

In contrast, the Lord used Peter to cast the gospel net on the day of Pentecost to catch 3,000 souls.   Again in Jerusalem through Peter's preaching many believed and the number of the men grew to about 5,000.

Andrew and Simon Bar-Jonas had learned well from the Maker of Men-fishers.

Are we willing to follow Jesus and let Him make us into fishers of men ?

February 14
Christ portrayed in Melchizedek

'And Melchizedek king of Salem brought forth bread and wine; and he was the priest of the most high God.'   (Gen. 14. 18.).

The identity of Melchizedek   is shrouded in mystery, for good reason.   In the New Testament, the writer to the Hebrews explains this. (Heb. 7. 1 - 4.).   Melchizedek's parentage, genealogy and personal history are not known and therefore he is an accurate type of the Son of God, our Lord Jesus.   Also, Melchizedek   was priest of the Most High God.

Abram was returning, having routed the armies of the eastern kings and recovered his nephew Lot with all his possessions.   It was a signal victory wrought by God through His servant who trusted in Him.   A band of shepherds overcame against a great army flushed with success.   But after all his strenuous exertion, Abram was now weary. They had arrived in the valley of the Kedron to the east of Jerusalem, which was also called the king's   dale.   It was an apt name, since two kings met Abram there;   the king of Sodom and the king of Salem.

The king of Sodom wanted the souls but the king of Salem brought solace in the form of bread and wine.   He also brought spiritual blessing to Abram from the Most High God, Possessor of   heaven and earth.   Melchizedek then praised God for delivering Abram's enemies into his hand.   In turn, and out of gratitude to God, Abram gave Melchizedek   a tenth of everything.

With this refreshment and encouragement, the man of faith was able to face the king of Sodom and resist his temptation to keep the goods.   Abram had raised his hand to Jehovah,   the Most High God and given his promise to take nothing that belonged to the king of Sodom.   Meeting with Melchizedek was what mattered.

Do we know the blessing of our Heavenly   Melchizedek   as He brings us bread and wine ?

February 15

Judge of the living and the dead

' "And He commanded us to preach to the people and to testify that He is the One whom God has appointed as Judge of the living and the dead." ' (Acts 10. 42.).

The apostle Peter and six other Jewish Christians were in the house of Cornelius, a Gentile centurion. The room was full with family and friends. Peter preached a message that was never finished; God, the Holy Spirit, intervened, as He fell on all who were listening to the 'word'.

The content of the 'word' declared by Peter was Jesus of Nazareth; how God anointed Him and was with Him to defeat the devil, by doing many deeds of kindness and working mighty miracles of healing. Then Peter testified to what the Christ's own kinsmen did to Him: They killed Him by hanging Him on a tree. But God raised Him from the dead on the third day and He was seen by Peter and other chosen witnesses. "We ate and drank with Him," said Peter, "after He rose from the dead."

Then Peter obeyed His Lord's command, not only to preach the good news to the people, but also to warn of coming judgment. God has appointed His Son Jesus to judge the living and the dead.

The first to be judged will be the church because judgment must begin at the house of God. This will take place at the 'Bema' or 'Judgment Seat' of Christ after our Lord's return to the air for us. This is the judgment of the living; to reward the saints for faithful service. Some will suffer loss, not of salvation, but of reward.

At our Lord's return to the earth with His saints to reign as King, He will judge the living nations. The unrighteous will go away to eternal punishment but the righteous to eternal life.

The 'dead' will be judged at the end of time before a great white throne. Their lot is the lake of fire.

Are you ready to stand before the Judge ?

February 16

Eliakim, the nail

'And it shall come to pass in that day, that I will call my servant Eliakim, the son of Hilkiah ---- and I will fasten Him as a Nail in a sure place; ---.' *(Isaiah 22. 20, 23.).*

The day did come when Eliakim was made steward of the royal palace, in the place of Shebna, the traitor.   The Jews said that he was in treacherous liaison with the king of Assyria and had agreed to deliver the city of Jerusalem into his hands.   Shebna was motivated by pride, vanity and self-sufficiency.   But Eliakim was invested with his robe, (the emblem of honour),   his sash,   (the emblem of power), and his authority. Shebna was demoted to the office of scribe (Isa. 36. 3.) and ceased to be steward.

In contrast, Eliakim became a father-figure to the inhabitants of Jerusalem and to the house of   Judah.   God placed on his shoulder the key of the house of David and fastened him as a nail in a sure   place.

But the final fulfilment of this prophecy is found in our Lord Jesus, the true Eliakim (meaning God will establish) the Son of   Hilkiah (meaning Jehovah's portion).   He is Son over the house of God, possessor of the key of David.   'What He opens, no one can shut, and what He shuts no one can open.' (Rev. 3. 7.).   He will oust the Anti-Christ,   the antitype of Shebna, and consign him to the lake of fire.

Our Lord is like a peg in a firm place.   He bears all the glory, whether it be the throne and the house of   His Father or that of   His servants, both greater or lesser;   golden vessels or goat skins.   So we can trust all to the One Who can never fail.   He bore our sorrows on the Tree, but now He bears the glory on the Throne.

Are we rejoicing in that security which is ours in Him, the Nail in a sure place ?

February 17

'And (they) were beyond measure astonished, saying, "He hath done all things well: He maketh both the deaf to hear and the dumb to speak." ' (Mk. 7. 37.).

God, the Son, did all things well in creation. On the sixth day, 'He saw everything that He had made, and behold, it was very good.' Although it is now marred by sin, we can observe that perfection in creation, whether we view it macroscopically or microscopically. The beauty and perfume of a rose, and the wonder of a new-born babe. All of creation witnesses to the well-doing of a Creator; it could never have 'evolved' by chance.

Watch the well-doing of the Son-Incarnate, as He makes the deaf to hear, the dumb to speak, the dead to live and the demons to depart. Those who observed Him at work had reason to be utterly astonished. The sinless Son of God was here to undo the works of Satan. Yet some were so blind that they attributed His work to Beelzebub, the prince of demons.

So sinful men put the holy Son on a Cross. But there, He completed the redemptive work that He had come to do. We hear His cry, 'Finished!', and we wonder afresh at the well-doing of our Saviour, for God and for us. We rest, by faith, on that finished work.

Our Lord is still doing His perfect work in the hearts of those who trust Him for salvation. It is a work of regeneration, as He makes all things new. He is presently making the spiritually deaf to hear and the spiritually dumb to speak, and the living shall praise Him eternally.

"And above the rest this note shall swell,
My Jesus has done all things well."

'He Who began a good work in you will perfect it until the day of Christ Jesus.' (Phil. 1. 6.).

Has He begun a good work in you ?

February 18

'Then the Jews answered Him, saying, "For a good work we stone Thee not; but for blasphemy; and because that Thou, being a man, makest Thyself God." ' (Jn. 10. 33.).

It was December in Jerusalem during the Feast of Dedication. For eight days, the people commemorated the cleansing of the Temple and altar by Judas Maccabaeus in 165 or 164 B.C., three years after their defilement by Antiochus Epiphanes.

Jesus was walking in the shelter of Solomon's Porch on the east side of the Temple court when the Jews surrounded Him. They said to Him, "If you are the Christ, say so to us openly." When our Lord affirmed that it was so, concluding with the amazing statement, "I and the Father are one," the Jews took up stones to stone Him, because they were aware of His claim to Deity. He, being a Man, made Himself God. He had blasphemed the Name of Jehovah; therefore He must surely be put to death. All the assembly should certainly stone Him. (Lev. 24. 16.).

Without doubt, He was and is a Man. While here among men, He knew what it was to be hungry and thirsty, hot and weary. He was moved to tears at the tomb of Lazarus and He wept over the fate of Jerusalem. As He prayed in Gethsemane, His sweat became as great drops of blood, falling down upon the earth. He suffered death as a Man, to rid us of sin's penalty and power.

It is also beyond all controversy that He not only made Himself God, but that He was and is God of very God. "I am the Son of God," He said to them. What the Jews said of Him was true, that He being a Man made Himself God. But it was more true to say that He, being God, made Himself Man to accomplish our redemption!

What is our reaction to the God-Man ? To reject Him or to receive Him ?

February 19
A worm

'But I am a Worm and no man; a reproach of men and despised of the people.'
(Ps. 22. 6.).

The experiences described in the psalm far transcend those of David, as he endured the wrath of King Saul. Indeed, they describe graphically the sufferings of our Lord on the Cross.

Even in the heading of the psalm, there is an allusion to our Saviour's sorrows, as, like the hind of the morning, He is hounded by His persecutors. In His infancy, it was Herod who led the hunt. Then Satan confronted Him personally in the wilderness temptation. Eventually men, energised by Satan, conspired to drag Him to His death.

The enemies of God's Son are likened by Him to animals. "Many bulls have encompassed Me. Strong ones of Bashan have beset Me around," He said, as He hung there on the Cross. It was an apt description of the proud Pharisees who had engineered His destruction. But Satan, like a ravening and a roaring lion, was the instigator of it all. He cried to His God, "Save Me from the lion's mouth," and was heard because of His piety.

Gentile dogs encompassed Him, as the Roman soldiers took Him and impaled Him to the Tree. He cried to God for deliverance from the power of Pontius Pilate (v. 20.) and His prayer was answered when the mighty power of God brought Him up from the dead. He was rescued from the horns of the wild oxen, the savage Sadducees who refused to believe in resurrection.

In His agony, He describes Himself as a Worm, to be crushed underfoot by His enemies without thought of pity or remorse. But from that crushing, a glorious crimson flood was produced to cleanse guilty sinners and clothe them in the royal robes of righteousness.

Are we willing, in our turn, to bear His reproach and be crushed under the heel of His enemies ?

February20
The law - giver

'But seeing the multitudes, He went up into the mountain, and having sat down, His disciples came to Him, and He opened His mouth and taught them -----.'
(Mat. 5. 1, 2.).

'And it came to pass, when Jesus had ended these sayings, the people was astonished at His doctrine; for He taught them as One having authority and not as the scribes.' (Mat. 7. 28, 29.).

The King had come with the offer of His Kingdom. Now He sits on His 'mountain - throne' and teaches His disciples the laws of that Kingdom.   His concern is not for political issues, but for the ethical and moral principles which govern the Kingdom. Since His people, the Jews, rejected their King and His Kingdom, these principles will not be put into practice fully until the King returns to set up His millennial reign.

He begins by revealing the secret of Kingdom happiness for the deprived, the righteous and the persecuted. (5. 1 - 12.).   Then He depicts Kingdom disciples as salt (of the earth), light (of the world), a city (on a mountain) and a lamp (in the house), (5. 13 - 16.).

He follows this by a description of Kingdom laws which fulfil the Old Testament, (5. 17 - 20.), surpass the Mosaic law (5. 21 - 48) in matters such as murder, adultery, perjury, retaliation and love. (5. 21 - 48.).   His laws regulate Kingdom practice in giving, praying, fasting, saving, eating, drinking, clothing, judging, asking (the Father) and everything. (6. 1 - 7, 11.).

Finally, there are contrasts in Kingdom truth.   Narrow and wide gates and ways; False prophets and wolves like sheep: Good and bad fruit and trees: False and true servants: Wise and foolish builders using good and bad foundations: The Authoritative teaching of Jesus and that of the scribes. (7. 12 - 29.).   Small wonder that the people were astonished at His doctrine.   Such a standard of perfection was unattainable (5. 48.), except by the King.

Have we applied for the King's pardon and received power to serve Him ?

The angel of Jehovah to Hagar

'And she called the Name of Jehovah that spake unto her, Thou God seest me; for she said, "Have I also here looked after Him that seest me." ' (Gen. 16. 13.).

'And God heard the voice of the lad' and the Angel of God called to Hagar from heaven and said unto her, "What aileth thee, Hagar? Fear not, for God hath heard the voice of the lad where he is." ' (21. 17.).

Here is the first mention of the Angel of Jehovah in the Old Testament. Evidently, He was a divine Person, none other than God appearing in human form. Therefore these manifestations are known as Christophanies or Huiophanies, that is, pre-incarnate appearances of the Son of God.

Sarai, Abram's wife, had given her maid-servant Hagar to him to build her a family. But when Hagar (meaning flight or wanderer) conceived, she despised her mistress, who reacted by mistreating her. Hagar, true to the meaning of her name, fled. The Angel of Jehovah found her near a spring in the desert and told her to return to her mistress. He also said that she would bear a son and instructed her to name him Ishmael (meaning 'God hears') because the Lord had heard of her misery. He also promised that her descendants would be numerous.

About sixteen years later, Hagar was again a fugitive in the desert but this time her son was with her. Again, the Angel of Jehovah came to her aid, calling to her from heaven, and opening her eyes to see a well of water. God's promise was re-iterated that He would make Ishmael into a great nation. The promise was fulfilled and many claim descent from Ishmael today.

Jehovah's Messenger had a deep concern for Hagar, the slave-girl and her son. Indeed, God was with the lad as he grew up. That same God cares deeply for us - enough to truly become human and die for us.

Can you, by faith say, as Hagar said, "I have seen the One Who sees me." ?

February22
The Lord Jesus Christ

' "So if God gave them the same gift as He gave us, who believed on the Lord Jesus Christ; what was I, that I could withstand God." ' (Acts 11. 17.).

This is one of more than fifty occurrences of our Saviour's compound Name in the New Testament Scriptures.

His divine Name is Lord, which is the equivalent of the Hebrew Name of God, Jehovah. His human Name is Jesus, which reminds us of His Saviourhood. Christ or Messiah is His official Name, as the One Whom God appointed and anointed to accomplish the work of Prophet, Priest and King, in that precise order.

When we place our confidence in the Lord Jesus Christ as our Saviour, then, instantly, we become the recipients of all God's blessings in Him. We receive grace, mercy and peace from God, the Father, and our Lord Jesus Christ. Judgment is what we deserve from God because of our sins against Him. But mercy withholds what we deserve: In contrast, God's grace gives us what we don't deserve, namely, eternal life in Jesus Christ our Lord. We then have the assurance that nothing can separate us from the love of God which is in Christ Jesus our Lord.

Through our Lord Jesus Christ, we have peace, joy and eternal life, all because of the Cross of our Lord Jesus Christ. God who gives us the victory through our Lord Jesus Christ. He has called us into fellowship with His Son, Jesus Christ our Lord.

Meantime, we await the coming and appearing of our Lord Jesus Christ, when our salvation will be completed. Then we shall share in the glory of our Lord Jesus Christ. We can use the salutation of the Apostle Paul when he wrote, 'Grace to all who love our Lord Jesus Christ with an undying love.'

Do we pay attention to the sound words of our Lord Jesus Christ? (1 Tim. 6.3.).

February 23

'Therefore, thus saith the Lord God, "Behold, I lay in Zion for a foundation a Stone, a tried Stone, a precious corner Stone, a sure Foundation; he that believeth shall not make haste." ' (Isaiah 28.16.).

The context surrounding the above verse describes two contrasting men, Satan's man and God's Man. The man empowered by Satan is called 'Death and Sheol' (see Rev. 6.8.), while the Man chosen by God is 'the Resurrection and the Life', our Lord Jesus Christ. The national leaders, based in Jerusalem, will make a covenant with the coming prince, the Antichrist. But this agreement will be based on lies and deceit.

In contrast, Adonai Jehovah introduces His plan, which is centred in a Stone, none other than His Son, our Lord Jesus. This Stone had first to be tested in every vicissitude of life, by God, Satan and men. The Stone emerged from this trial faultless and flawless. The Stone then had to be laid in Zion as the Foundation of a building God was planning: This was done at Golgotha when the costly cornerstone of the Building was well-laid. The Resurrection provides a sure foundation for the Building of God, the Church. Faith in Christ, the Living Stone, adds us, as living stones, to the Building founded on Him. We shall never be moved from that secure place. All else that is not His, all liars and deceivers, will be swept away at His return to the earth. There will be no hiding place in that Day.

Meantime, the Building continues to grow until the penultimate stone is added. Then the final Capstone will be brought out with shoutings: "Grace, grace unto it!" for our Lord shall have the pre-eminence as First and Final Stone in God's Building, the Church.

Are you waiting for the second advent of the Stone ?

February24

'And when He was gone forth into the way, there came one running, and kneeled to Him and asked Him, "Good Teacher, what shall I do that I may inherit eternal life?" '
(Mk. 10.17.).

This young man appeared to be sincere in his request regarding eternal life. He was in a hurry - he came running; he was reverent - he was kneeling to Jesus; he came to the right Person - God's unique Son; he addressed our Lord as 'good teacher' - most appropriate in the circumstances, but he didn't realise how appropriate!

This is why Jesus said to him, "Why do you call Me good? There is none good but One, only God." The young ruler could not accept the implication, that he was face-to-face with Immanuel, God with us. So, in his reply to our Lord, he omitted the 'good' and called Him 'teacher' only, (v. 20).

As a Teacher, the Lord Jesus surpassed all others. He was, and is, the very embodiment of wisdom. He taught as One with authority, and not as the scribes of His day. His teaching was profound yet simple. The common people heard Him gladly. Also, in His goodness, He was perfect. At the outset of our Lord's public ministry, the Father declared His delight in His Son.

This episode in Mark 10 illustrates our Lord's teaching technique. He responded exactly to the approach made by the young man. He wanted to do something to inherit eternal life. So Jesus said, in effect, "You must keep the Law." But no-one could do that perfectly, save Jesus only, the 'Good' Teacher. The wealthy young man showed his limitation, when challenged by the Lord to renounce his wealth and follow Him. His possessions were more important to him than a place in God's kingdom. He was breaking the first commandment since possessions were his god.

Do we obey the teaching of the 'Good Teacher' ?

February 25

'Jesus said unto her, "I am the Resurrection and the Life; he that believeth in Me, though he were dead, yet shall he live; and whosoever liveth and believeth in Me, shall never die. Believest thou this ?" ' (John 11. 25, 26.).

Jesus' friend Lazarus had died; the Lord had already revealed this to His disciples where they were, beyond Jordan. When they approached the outskirts of Bethany, they were told that Lazarus had been dead for four days. Mary and Martha, the dead man's two sisters, reacted differently to the news of our Lord's arrival. Mary sat in the house, while Martha went to meet the Master.

In the dialogue which followed, between Martha and Jesus, He made the amazing claim to be 'the Resurrection and the Life'. His claim was put to the test and proved almost immediately, when our Lord commanded Lazarus to come out of the tomb. The dead came out, bound feet and hands with grave clothes and his face bound around with a napkin. "Loose him and let him go," Jesus said to them.

A further and even more convincing proof of our Lord's claim was given some time later. He was taken by wicked men, crucified and slain. His body was laid in the new tomb of Joseph of Arimathea. After three days, He rose from the dead and appeared to His disciples. He showed them that He was alive by many infallible proofs.

The next great proof of our Lord's claim awaits His return to the air. Then, the bodies of believers of this present era of grace will be raised. Thus our Lord's words, "he who believes on Me, thought he has died (physically), shall live (physically)", shall find fulfilment. His next statement shall also be fulfilled; "and everyone who lives (physically) and believes on Me, shall never, forever, die (physically). Those believers who are alive at the coming of our Lord Jesus shall have their bodies transformed and then translated to meet Him in the air. They shall never need to die: What a glorious experience!

Do you believe this ? See John 11.27.

February26

'The Lord is my Shepherd; I shall not want.' (Ps. 23. 1.).

The author of this Psalm is David, king of Israel. But he was a shepherd before he became a sovereign. Indeed, he was summoned from shepherding to be anointed as king by Samuel, the prophet. However, in this Psalm, he changes his role from shepherd to sheep, and the Lord is his Shepherd.

We possess the key to a contented life when the Lord is our Shepherd. There is none greater than Jehovah; the covenant-keeping God, who became Jesus to be our Shepherd. But the Shepherd must become my Shepherd by an act of faith in Him on my part. Then, and only then, do I know the secret of a truly happy life.

When we accept the Lord Jesus as our Shepherd, we are then assured of needing nothing else. He gives us luscious food to eat and living water to drink from His Word. He revives our souls and shows us the right way to go. He is always there as our Feeder and Leader. There is no-one more loving than He.

Also, if the Lord is my Shepherd, I have the key to a victorious death, since, in its dark valley, "I will fear no evil for Thou are with me." It is noticeable that David speaks of the Lord here in the first person ("Thou art with me") and not, as hitherto, in the third person ("He is with me."). I, like the Psalmist, can also be assured that the Lord will guard me with His rod and guide me with His staff. He, who has defeated all our foes through death and resurrection, will give us the victory in death.

Again, because the Lord is my Shepherd, I have the key to a glorious eternity: "I will dwell in the house of the Lord for ever". There is complete assurance of absolute shelter and eternal bliss.

Can we say, then, that "Jehovah - Jesus is my Shepherd" ?

February27

'And, behold, there came a leper and worshipped Him, saying, "Lord, if Thou wilt, Thou canst make me clean." ' *(Mat. 8. 2.)*

Our Lord Jesus, while here among men, received homage from many, as was His right. At His birth, wise men came from the east to Jerusalem to worship Him. When they were led to the house, they fell down before Him and did Him homage. Then they presented to Him gifts fit for a King; gold, frankincense and myrhh (2. 11.). Wise men still worship the King.

After the King had instructed His followers in the laws of His Kingdom, He descended from the mountain. It was then, that a leper came up to Him and worshipped Him, confident that He could heal him. The King still receives homage from spiritual lepers whom He heals.

Jairus, a ruler of the synagogue, came to Jesus and worshipped Him, beseeching His help for his twelve years old daughter who was dying, if not already dead. The Saviour raised the girl to life and restored her to her parents. (9. 18-25).

Jesus came towards the storm-tossed disciples in the boat, walking on the water. Peter had also walked toward Him at His command, although subsequently he had to be rescued by the Lord. When they entered the boat, the wind abated. Then the disciples came and worshipped Him, saying, "Truly, Thou art the Son of God." (14. 33.).

A Canaanitish woman came and worshipped Him, saying, "Lord, help me." Jesus commended her faith and healed her daughter (15. 25.).

The mother of the sons of Zebedee also worshipped Him, as she came with her request to Jesus (20. 20.). The risen Christ was worshipped by the women returning from the empty tomb and by the disciples who met with Him on the mountain. (28. 9, 17.).

How and when do we worship the King ?

February 28

'And Jehovah appeared unto him by the oaks of Mamre; and he sat in the tent door in the heat of the day.' (Gen. 18. 1.).

Abraham was a tent-dweller, a stranger in a land promised to him and his seed by Jehovah-God. He had pitched his tent by the terebinths of Mamre, the Amorites, on the heights west of the Dead Sea. As he sat at the entrance to his tent, suddenly he was confronted by three 'men'. It soon became apparent that one of the trio was none other than Jehovah-God in human form, namely, a Christophany.

Rest and refreshment were quickly provided for his guests by the patriarch, now 100 years old. "Rest yourselves under the tree," he said. A veritable banquet was prepared for the visitors by Abraham, helped by his wife and his servant. First, their feet must be washed with water and then the meal was served.

There were bread cakes, baked by Sarah from 3 'seahs' (about 20 litres) of fine flour; a tender, choice calf with thick and sweet milk to drink. They partook of what was prepared for them 'under the tree.' But now God has found eternal rest and satisfaction, as we have, 'under the Tree', the Cross of Jesus.

After the provision came the promise of a son. Sarah was in the tent door when she heard that she would have a son, and she laughed within herself. Then Jehovah said, "Is anything too hard for Jehovah?" Of course, the answer is "No!" Not even life from the dead, and Sarah did conceive and bear a son!

Then God revealed to His friend His thoughts concerning Sodom and Gomorrah. Abraham pleaded with the Lord to spare Sodom even if only 10 righteous were found there. God answered his prayer be rescuing righteous Lot, Abraham's nephew, and his two daughters before it was destroyed.

How can we please and refresh our Lord?

February 29
Another king Jesus

' "These that have turned the world upside down are come hither also, whom Jason hath received; and these all do contrary to the decrees of Caesar, saying that there is another king, Jesus." ' (Acts 17. 7.).

Paul and his companions had arrived in the sea-port city of Thessalonica, where there was a Jewish synagogue.   Again, Paul took the opportunity of going there and witnessing to his fellow-Jews concerning Jesus.   He did this on three Sabbath days.

Firstly, he used the Old Testament Scriptures to explain and give evidence that Messiah had to suffer and rise again from the dead.   Undoubtedly, such Scriptures as Psalms 2, 16, 22, and Isaiah 53 would come to mind.   The Jews had a problem with the two views of Messiah presented in the Old Testament; a Messiah suffering and a Messiah reigning.   So some concluded that there must be two Messiahs.   Even John Baptist in prison asked the question, "Art thou he who should come or do we look for another?"

Then the apostle claimed that Jesus of Nazareth was none other than the Messiah. He, God's Anointed, had suffered death for our sins and had risen from the tomb. Saul of Tarsus had seen that Blaze of Light and heard that Voice of Love on the Damascus road. Now, He is a Sovereign at the right hand of God, waiting to return as reigning Messiah on the earth.

So Paul's accusers were right when they charged the Lord's servants of claiming that there is another Emperor of a different kind to Caesar. In this present era, our Lord's kingdom is a spiritual and heavenly one, which all who own His sovereignty can enter by faith in Him. His is a kingdom of love and light.

Do we walk worthy of God Who calls us into His kingdom and glory?
(1 Thes. 2. 12.).

March 1

'And I said, "Who art Thou, Lord?" And He said, "I am Jesus whom thou persecutest."
' (Acts 26.15.).

Paul the apostle was a prisoner of Rome in Caesarea by the sea. A new procurator, Portius Festus, had been appointed. On being summoned into his presence for judgment, Paul, as a Roman citizen, appealed to Caesar as the ultimate human judge.

Some days later, king Agrippa and his sister Bernice were paying a courtesy call on the new procurator. Festus discussed Paul's case with the king and expressed a wish to hear Paul. The next day, Paul was brought before the dignitaries and given permission to speak.

Paul gave a brief account of his early days as a devout Pharisee. Then he described how he was convinced that he ought to do all that was possible to oppose the name of Jesus of Nazareth. Old Jacob's prophecy concerning his son Benjamin was mirrored in Saul, a Benjamite. He was like a wolf, breathing out threatenings and slaughter against those of 'the Way'. (Gen. 49.27.).

But on the road to Damascus, he saw that Light from heaven, brighter than the sun, and heard that Voice in Aramaic, saying, "Saul, Saul, why do you persecute Me?" In that instant, Saul knew that Jesus, the Crucified, was alive and risen from the dead; from that moment his life was yielded up to serve the Saviour.

Thus, from the beginning of his spiritual career, he was made aware of the bond between Christ and Christians, between the Head and the Church, the mystical body of Christ. Saul was persecuting the saints, but Jesus said, "You are persecuting Me!" The apostle Paul became the foremost proponent of this truth regarding Christ and the Church in the New Testament epistles.

Are we fully aware of this fact, that any action against a saint on earth is also felt by the Saviour in heaven?

March 2
The hiding place

'Behold, a king shall reign in righteousness, and princes shall rule in judgment; and a Man shall be as an hiding place from the wind, and a covert from the tempest; as rivers of water in a dry place, as the shadow of a great rock in a weary land.'
(Isa. 32. 1,2.).

This passage looks forward to a time of peace and prosperity on earth for God's earthly people, Israel (vs. 16-18.). The King is easily identified as our Lord Jesus Christ, as He comes to set up His millennial kingdom on earth. He alone, as the heavenly Melchisedek, can reign in righteousness. But our Lord will have others with Him during this time. He gave this promise that, "you who have followed Me, in the regeneration, when the Son of Man shall sit down upon His throne of glory, you also shall sit upon twelve thrones, judging the twelve tribes of Israel."
(Mat. 19. 28.). So princes shall rule justly, and the saints will judge the world.
(1 Cor. 6. 2.).

In that day, each will be like his Lord, giving shelter and succour to the needy. But, pre-eminently, He is the true Hiding Place from the wind of adversity, even now. There was no refuge for Him, when exposed to the awful storm of God's judgment on the Cross. He was willing to endure and exhaust that tempest, so that we might find eternal safety and security in Him.

As in that day to come, so now, we who are the King's servants can offer refuge and shelter to others, who are battling against the storms of life. More than that, the Saviour said that those who believe in Him shall supply streams of living water to the thirsty souls around them. (John 7. 38.).

Have you sought refuge in Christ and, as a consequence, are you offering that Hiding Place to others?

March 3

'And Jesus answered and said unto him, "What wilt thou that I should do unto thee?"
The blind man said unto Him, "Lord, (i.e. Rabboni), that I might receive my sight." '
(Mark 10. 51.).

Our Lord Jesus was passing through Jericho. He was on His way to Jerusalem for the last time, to suffer and die there on a Cross outside its walls.

Because of its pleasant site in the Jordan valley, Jericho was a very desirable city in which to live. Indeed, it is named 'the city of palm trees' in the fifth book of Moses (Deuteronomy). It is reckoned that about 12,000 priests lived there, out of a total population of around 100,000. But here was a different kind of Priest on His way through Jericho, 'to give His life a ransom for many'. He alone could offer Himself to God as a perfect sacrifice for sins.

Mark, the Gospel writer, then introduces us to a blind beggar, Bartimaeus, the son of Timaeus. In Aramaic, Timaeus means 'unclean', while in Greek it means 'esteemed'. So the 'son of the unclean' can become the 'son of the esteemed'
through an encounter with Jesus, the Son of Man, the Son of David.

The continual cry of Bartimaeus for mercy is heard by Jesus, Who stands still and summons him. Now he must express exactly what he wishes the Lord to do for him. This he does, giving Jesus the most reverential title he knew: "Rabboni, that I may see." (At that time, the titles given to teachers were, in ascending order of rank, Rab, Rabbi, Rabban and Rabboni.)

The blind man was acknowledging Jesus to be his Lord and Master. This act of faith resulted in his salvation. He received his sight and followed Jesus in the way. We too who are blinded by sin and the sons of the unclean, can be given spiritual sight and become sons of esteem; indeed, sons of God and heirs of salvation, by faith in Rabboni, our Lord and Master.

Do we recognise the Risen Christ as our 'Rabboni'? (John 20. 16.).

March 4
The sympathetic Son of God

'When Jesus therefore saw her weeping, and the Jews also weeping, who came with her, he groaned in the spirit and was troubled, and said, "Where have ye laid him?" They said unto Him, "Lord, come and see." Jesus wept.' (John 11. 33-35.).

Lazarus, the brother of Martha and Mary, was dead. After some delay, Jesus came to Bethany and was met by Martha, who, in turn, told Mary that the Teacher was asking for her. Mary arose quickly, went to Him and fell at His feet weeping.

Our Lord responded to this expression of grief in complete and utter sympathy. He was deeply moved, even to the point of indignation, in spirit, as He recognised the ravages which sin had wrought in the human experience of death. In His groaning, He showed His deep antagonism to the power of evil in death. Also, He was troubled in soul, or, as the text reads literally, He troubled Himself: God became Man, A Man of sorrows Who made grief His friend. He troubled Himself, even to enter into death for us. Moreover, our Lord was moved physically, to the point of shedding tears. It is unusual for a man to weep in public, but Jesus wept. The onlookers saw the tears and concluded that they sprang from His love for Lazarus, which was surely true (v. 5.).

But there is reason to believe that even when our Lord was manifesting His grief, Lazarus was again in the tabernacle of his body. Firstly, Jesus asked, "Where have you laid him?" Secondly, at the tomb, He said, "Father, I thank Thee that Thou hast heard Me ---." Thirdly, He commanded Lazarus to 'come out' of the burial place, the inference being that he was already in the body.

Also, the Son of God knew that He had called Lazarus from a realm of bliss and purity, back into a world of sadness and misery, only to die again in a few short years. Surely, this was reason enough for the Saviour's sorrow.

Have you ever thought of how much Jesus 'troubled Himself' on your account?   See John 12. 27;   14. 1.

March 5

'Lift up your heads, O ye gates, and be ye lift up, ye ancient doors, and the King of glory shall come in.   Who is this King of glory?   Jehovah strong and mighty, Jehovah mighty in battle.   Lift up your heads, O ye gates;   even lift them up, ye ancient doors, and the King of Glory   shall come in.   Who is this King of Glory?   Jehovah of hosts, He is the King of Glory.   Selah.'
(Psalm 24. 7-10.).

This Psalm was written by David, probably to celebrate the occasion of bringing the ark of the covenant into the newly captured fortress of Zion.   The ark was the symbol of Jehovah's presence with His people.

The Psalm describes the deeds of Jehovah: Firstly, we are reminded of His mighty power in creation.   Particular reference is made to the earth and its inhabitants, all of which belongs to Jehovah.   He established the earth upon the waters, which were then unleashed at the time of Noah, and all the fountains of the great deep burst forth.

Then David re-iterates the question of the men of   Beth-shemesh when they looked into the ark of Jehovah and He smote them (1 Sam. 6. 19,20.).   "-----, and who shall stand in His holy place?"   Only Jehovah-Jesus can attain to God's perfect standard, with His moral purity in consecration to His Father.   His righteousness was vindicated by His resurrection out from among the dead.   But, He has also a progeny, who, Jacob-like, cling to Him, claim His grace and seek His face.

Lastly, we have Jehovah-Jesus exercising His martial power in conflict as He returns with His saints to vanquish all His foes and set up His millennial kingdom.   Who is this King of Glory Who enters the ancient gates of Jerusalem as Victor?   None other than Jehovah of hosts, strong and mighty in battle.

Have you sought the face of Jesus, King of glory, and entered within the circle of His favour?

March6

'And, behold, there came a leper and worshipped Him, saying, "Lord, if Thou wilt, Thou canst make me clean."   And Jesus put forth His hand, and touched him, saying, "I will; be thou clean."   and immediately his leprosy was cleansed.'
(Mat. 8. 2, 3.).

In his approach to Jesus, the leper addressed Him as Lord, thus showing his reverence and respect for the Saviour.   But the Greek word translated as 'Lord' in English was used in a variety of contexts in the New Testament.

A bond-slave would look upon his master as his Lord. (Mat. 6. 24.).   We, as bond-slaves of   Jesus Christ, willingly recognise Him as our Lord.   The apostle Paul described himself in this way.

The owner of a vineyard was called its lord. (Mat. 20. 8.).   It was his possession and property.   In a spiritual sense we belong to our Lord Jesus, Who has bought us by His blood and made us His own.   In this context too, He is Lord.

When the chief priests and Pharisees asked Pilate, the Roman governor, to make the burial place of our Lord Jesus secure, they addressed him as Lord.   (Mat. 27. 63.).   Even the Roman emperor was called Lord by his subjects. (Acts. 25. 26.).   We, as subjects of the King of Kings, delight to call Jesus Lord.

But, at the highest level, the title was used of God.   For example, John Baptist is described as the voice of one crying in the wilderness, "Prepare ye the way of the Lord." (Mat. 3. 3.).   The Old Testament quote is from Isaiah 40. 3., where Jehovah, the special Name of God, is used.   Thus 'Jehovah' in Hebrew is translated 'Lord', with the text clearly referring to Jesus, the Messiah.   Later on, in the days of the early church, this fact was attested to again and again in the literature, that Jesus is Jehovah-Lord. (Rom. 10. 9; Phil. 2. 11.): Perfect Humanity in absolute Deity.

Have you confessed that Jesus, risen from the dead, is LORD ?
What eternal consequence follows?

March 7

The angel of Jehovah on mount Moriah

'And the Angel of Jehovah called unto him out of heaven and said, "Abraham, Abraham:" And he said, "Here am I." And He said, "Lay not thine hand upon the lad, neither do thou anything unto him; for now I know that thou fearest God, seeing thou hast not withheld thy son, thine only (son) from Me." ' (Gen. 22. 11, 12.).

God had fulfilled His promise to Abraham and had given him a son, Isaac, through Sarah, his wife. Now that same son, his only one, whom he loved, was lying bound on the wood of an altar built by his father on Mount Moriah.

But this had been the explicit command of God to Abraham, in this supreme test of his faith in God. Abraham had obeyed God's command implicitly. Now Isaac, although in the full vigour of youth, had allowed his father to take him, bind him, and lay him on the altar.

Then, as Abraham reached out for the knife to slaughter his son, the Angel of Jehovah called to him from heaven "Abraham, Abraham! Do not lay a hand on the lad and do nothing to him; for now I know that you reverence God, since you have not withheld your son, your only son from Me." It is therefore apparent from this statement that the Angel of Jehovah is God; and from other considerations, there is reason to believe that He is God, the Son. And He knew that He must walk up that same mountain many centuries later, in Manhood, carrying a wooden Cross, to become the Lamb of God's providing.

The outcome of the incarnation, death and resurrection of God's Son is seen in the second statement of the Angel of Jehovah to Abraham. "In thy Seed, shall all the nations of the earth be blessed."

Are you enjoying the blessings of salvation, through faith in Abraham's Seed, the Son of God ?

March 8
The heavenly vision

' " *Whereupon O King Agrippa, I was not disobedient unto the Heavenly Vision, but showed first unto them of Damascus and at Jerusalem and throughout all the coasts of Judaea and then to the Gentiles, that they should repent and turn to God, and do works meet for repentance." ' (Acts 26. 19,20.)*

What was this 'Heavenly Vision' which Saul of Tarsus saw on the Damascus highway? Luke, the narrator, describes it as a light from heaven shining round about Saul. (Acts 9.3.) In his defence before the Jews in Jerusalem, Paul speaks of it as a great light. (22. 6.). Here, in Caesarea, he tells king Agrippa that the light was "above the brightness of the sun, shining round about me and my companions". The event took place when the sun was at its zenith.

Saul was given a glimpse of the glory of the ascended Christ, and he fell to the ground, blinded.

The Heavenly Vision was also vocal and verbal. This Person Whom Saul was persecuting likened him to an obdurate ox which was refusing to obey its owner's commands. "It is hard for you to kick against the goads". Having revealed His identity in answer to Saul's query, the Lord Jesus gave Saul certain instructions. The Lord had appeared to him for a particular purpose; to appoint him as a servant and a witness of what he had seen of the Lord and what He would later reveal to him. In this commission, there was also the promise of deliverance from both Jews and Gentiles.

Saul's response to the revelation was complete and enduring: He was not disobedient to the 'Heavenly Vision'. With God's help, he remained faithful, right on to the end of His life.

How does our obedience compare with that of Paul, we who have the same revelation? (Heb. 2. 9.).

March 9

' "Behold My Servant, Whom I uphold; Mine Elect, in Whom My soul delighteth. I have put My Spirit upon Him: He shall bring forth judgment to the Gentiles" '.
(Isa. 42. 1.).

Other servants of Jehovah-God have already been mentioned by Isaiah in his prophecy, such as king David (37. 35.) and the nation Israel (41. 8.). These, and all others, are eclipsed by Jehovah's perfect Servant, our Lord Jesus Christ. He is the glorious Subject in this Servant-Song, the first of four in the book of Isaiah. The others are found in 49. 5,6; 50. 4-10 and 52. 13 to 53. 12, respectively. Matthew in his Gospel (Mat. 12. 17-21) quotes from Isaiah 42. 1-4, and shows that it is a prophecy concerning our Lord Jesus.

Firstly, Jehovah introduces His Servant as His chosen One whom He upholds. His whole being delights in Him. The baptism of our Lord Jesus in Jordan immediately springs to mind, with subsequent events. The Father's approbation of the Servant-Son, and the descent of the Spirit as a Dove alighting on Him.

Then the Servant's mission is mentioned briefly. "He will bring forth judgment (or justice) to the nations." The fulfilment of this awaits the return of the Servant-Sovereign to earth, to rule with an iron sceptre over the nations.

Next, the Servant's method is described. Initially, His work is characterised by grace and gentleness, not bruising the broken reed nor quenching the smoking flax in the lamp. Finally, His work is characterised by justice and judgment. He, Who patiently endured the judgment and wrath of God against sin on the Cross, "will ı ot fail (i.e. burn dimly) nor be discouraged (i.e. bruised like a reed) until He establishes justice on earth", at His return. "The coastlands will wait expectantly for His instruction".

Do we, presently, follow the instructions of Jehovah's gentle Servant, as we hear His voice in the quietness of our heart ?

March10

' "Watch therefore; for ye know not when the Master of the House cometh, at evening or at midnight, or at the cock-crowing or in the morning; lest coming suddenly He finds you sleeping." ' (Mark 13. 35, 36.).

The Master, or Lord, of the House is Jesus, our Saviour.   After His death and resurrection,   He went on a journey back to His Father in Glory.   The House, or Household, is the true church, the company of the redeemed.

We are His bond-slaves, bought by His precious blood and pledged to serve Him.   He has given to us the authority to act on His behalf in the House.   Each of us has a task to do, which the Lord has assigned to us.   When we received the gift of eternal life, by faith in our Lord Jesus, we also were endowed with God-given abilities.   These were given for the benefit of the church, the family of God.   It is our responsibility to discover our spiritual gifts and use them for the building up of the church.

Our Lord makes special mention here of the door-keeper.   Obviously, his task was to check the credentials of those seeking admittance, and, more importantly, to recognise and welcome the Master at His return.   The door-keeper must therefore be alert and vigilant at all times, especially during the hours of darkness.   The Lord Jesus exhorts us to watch for Him, as the darkness increases and then as the dawn approaches.   He is coming as the Bright and Morning Star to guide His own to Glory and, subsequently, as the Sun of Righteousness to rule the world.

The Lord warns against the danger of being (spiritually) asleep when He returns. Paul re-iterates the warning: 'It is already the hour for you to wake up out of slumber, because our salvation is nearer now than when we first believed.'
(Rom. 13. 11.).

When the Lord of the House returns, will He find us watching and working for Him ?

March 11

'And one of them, named Caiaphas, being the high priest that same year, said unto them, "Ye know nothing at all nor consider that it is expedient for us, that one man should die for the people, and that the whole nation perish not." And this spake he not of himself; but being high priest that year, he prophesied that Jesus should die for the nation; and not for that nation only, but that also He should gather in one the children of God that were scattered abroad.' (John 11. 49-52).

When news of the raising of Lazarus reached the Jewish rulers in Jerusalem, they quickly convened a council meeting. Both the Sadducees and the Pharisees were alarmed at the miraculous things which Jesus was performing. They were concerned for their own self-interest. "The Romans will come and take away both our place (the Temple) and our nation," they said. Self-interest can easily displace interest in the things of the Lord.

Then Caiaphas, the high priest for that year, gave his judgment on the matter. Although he was not aware of it, he was prophesying. To save the whole nation, one man must die, he said in effect. God used this man to utter such words, just as He did with Balaam (Nu. 22. 38.), with this great difference. Balaam was a heathen diviner; Joseph Caiaphas was a Jewish high priest, a son of Aaron, the son of Levi. But he prophesied of another Priest, of a higher order, that of Melchisedek, Who is also Prophet and Prince, and the Lamb of God, Who took away the sin of the world.

John, the evangelist, adds his own foot-note to the prophecy. He explains that Christ's death was not only for the Jews but also the Gentiles; that there would be one flock and one Shepherd.

Can you make this confession: "I am a guilty sinner, but Jesus died for me"?

March12

'Deliver me not over into the will of mine enemies; for false witnesses are risen up against me, and such as breathe out cruelty.' (Psalm 27. 12.).

'False witnesses did rise up; they laid to my charge things that I knew not. They rewarded me evil for good to the spoiling of my soul.' (Psalm 35. 11, 12.).

To slander someone is to give a false or malicious report about that person. In Scots law, it matters not whether the defamation is spoken or written - it is still slander.

David was fleeing for his life before King Saul and three thousand men chosen from all Israel. David and his men were in the inner recesses of a cave when Saul also entered. Despite his men's protestations, David spared Saul but cut off the edge of the king's robe. Later, when confronting Saul with the evidence of his integrity, David said to him, "Why do you listen to the words of men, saying, 'Behold, David seeks to harm you?' " (1 Sam 24. 9.). So David knew what it was to be slandered.

But David had a Son Who is also his Lord. Towards the end of His earthly sojourn, He too was the Subject of slanderous attack. Our Lord Jesus had been arrested and taken to Caiaphas, the high priest, where the scribes and elders were assembled. They kept trying to obtain false testimony against Jesus, so that they might put Him to death.

Literally thousands would have been able to give true testimony on behalf of Jesus, such as the nobleman whose son Jesus healed; Jairus, whose daughter Jesus raised from the dead; the centurion, whose servant was healed and many, many more. These were never sought by the Sanhedrin. But they found two who falsely accused Jesus of saying that He was able to destroy the Temple and rebuild it in three days. Of course, our Lord was referring to His own body in this statement which they were quoting inaccurately. (John 2. 19.).

Are we willing to be true witnesses to Jesus? (Acts 1. 8.).

March 13

A man under authority

'And the centurion answered and said, "Lord, I am not worthy that Thou shouldest come under my roof; but speak the word only and my servant shall be healed.   For I also am a man under authority, having soldiers under me; and I say to this man, "Go," and he goeth, and to another, "Come," and he cometh; and to my bond-servant, "Do this, and he doeth it." ' (Mat. 8. 8, 9.) See also Luke 7. 8.

A centurion in the Roman army commanded 100 men;   he was under the authority of a tribune. (Acts. 21. 31.).   Favourable mention is made of centurions in the New Testament.   The centurion at the Cross confessed Jesus to be a righteous Man, the Son of God.   The centurion, Cornelius of Caesarea, received the witness of Peter and the gift of   the Holy Spirit.   A centurion called Julius treated Paul with consideration during his journey, as a prisoner, to Rome: He also protected him from being killed by the soldiers during the ship-wreck on Malta.   Our Lord Jesus commended the centurion of Capernaum for his faith.   Jesus was astonished and said, "I have not found such great faith in Israel".

This centurion had come to realise that Jesus was also a Man under authority, the ultimate authority of heaven and therefore fitted to exercise authority on earth.   The Son of   God in Manhood continually and consistently accepted the authority of   His Father.   "I do always the things that please Him," He said: Even if it meant laying down His life, which it did.   He had authority to lay it down and to take it up again. He had received this commandment from His Father.   He said to the Father in the garden of Gethsemane, "Not My will but Thine be done" and He accomplished that, in His death on the Cross.   Now risen from the dead, He possesses all authority in heaven and on earth.

How does our faith in the Man with authority compare with that of the centurion of Capernaum ?

March 14

'And Isaac went out to meditate in the field at the eventide; and saw and, behold, the camels were coming; and Rebeka lifted up her eyes and when she saw Isaac, she lighted off the camel.' (Gen. 24. 63, 64.)

Much of the experience of our Lord Jesus is pre-figured in the life of Isaac. Both sons were named by God before they were born. Both their conceptions were contrary to nature since Sarah, the mother of Isaac, was past child-bearing, and Mary was a virgin. Both sons were promised by God; in Isaac's case both his father and mother were given the promise, while the promise of the woman's seed was first given in the garden of Eden. This promise was repeated again and again subsequently. (Isa. 7. 14; 9. 6.). The birth of both sons occurred at a Divinely-appointed time. (Gen. 21. 2; Gal. 4. 4.). Isaac, whom he loved, was Abraham's only son, by Sarah. Jesus was God's unique Son, His well-beloved.

Both sons, Isaac and Jesus, were brought by their fathers to the same place, Moriah, to be offered as sacrifices to God. Both carried the wood on which they were laid in submission to their father's will. 'Abraham reasoned that God could raise the dead, and figuratively speaking, he did receive Isaac back from death.' (Heb. 11. 19.).
But there was no substitute for the Son of God, no ram caught in a thicket, since He alone could be our Substitute, dying in our place.

As Abraham did for his son, so now the Father sends His servant to find a bride for His beloved Son, risen from the dead and now in the Father's house. One day soon, the Lord will meet His bride, the church, and take us home to be with Him for ever.

"He and I, in that bright glory, one deep joy shall share:
Mine to be for ever with Him; His that I am there."

Are we longing to meet with our Heavenly Isaac, Whom having not seen, we love ?

March 15

'But not as the offence, so also is the free gift. For if through the offence of one many be dead, much more the grace of God, and the gift by grace, which is by the one Man, Jesus Christ, hath abounded unto many.' *(Rom. 5. 15.).*

The one Man, Jesus Christ, has become the Head of a new spiritual race of human beings. The contrast between Adam and Christ is clear here: Adam's act of disobedience to God's stated command has plunged the whole human race into sin, and as a consequence, death, both physical and spiritual. We were all in Adam when he sinned, and therefore we have all inherited his sin. Thus one man, Adam, became the head of a sinful, dead humanity.

But another Man, the second Man, the Lord out of heaven entered this scene. His mission was to bring God's grace in salvation to mankind; hence His name, Jesus. So the grace of God that brings salvation appeared to all men in a new kind of Humanity; perfect, pure, sinless and flawless.

The order of our Lord's two names, 'Jesus Christ' in our text is significant. Just as Adam, by one disobedient act, became head of a ruined humanity, so Jesus, by His obedient act of submitting Himself to death for our sins, was made by God both Lord and Christ, in His resurrection glory. Hence the order, 'Jesus Christ'.

What is this free gift of God's grace which is by one Man, Jesus Christ? It is a new kind of life, eternal life, received by faith in Christ, on our part. For He is the true God and Eternal Life. Just as, in Adam, we inherited an old sinful nature, so in Christ, we, by God's grace, receive a new spiritual nature. We become a new creation in Christ; the old has gone and the new has come.

Have you received the gift of God's grace, eternal life? Then thank Him for it.

March16

' "Come ye near unto Me, hear ye this: I have not spoken in secret from the beginning; from the time that it was, there am I; and now the Lord Jehovah, and His Spirit, hath sent Me." ' (Isa. 48. 16.).

Here is one of the most remarkable statements of the truth of the Trinity of God, found in the Old Testament Scriptures.

The immediate context for the above verse begins at v. 12, where Israel is reminded of the God Who called them. They are exhorted to listen to the One Who is always the Same, the First and the Last, the Beginning and Ending of all things. These titles belong to God, the Son, (Rev. 1. 17; 22. 13.), Who is Jesus Christ, the Same, yesterday and today and to the ages to come.

Israel is also counselled to remember their Creator; He established the earth and spread abroad the heavens, by His hand, His right hand. They, the earth and the heavens, are mute witnesses to the mighty power of God, the Son. All things have been created by Him and for Him; and He is before all and by Him all things cohere. (Col. 1. 16, 17.).

Then Israel must listen to a public announcement by this Same One. He has chosen and named Cyrus, King of Persia, to execute His pleasure on Babylon and on the Chaldeans. (Isa. 44. 28; 45. 1.). This prophetic word was given long before Cyrus was born: Its fulfilment is found in Ezra 1. 1-4, when Cyrus decreed that the Jews should return to Jerusalem to rebuild the Temple.

Finally, there is an even more remarkable revelation. The One who is addressing Israel in these strong terms, is also being sent on an infinitely more important mission by Adonai Jehovah, together with His Spirit! It was a mission of mercy and salvation. The Father sent the Son to be the Saviour of the world. He came to set Satan's captives free, in order that a heavenly, not earthly, temple, the Church, would be built.

Are you willing to be sent by the Son on missions of mercy?

March 17
The smitten shepherd

'And Jesus saith unto them, "All ye shall be offended because of Me this night; for it is written, 'I will smite the Shepherd, and the sheep shall be scattered.' But after that I am risen, I will go before you into Galilee." ' (Mark 14. 27, 28.).

The last supper had ended and our Lord had instituted the feast of remembrance. The Lord Jesus and His disciples, with a notable exception, were now on their way to the garden of Gethsemane. The exception, of course, was Judas Iscariot who was already on his way to meet the Jewish officials and soldiers, in order to lead them to Jesus.

As they walked towards Gethsemane, across the brook Cedron, on the east side of Jerusalem, the Lord Jesus warned His disciples of what was going to happen. They would all be 'scandalised' because of Him that night. The Greek word 'skandalon' used here is the catch of a trap which makes it fall when touched.

Then the Saviour referred to the prophetic word in Zechariah (13. 7.). God would smite the Shepherd, His Fellow, and the sheep would be scattered. God's Shepherd must become God's Sacrifice, the Lamb Who alone could bear away the sin of the 'cosmos'.

When the armed band came and arrested Jesus, the 'sheep' were allowed to go away. In all probability, all, except Peter and John, sought refuge in Bethany. So the ancient prophecy was fulfilled. But the Lord did not leave them without hope. He told them that when He had risen from the dead, He would meet them in a prearranged place in Galilee. The scattered sheep would be gathered round the Shepherd again; and it happened just as He had promised. More than 500 brethren met Him on that occasion. (1 Cor. 15. 6; Mat. 28. 16-18.)

Can you say that the Smitten Shepherd is your Shepherd ?

March 18
The grain of wheat

' "Verily, verily, I say unto you, except the grain of wheat fall into the ground and die, it abideth alone; but if it die, it bringeth forth much fruit." ' (John 12. 24.)

Some Greeks, who had come to Jerusalem to worship at the time of Passover, desired to see Jesus. They shared their wishes with Philip, a Galilean, who in turn told Andrew, who then told Jesus. Our Lord replied to these Greeks, by saying in effect, "If you really want to see Me, you must follow Me to the Cross!"

In His response, Jesus spoke of the imminent glorification of the Son of Man, and by means of His death and resurrection! Then came this solemn saying, prefixed by the double 'Amen'; that, of necessity the grain of wheat must die to produce a harvest. We see this process in nature every year. The seed is sown and in the fullness of time, new life emerges from the dead seed.

In the illustration, our Lord Jesus was describing the absolute necessity of His death. If the grain of wheat is kept intact and not sown, it will remain alone and there would be no harvest to follow. If the Son of God had remained in heaven, none of the redeemed would be there. But God planned for an abundant harvest of redeemed beings to populate heaven. This demanded the death of the Seed, the Son of God become Son of Man.

Our Lord realised fully what this meant for Him. The awful sorrow that His soul would endure as He was lifted up and left alone to die on the Tree. But He did this willingly to glorify the Father's Name and lead a multitude to glory. Heaven will be full because the Son of God emptied Himself and entered into death.

Are you part of the rich harvest resulting from the death of 'the Grain of Wheat'? Then give thanks to God.

March 19

The rock

'Unto Thee will I cry, O Jehovah my Rock; be not silent to me; lest, if Thou be silent to me, I become like them that go down into the pit.' (Psalm 28. 1.).

When the Psalmist, David, called to Jehovah, his Rock, he expected a ready response. It was not just an echo of his own voice, reflected from the Rock. Our Lord Jesus is always attentive to the faintest, feeblest cry of his saints and His response is guaranteed.

The Psalms abound with references to the Lord as the Rock. The picture which it conjures up in the mind is that of strength, security, a sure foundation, shelter, safety and even sustenance. For instance in Psalm 31, David asks Jehovah to be a strong Rock to him, a House of defence to save him. Then he writes, "For Thou art my Rock and my Fortress; therefore, for Thy name's sake, lead me and guide me." In Psalm 40 he testifies that Jehovah brought him up out of the pit of destruction, out of the miry clay and set his feet upon a Rock and gave him a firm place to stand. Again, in Psalm 62, he says, "My soul finds rest in God alone; my Salvation comes from Him. He alone, is my Rock and my Salvation, my Fortress, I will never be shaken."

Asaph, in Psalm 73, writes, "My flesh and my heart may fail, but God is the Rock of my heart and my portion for ever". The same author reminds Israel, in Psalm 78, that Jehovah brought streams out of the Rock to quench the people's thirst in the wilderness: That Rock was Christ. Again, God promises honey from the Rock, for those who will follow His ways. (Ps. 81. 16.).

But there is an all-important personal note struck again and again in the Psalms. "Jehovah, my Rock," the psalmist says.

Is the Psalmist's Rock, your Rock ?

March20

'And a certain scribe came and said unto Him, "Teacher, I will follow Thee wherever Thou goest." ' (Mat. 8. 19.)

That our Lord was a consummate teacher is beyond question.   Even His enemies, Herodians, Sadducees and Pharisees, addressed Him as such. (Mat. 22. 16, 24, 36.). Also, the Lord Jesus described Himself as such (Mat. 26. 18.), and it was so.   Prior to the incident involving the scribe, Matthew records how our Lord, with a word, drove out the spirits from the demon-possessed with a word; and teachers use words.

Jesus had given orders to cross to the other side of the lake.   It was then that the scribe approached the Lord with his offer of allegiance.   He was also a teacher of the Rabbinical law, and no doubt well-respected by all.   He must have been greatly impressed by Jesus of Nazareth, to make this decision to follow Him.   There was no apparent reservation in his commitment - he was willing to follow the Teacher no matter where.   This was a very commendable desire, but he had no knowledge of the future rejection of the Galilean Teacher by the Jewish authorities and subsequent crucifixion.

Our Lord as Teacher, instructed him.   First He gave him a lesson from Nature; that foxes have lairs and birds have nests in which they rest.   The Son of God had made that provision for them in creation but now the lesson continued; that the Son of God become Son of Man has nowhere to lay His head.   It was a voluntary act of renunciation - to leave the splendour of Heaven and become the Stranger of Galilee. Although His dwelling-place was ever the bosom of the Father, He had no fixed abode here on earth.   Here was tough, practical teaching indeed which probed the scribe's motives in seeking to follow Jesus.

'Not for ease or worldly pleasure; not for fame my prayer shall be;
Gladly will I toil and suffer: Only let me walk with Thee.'

Can we accept this kind of teaching from the Teacher?

March21
The ladder

'And he (Jacob) dreamed, and behold a Ladder set up on the earth, and the top of it reached to heaven, and behold the angels of God ascending and descending on it.' (Gen. 28. 12.)

Jacob had set out on his journey to the plain of Aram, in Syria, to take a wife from the daughters of Laban, his mother's brother. It is estimated that he was 77 years of age. During that first day, he travelled more than 50 miles of his 850 mile journey, and stopped at a place called Luz. The sun had already set when he lay down to sleep, with a stone which he had selected for a pillow.

As he slept, God graciously communicated with him in a dream. Jacob saw this ladder or stairway resting on the earth and reaching to heaven. Here was the way from earth to heaven for weary travellers as well as angels; and Jesus is the only Way - "No one comes to the Father but by Me," He said. Earthlings can only gain access to heaven through the mediation of Christ and His Cross. He is the Ladder that Jacob saw. He enables the angels to do their work of bringing information to heaven and help to earth.

Then Jehovah God repeated the promise made to Jacob's father and grand-father, with the added pledge of His Presence and protection. When Jacob awoke, he said, "This is none other than the house of God; this is the gate of heaven." He called the place 'Bethel', meaning 'House of God'.

The Lord Jesus used this episode from Jacob's history in his encounter with Nathanael. He said, "Amen, Amen, I say unto you (all), henceforth you shall see the heaven opened, and the angels of God ascending and descending on the Son of Man." (John 1. 51.). Israel will one day enjoy the mediatorial presence of the Son of Man, when He sets up His earthly kingdom.

Which ladder are you on? The One Jacob saw, or one of worldly origin?

March22

'For whom He did foreknow, He also did predestinate to be conformed to the image of His Son, that He might be the Firstborn among many brethren.' (Rom. 8. 29.)

Those who love God know that He is working in their circumstances for the saints' good and the Son's glory. They received, by faith, the Gift of the Holy Spirit, and consequently the love of God was poured out within their hearts (5. 5.). Thus, they became the recipients of Divine love. God called them, they obeyed, and were saved by His grace.

Now the apostle Paul outlines the out-working of God's purpose for the good of the saints. Seven items are mentioned, all originating in the heart of God. He foreknew and fore-ordained us, to be conformed to the likeness of His Son, and become His brethren. He called us, justified us and glorified us, as if the process was already completed. It is evident that God foreknew and fore-ordained us in eternity past. (Eph. 1. 4, 5.). Our calling, becoming the Lord's brethren, and justification took place in our individual experience in time. Conformity to the Son's image, and glorification are still in the future, awaiting the Lord's return to the air to receive from the world His own. (1 Thess. 4. 16, 17; Phil. 3. 21.). But in the mind of God, the process is accomplished, since the work of redemption is perfect and complete. Christ has died and risen and gone above to the Father's right hand; and where He is, we are also, by God's matchless grace.

Although there are, and will be, 'many brethren', yet our Lord is unique as 'Firstborn'. We have been welcomed into the family of God, and are indeed the sons of God, having received the Spirit of adoption as sons by which we cry, "Abba, Father!" But our Lord Jesus is the unique Son of the Father from eternity, and doubly so by His physical resurrection, as Firstborn from the dead.

As we follow the Firstborn, what family characteristics do we display, to demonstrate that we are His brethren?

March 23

'The Lord JEHOVAH hath given Me the tongue of the learned, that I should know how to speak a word in season to him that is weary: He wakeneth (Me) morning by morning, He wakeneth Mine ear to hear as the learned. The Lord JEHOVAH hath opened Mine ear, and I was not rebellious, neither turned away back. I gave My back to the smiter, and My cheeks to them that plucked off the hair; I hid not My face from shame and spitting.' (Isaiah 50. 4-6.)

Three different Speakers are identifiable in this chapter of Isaiah. The first is Jehovah (vs. 1 - 3.), asking the nation Israel a series of questions and reminding the people of His power. The second is Jehovah's Servant (vs. 4 - 9.), describing the path of obedience he must follow to redeem His people. Thus these two Speakers may be identified as God the Father and God the Son. The third Speaker is discerned then as God, the Spirit (vs. 10. 11.), instructing the remnant who fear Jehovah and predicting doom on the others who walk in their own way.

The Servant speaks of His dependence on Adonai Jehovah, His sovereign Lord. As a result, He was an instructed Preacher and a diligent Listener to all the Father's words. In obedience to the Father, He became a willing Sufferer, even unto death, and subsequently through resurrection, a vindicated Victor. "Behold, Adonai Jehovah helps Me," He says, "Who is he that will condemn Me?" The unspoken answer is, "No-one!" The same question is asked by the saints, (Rom. 8. 34.) with the same reply.

The true and perfect humanity of the obedient Servant is stressed here. He speaks of His instructed tongue and opened ear; His scourged back, torn cheeks and bespattered face. He set His face like a flint to endure this suffering, and far more besides, in obedience to the Father's will, and for our eternal weal.

God's perfect Servant obeyed implicitly the voice of His sovereign Lord.

Do we obey the voice of His Servant, Jesus (v. 10.) as we hear His voice, morning by morning.

March 24

'And He (Jesus) said unto them (the 'Eleven'), "Go ye into all the world, and preach the gospel to all creation. He that believeth and is baptised shall be saved; but he that believeth not shall be condemned." ' (Mark 16. 15, 16.).

The risen Christ was about to return to the right hand of God in heaven (v. 19.). Before doing so, He commissioned His disciples for the work which He expected them to do.

Firstly, the Lord Jesus told them to go. If they had stayed in Jerusalem or even Judea, the growth of the church would have suffered. Then they were to go into all the world. Hitherto they had been sent to the lost sheep of the house of Israel, and not to the Gentiles nor even the Samaritans. Now the scope of the commission is enlarged to embrace the whole world of Jews and Gentiles alike. All of humanity must be given the opportunity of hearing this vital message of God's good news.

They were commissioned to preach the Gospel; that Christ (Who is God manifest in flesh) died for our sins, He was buried and that He was raised the third day. The response to this message was all-important. Faith in Christ, demonstrated by the baptism of the believer, brought salvation: Unbelief resulted in condemnation. It is clear from many other Scriptures that salvation is obtained by faith alone, and not by works, even water baptism. But here, in the Gospel of Mark, it is fitting that the followers of God's Perfect Servant Jesus (the Subject of this Gospel) should also be obedient servants in the matter of baptism. Again, unbelief is the only criterion for condemnation, and not lack of baptism.

That our Lord's commission was carried out by His followers is clear from Col. 1. 6, 23.

Are we as diligent as these early disciples in obeying our Lord's commission?

March 25
The Lord and teacher

' "If I then, the Lord and the Teacher, washed your feet, you ought also to wash one another's feet." ' (John 13. 14.).

This double description of our Lord Jesus is set in the sequence of events associated with the 'Last Supper'.   God's Son was the Host and His disciples were His guests, although the table was borrowed and so was the guest-chamber.

Then a remarkable thing happened during the supper.   The Lord Jesus rose, laid aside His garments, took a towel and girded Himself with it.   Then He poured water into a basin, and began to wash the disciples' feet, wiping them with the towel which was wrapped around Him.   It was the task allotted to the lowest house-servant, and here it is done by the Lord of Glory.

It is a symbol of the stupendous stoop of the Son of God from Glory's heights to this world's depths, to take a bondman's place and endure a criminal's death on a Cross in love for His own.   He loved them to the uttermost!

After He had resumed His position at the table, our Lord said to His disciples,   "You call Me the Teacher and the Lord and you are right, for I am."   It was the common mode of address used by disciples of their teacher.   But the Lord Jesus, in verifying the accuracy of such a description of Himself, added to it a Divine dimension in these final words, 'I am'.   The Lord and the Teacher was none other than the great 'I AM', Who revealed Himself as such to Moses out of the bush that burned but was not consumed.

If the Lord and Teacher was willing to humble Himself in such a manner, in order to minister to others, how much more should His followers do likewise.

What is entailed in 'washing one another's feet', spiritually?

March 26
The expiring one

'Into Thine hand I commit my spirit.'   (Psalm 31. 5.).
'And when Jesus had cried with a loud voice, He said, "Father, into Thy hands I commit My spirit"; and having said this, He expired.' (Luke 23. 46.)

In his affliction, the psalmist David was able to commit his spirit to Jehovah, God of Truth.   More than a millennium later, Jehovah-Jesus, the Truth, used these self-same words before expiring on the Tree.   It is understood that Jewish mothers taught their children to say the above prayer before they went to bed for the night.   Just as some mothers even today teach their children to say at bed-time:-

"This night, as I lie down to sleep,
 I pray Thee, Lord, my soul to keep.
 If I should die before I wake,
 I pray Thee, Lord, my soul to take
 To Heaven, for Jesus' sake."

In this final saying of seven uttered by our Lord while on the Cross, He again, as at the beginning of His ordeal, addresses the Father: And having spoken these words, He expired.

Note when He expired;   it was when the work of atonement was completed and His sufferings had ended.   He had cried with a loud voice, "Finished!".   It was the ninth hour, (that is three o'clock in the afternoon), when the three hours of darkness ended.

Note, too, where He expired;   it was at Golgotha, on Mount Moriah where Abraham was stopped by Jehovah from sacrificing his son Isaac, and the promise was made that in the Mount of Jehovah, it (the Sacrifice) would be provided.   That promise was now fulfilled.

Note again, how He expired;   it was a voluntary act, in accordance with His own words,   "No one takes My life from Me I have authority to lay it down and take it again."   Our Lord relinquished His life because He willed it, when He willed, and how He willed.

What comparisons and contrasts are there between the death of our Lord and Stephen. (Acts 7. 59, 60.)?

86

March27

'But the men marvelled, saying, "What manner of Man is this, that even the winds and the sea obey Him!" ' (Mat. 8. 27.)

Another busy day was drawing to a close by the Galilean lake-side, with the crowds still thronging around the Saviour. "Let us go to the other side," He said to the disciples. So they embarked and set sail for the eastern shore of the lake.

Suddenly, a furious storm arose, with a great agitation of the water, so that the ship was covered by the waves. In stark contrast to all this commotion of the elements, our Lord was asleep. He who, as God, neither slumbers nor sleeps (Ps. 121. 4.), yet as Man, was subject to fatigue.

The disciples came to Him and awoke Him, saying "Lord, save us, we are perishing!" He was their only hope in the midst of that maelstrom which, as they feared, was about to overwhelm them. The Lord rebuked them for their great fear and little faith. In a time of trial, the psalmist David said to God, "What time I am afraid, I will trust in Thee." (Ps. 56. 3.).

Then our Lord Jesus arose, rebuked the wind and the sea, and there was a great calm. The men marvelled saying, "What kind (of man) is this ---!" The answer to their question was patently obvious. They were confronted with the God-Man, Someone possessed of holy humanity, yet also retaining absolute Deity. This same One would soon enter into an infinitely greater storm on Golgotha's summit, and rise triumphantly to rebuke all His foes, and even the fears of His friends and followers.

He who rebuked the Red Sea (Ps. 106. 9; Nahum 1. 4.) is the same One who rebuked the wind and the waves of the Sea of Galilee.

Shall we let this kind of Man calm our fears and increase our faith?

March28

' "And thy seed shall be as the dust of the earth, and thou shalt spread abroad to the west, and to the east, and to the north, and to the south; and in thee and in thy seed shall all the families of the earth be blessed." ' (Gen. 28. 14.)

During his first night away from home, Jacob had a dream. In it, he saw Jehovah standing above a ladder or ramp. He spoke to Jacob, identifying Himself as the God of Abraham and of Isaac. Then He made a series of promise to Jacob.

Firstly, God covenanted to give to him and to his descendants the land on which Jacob was lying, namely the land of Canaan. The final fulfilment of this promise awaits realisation. Secondly, God predicted that Jacob's progeny would become so numerous as to be 'like the dust of the earth'. There are about twenty million Jews in the world today. Thirdly, there would be a dispersion of Israel in every direction: This has happened, with millions of Jews in North and South America, and Russia, with substantial numbers in some parts of Europe and elsewhere.

The fourth statement promised blessing for all the families of the earth in Jacob and his seed. Such a universal blessing will only come through Messiah Jesus, at His return to reign, but resulting from His first advent to redeem.

Abraham, Isaac and Jacob will be raised to share with the Son of Abraham, the promised Seed, in millennial bliss. The faithful remnant of Israel will also be there, together with a great multitude of Gentile believers having come out of the Great Tribulation. We, too, who have believed in Christ Jesus in this era, have been blessed in Jacob's seed. We are sons of God and Abraham's spiritual seed, heirs according to promise.

What other promises did God give to Jacob in his dream that night? Which of them apply to us today?

March 29

'For I could wish that I myself were accursed from Christ for my brethren, my kinsmen according to the flesh; who are Israelites, whose is the adoption, and the glory, and the covenants, and the giving of the law, and the temple worship, and the promises; whose are the fathers, and of whom as concerning the flesh (is) the Christ, Who is God over all blessed for ever, Amen.' (Rom 9. 3-5.)

The apostle Paul now deals with the problem of his own people, the Jews, in this part of his letter (chapters 9 to 11.). He explains how God chose Israel, in the past, as a nation (ch. 9.), why He rejects them in the present (ch. 10.), and how He will re-instate them in the future (ch. 11.).

But here, he lists the great privileges conferred upon his earthly people. They are Israelites, descendants of Jacob whom God dubbed 'Israel' (meaning 'he struggles with God') at Peniel. God adopted the nation as His sons, setting them aside from all other nations. He presenced Himself among them as the Shekinah glory of the tabernacle. He made covenants with them through Abraham, Moses and David. He gave them the law to regulate their lives, both individually and corporately. He also gave them the Levitical system by which they could approach Him in worship. He gave them the promises and the patriarchs.

But their supreme privilege was the coming of Immanuel, Jesus Christ. Here, the apostle points out our Lord's true humanity and essential Deity. That Jesus of Nazareth is the Christ is beyond dispute. In this letter already, the apostle has joined these two Names together some twenty times. Also beyond dispute is the equating of the Christ with God here in our text, with His supremacy emphasised, as being over all blessed for ever.

Are we among those who will bless the Christ-God for ever?

March 30

'How beautiful upon the mountains are the feet of Him that bringeth good tidings, that publisheth peace; that bringeth good tidings of good, that publisheth salvation; that saith unto Zion, "Thy God reigneth!" ' (Isa.. 52. 7.)

This section of the prophecy (vs. 7-10) consists of three connected events, which are, in order, the messenger running towards Zion, the watchmen waiting in Zion and Jehovah redeeming Zion.

The messenger racing towards the city is described as having beautiful feet. This is because of the function they are performing. They are bringing the herald with his message of good news. Although John Baptist performed this function, preparing the way for Jesus-Messiah, He was pre-eminently the Bearer of glad tidings having beautiful feet. He had to traverse mountains of misunderstanding, reproach and disbelief as He ascended Mount Zion and eventually the hill Calvary, where they impaled His beautiful feet on a Cross.

But the message was delivered; a message of peace through the blood of His Cross, of well-being and salvation for all who believe on Him. This message must be brought to all mankind in this present era, too, by others who have beautiful feet, but for them, there is no mention of mountains! (Rom. 10. 15.)

In a future day, after Jehovah has chastised His earthly people, the Jews, and Jerusalem has drunk from His hand the cup of His anger, He will send His Messenger again to Zion with this message of peace and salvation. Then the watchmen will rejoice as they see with their own eyes Jehovah returning, redeeming and reigning: That same One with beautiful feet. All the nations will see His mighty power in that day of deliverance and His people, Israel, will be comforted.

How beautiful are your feet?

March 31
The risen one

'And the angel answered and said to the women, "Fear not, for I know that you seek Jesus Who was crucified. He is not here, for He is risen, as He said. Come, see the place where the Lord lay," ' (Mat. 28. 5,6)

Faithful women made their way to the tomb, as the first day of a new week began to dawn. The included Mary Magdalene, Mary the wife of Cleophas, Salome wife of Zebedee, and Joanna. They had brought spices to anoint the body of Jesus.

As they approached the garden tomb, a question arose in the minds of the women. Who was going to move the great stone away from the entrance? But when they looked, they saw that it had been rolled already. It was the work of an angel.

After he had quelled their fears, he revealed to them the tremendous truth. Christ has risen from the dead. The tomb was empty. The angel reminded the women that it was as 'the Lord has said'.

It was 'as He said' to His Father prophetically, reminding Him of His sure promise, not to allow His Holy One to see corruption (Ps. 16. 10.).

It was 'as He said' to the Jews allegorically, when He promised to raise up the Temple of His body in three days. (Jn. 2. 19.).

It was 'as He said' to His own plainly, when He told them repeatedly that He would rise again after three days. (Mk. 8. 31; 9.8; 10.34.).

What are the practical implications to yourself, resulting from the resurrection of Christ? See, for instance, 1 Corinthians 15. 20.

April 1

'Jesus says to him, "I am the Way, and the Truth, and the Life; no one comes to the Father unless by Me." ' (Jn. 14. 6.)

Here is the sixth self-description and claim of our Lord Jesus in the Gospel of John. The Lord was replying to a question put to Him by Thomas who had said, "Lord, we know not where Thou goest and how can we know the way?"

In His reply, the Saviour asserted that He is the Way, the only Way, to the Father's house and the Father's heart.   There is only one Way to heaven, the Lord Jesus Christ Himself.   He is that new and living Way into the holy of holies, which He has dedicated for us who believe in Him, by the shedding of His blood and through the rending of the veil of His flesh. (Heb. 10. 19, 20.).   This is a Way of more surpassing excellence, the Way of love and the Way of truth. (2 Peter 2. 2.).   All other ways lead downward; this Way takes us upward, heavenward and homeward.

Our Lord Jesus is also the Truth.   The truth is not only in Him (Eph. 4. 21.), but He is the embodiment of truth.   The Truth concerning the Way to the Father's house and all other matters besides.   This is in contrast to Satan, who is a liar and the father of lies. (Jn. 8. 44.).   This Truth and the knowledge of Him sets us free from Satan's bondage, to walk in the narrow way up to Glory. (v. 32).

Not only so, but our Lord is the Life.   He is the Originator of both physical and spiritual life. (Jn. 1. 4.).   He is also its Sustainer, for in Him we live and move and exist.   Moreover, He is the giver of Life, for He is the true God and Eternal Life. (1 Jn. 5. 20).   He gives His sheep that Eternal Life, those who hear His voice and follow Him. (Jn. 10. 28).   So we must follow Him, Who is the Way, know Him, Who is the Truth and receive Him, Who is the Life.

Can you say that you are one of those of the Way? (Acts 9. 2.).

April2

'Many are the afflictions of the righteous, but Jehovah delivers him out of them all: He keeps all His bones; not one of them is broken.' (Ps. 34. 19, 20.).

The theme of deliverance is prominent in this psalm. David sought Jehovah, and He answered him and delivered him from all his fears (v. 4.). Again, he called and Jehovah heard and saved him out of all his troubles (v. 6.). Those who fear Jehovah can reply on His angel to bring deliverance. It was certainly so for Elisha the prophet, when besieged by a great host of Syrians with horses and chariots. Jehovah opened the eyes of the young man with Elisha and 'behold, the mountain was full of horses and chariots of fire round about Elisha'. (2 Kings 6. 17.). Jehovah hears the cry of the broken-hearted and those with contrite spirits, and comes to them with salvation and deliverance. (Ps. 34. 17, 18.).

At this point in the psalm, David's experience is eclipsed by that of the Lord Jesus, his Son and Lord. His afflictions as He journeyed to the Cross were manifold. There was the ordeal in Gethsemane as the blood-like sweat fell from Him. Then the betrayal by Judas Iscariot and the binding by the armed band. This was followed by buffeting, scourging by Pilate, and the mock coronation by the soldiers; then the carrying of the cross and the horrors of crucifixion. But the ultimate affliction was His abandonment by God, when He laid upon His holy Son the iniquity of us all.

But further indignity was not permitted after His death. Unlike the two crucified with Him, His legs were not broken, thus fulfilling the type of the Paschal Lamb
(Ex. 12. 46.), as well as the prophecy in the psalm. Then, on the third day came total deliverance from death, hell and the grave. Hallelujah, Christ arose!

Have you cried to Him for deliverance from all your fears and troubles?

April 3

'And behold, they brought to Him a paralytic, laid upon a bed; and Jesus, seeing their faith, said to the paralytic, "Be of good courage, child; thy sins are forgiven." '
(Mat. 9. 2.)

The man's condition was helpless, reminding us of the spiritual helplessness induced in all of us by sin. (Rom. 5. 6.). His only hope was to get to Jesus, which he did, with the help of His four faithful friends. They were united in their determination to bring him to the Saviour. They surmounted every obstacle in their path, even breaking up the roof in the house where Jesus was. They had the necessary tackle to lower their friend through the hole to the feet of Jesus. But above all, they had faith that the Lord could and would heal their friend.

What transpired was beyond their expectation. When the Lord Jesus saw the faith of the five, he said to the helpless one, "Thy sins are forgiven." God is always delighted with faith and honours it.

Our Lord also saw the thoughts of some scribes who were there. Their theology was right, that only God can forgive sins, but their conclusion was wrong, that Jesus blasphemed, because Jesus is God. But forgiveness is only to be found on earth, because in heaven all there are already forgiven; and it cannot be obtained in hell since all there have rejected forgiveness.

But forgiveness of sins could only be granted on the basis of the shedding of the precious blood of God's lamb. So our Lord was sealing His own death warrant when He spoke that word of forgiveness to the man. Then the easier word was spoken; the command to rise, take up his bed and go to his house, which he did.

On another occasion, the Saviour forgave the many sins of a woman, for she loved much. (Lk. 7. 47.). Her love and His new life proved the reality of sins forgiven.

Do I show that my sins are forgiven by my life and love for the Lord?

April 4
The divine wrestler

'And Jacob was left alone; and there wrestled a Man with him until the breaking of the day, -----. And He said, "Thy name shall be called no more Jacob, but Israel; for as a prince hast thou power with God and with men, and hast prevailed." '
(Gen. 32. 24, 28.)

Jacob was returning home to his father Isaac. He had fled from his uncle Laban after serving him for twenty years. Laban pursued him, but God warned him not to harm Jacob. But now Jacob was greatly afraid and distressed; news had reached him that his brother Esau was coming to meet him with 400 men.

So Jacob devised a plan; he divided his people into two troops, so that is Esau attacked one the other would escape. Then he prayed to Jehovah the God of his fathers for deliverance from the hand of Esau. He also sent on a gift of 580 domestic animals of different kinds in order to propitiate his brother.

Having done all that he could, Jacob was left alone in the night. Then he had a very personal encounter with the Angel (Hos. 12. 4.) as God, in human form, wrestled with him until the rising of the dawn. The contest ended when the Wrestler touched Jacob's thigh-joint and it was dislocated.

Jacob was never the same after that encounter. God gave him a new name, Israel, 'God's prince'. No longer the crooked, twisted, scheming supplanter, Jacob, dominated by selfish ambition, but now a prince with God.

Jacob called the name of the place Peniel, for he had seen God face to face, and his life was preserved. As he passed over Peniel, the sun rose upon him and he limped upon his hip. It was indicative of a new phase in the life of Jacob at 97 years of age; a man with a new name and a new vision.

Have you had a 'Peniel' encounter with God, giving you a new name and nature?

April 5

'For Christ is the end of the law for righteousness to every one who believes.'
(Rom. 10. 4.).

The apostle Paul had a deep heart-concern for his own nation, Israel. He longed and prayed for their salvation. In this respect, he is an example to us to do likewise for our nation. He recommends his own people for their zeal for God, but comments that it is not according to knowledge. They thought that righteousness could be attained by keeping the law, and it was true. (Lev. 18. 5). But sin within the human heart always prevents that goal from being achieved. For who can love God with all his heart, soul, mind and strength (and that continually) and love his neighbour as himself? No one! So the law should have condemned them, as it does us, and forced them to find God's righteousness in Christ.

But Christ is the end of the law, having fulfilled it perfectly and completely in His life, death and resurrection. During His life-time, as Jehovah's righteous Servant, He magnified the law and made it honourable (Isa. 42. 21.). He said to the Jews on one occasion "Which of you convinces Me of sin?" (Jn. 8. 46.). He and sin were complete strangers, walking on opposite sides of the street. Thus Christ was the end of the moral law.

He was also the end of the ceremonial law. The blood of bulls and goats could never remove sin, but the Blood of Jesus Christ, God's Son cleanses us from all and every sin. His one Sacrifice of Himself for sins is the Substance of which all the animal sacrifices of the past were the shadow.

Now the Risen Christ can impart His own righteousness to all who believe on Him and receive Him as their Saviour.

Have you ceased from striving after your own righteousness, and received, by faith, Christ and His perfect righteousness?

April 6
Jehovah's prudent servant

' "Behold, My Servant shall deal prudently; He shall be exalted and lifted up, and be very high." ' (Isa. 52. 13.).

This word translated 'prudent is very rarely used in the Old Testament. Huram, King of Tyre, in his letter to Solomon said, "Blessed be Jehovah the God of Israel, Who made heaven and earth, for He has given King David a wise son, endowed with prudence and understanding, who will build a house for Jehovah and a royal house for himself." (2 Chron. 2. 12.)   But a greater than Solomon, Jehovah's prudent Servant has come to build a spiritual house, the Church which will stand eternally.

When our Lord Jesus was 12 years old, His parents found their missing son in the temple, sitting in the midst of the teachers, listening to them and asking them questions: All were astonished at His understanding and answers.

This prudence characterised our Lord's ministry from beginning to end. For example, on one occasion the question of paying the temple tax was raised. So the Lord instructed Peter to go to the sea, cast a hook, catch a fish and in its mouth he would find a coin to pay the tax for both of them.

During His final trials, our Lord was sent by Pilate to Herod, who asked Him many questions but Jehovah's Servant answered him nothing, in accordance with Amos 5. 13, which enjoins the prudent to keep silence in an evil time. Our Lord's prudent dealings are clearly seen during these final hours of torment: Firstly, at the hands of men, who, among other indignities, struck His face repeatedly with their fists.   Then Jehovah laid on His Servant the iniquity of us all. Because of these awful sufferings, our Lord's face and form were terribly marred.

But the Servant, Who was lifted up to die, is now lifted up in Glory;   exalted, extolled and very high.   Indeed, the highest place in Heaven is His, and He is worthy.

Are you among those who now see and understand these prudent dealings of Jehovah's Servant? (Rom. 15. 21.).

April 7

'Then said Mary to the angel, "How can this be, since I do not know a man?" And the angel answered and said to her, "The Holy Spirit will come upon you, and the power of the Highest will overshadow you; therefore, also, that Holy Thing which is to be born shall be called the Son of God." ' (Luke 1. 34, 35.)

The motive of Mary's question to the angel was unlike that of Zacharias, the husband of her kinswoman, Elizabeth. His question, "How shall I know this?", sprang from disbelief. He could not accept Gabriel's revelation that his wife would bear a son (Lk. 1. 18.): They were both too old. Therefore he was struck dumb until the eighth day after the baby was born. After he had written that the child's name should be John (meaning Jehovah is gracious!), the dumb priest's 'mouth was opened immediately and his tongue, and he spoke, blessing God.' (v. 64.).

But Mary's query was made to obtain further necessary clarification. Although she was betrothed to Joseph, they had not yet come together. The angel therefore gave the necessary elucidation. The Holy Spirit would come upon her for conception; the power of the Highest would overshadow her for protection during the gestation period. This was holy work done on Mary by the members of the Holy Trinity in order that a Holy Thing or One should be born, Who is called Son of God.

Mary never wavered in her faith, but said to the angel, "Behold the handmaid of the Lord; be it to me according to your word." She was surely encouraged by Gabriel's remark that nothing shall be impossible with God (v. 37.).

In contrast to the dumb priest, Zacharias, the two women, Elizabeth and Mary, when they meet subsequently, are able to articulate their praise to God. It has to be noted that the Holy One or Thing born of Mary was also God, her Saviour, in whom her spirit rejoiced.

Can we match Mary's faith, as she willingly accepts God's will for her, despite obvious problems?

April8

' "If you love Me, keep my commandments and I will pray the Father, and He shall give you another Comforter/Helper that He may abide with you for ever." '
(John 14. 15, 16.).

The Saviour makes the solemn promise to ask the Father to give the disciples another Comforter or Helper. This promise was fulfilled on the Day of Pentecost, when the Holy Spirit came.   But the disciples already had a Helper, as the Greek word translated 'another' indicates.   This word means 'another of the same kind', that is, of the same kind as the Son.   So the Holy Trinity is involved here. The Father gives the Holy Spirit to replace the Son, Who returns to Heaven, after His resurrection appearances are completed.

The timely help of the Lord Jesus was a feature of His earthly ministry.   For example, when the disciples encountered rough weather, during a voyage across lake Gennesaret, Jesus came to them walking on the sea.   They received Him into the boat, and immediately the boat was at the land to which they were going. (Jn. 6. 21.).

Another striking example of our Lord's help in time of need is seen when He and His disciples were leaving the Garden of Gethsemane. He said to the arresting detachment guided by Judas, "If you are looking for Me, then let these men go."
(Jn. 18. 8.).

But the supreme example of our Lord as Helper of the helpless is found on the hill of Golgotha.   It was there, while we were still helpless, that, at the right time, Christ died, on the Cross, for the ungodly. (Rom. 5. 6.).

Then, on the resurrection day, He walked with the two on the way to Emmaus.   He helped them to understand the Scriptures, and then to recognise that He was alive from the dead. (Lk. 24. 27, 31.).

Have we received mercy and found grace to help in our time of need?   (Heb. 4. 16.).

April 9
The perfect one

'Mark the perfect (man) and behold the upright; for the end of (that) man is peace.' (Ps. 37. 37.).

The structure of this psalm follows an acrostic pattern with almost each couplet beginning with the required letter in alphabetical sequence. The couplet containing vs. 37 and 38 is under the letter 'shin', this being the first letter of the Hebrew word 'Shamar', translated 'mark' in English.

The theme of the psalm is the contrast between the wicked and the upright. Each group is headed up in one individual; that of the wicked in the wicked or lawless one (2 Thess. 2. 8.) who is yet to be revealed; that of the upright in the Perfect One, our Lord Jesus Christ.

Although there were some whom God called 'perfect' such as Noah and Job, they are not to be compared with the 'Perfect Man', Christ Jesus. He is perfect in His Godhead, having all the attributes of Deity. He is omnipotent, omniscient and omnipresent. He is Love and Light and Life.

He is also perfect in His Manhood, being Holy, harmless, undefiled, separate from sinners and exalted higher than the heavens. (Heb. 7. 26.). He was perfect in His obedience to the Father and in His faithfulness to God. In His Humanity and humiliation the Author of our salvation was made perfect through sufferings.
(Heb. 2. 10.).

Also, our Lord is perfect in His Saviourhood. His was a perfect Sacrifice, well-pleasing to God, as the Lamb of His providing. Redemption's work was done, fully and finally, on the Cross, as we hear Him cry "Finished!" And redemption's price was paid in the out-pouring of His precious Blood. This Man of Perfection and Peace will have a posterity.

Will you participate in that posterity when the Perfect One will be universally praised?

April 10

'And when the Pharisees saw it, they said to His disciples, "Why does your Teacher eat with the tax-gathers and sinners?" But when Jesus heard that, He said to them, "It is not the healthy who need a physician, but those who are ill." ' (Mat. 9. 11, 12.).

There are at least 27 specific acts of healing done by our Lord Jesus, recorded in the four Gospels. He treated the complete spectrum of illness.

When John Baptist was in prison, he sent two of his disciples with the question, "Are You He who should come, or do we look for another?" Jesus answered, "Go and show John again those things you hear and see: The blind receive their sight, and the lame walk, the lepers are cleansed, and the deaf hear, the dead are raised up, and the poor have the gospel preached to them." (Mat. 11. 3-5.). This was in fulfilment of the prophecies in Isaiah. (35. 5, 6; 61. 1, 2. Septuagint).

Many other people with different kinds of ailments were healed by the Lord Jesus. For instance, a centurion's paralysed servant; Peter's mother-in-law in a fevered condition; a woman with a haemorrhage; a man with a withered hand; an epileptic; a deformed woman; a man with dropsy. There was also the healing of Malchus' ear, sliced off by Peter.

There were others in a difference category who were healed, namely the demon possessed. There was the notable case of the Gaderene demoniac, as well as a blind and dumb demoniac. There was also the healing of a man with an unclean spirit in the synagogue in Capernaum. Then there was Mary Magdalene, from whom seven demons had gone out.

Matthew gives the terse comment on our Saviour's healing ministry, 'He healed them all.' (Mat. 12. 15.).

Have you experienced the healing touch of the Great Physician in your life?

April 11
Portrayed in Joseph

'And when all the land of Egypt was famished, the people cried out to the Pharaoh for bread; and Pharaoh said to all the Egyptians, "Go to Joseph; whatever he says to you, do." ' (Gen. 41. 55.).

Many fascinating parallels exist between the experiences of Joseph and those of our Lord Jesus Christ.

Joseph was considered to be a special son by his father, Jacob, who made him a coat of many colours. Jesus was the unique Son of the Father, and declared to be so by Him. Joseph was hated by his brethren because of his revelation to them of his dreams. Jesus was hated without a cause. Joseph sought the welfare of his brethren, who threw him into a pit, then sold him for 20 silver pieces, at the instigation of Judah. Jesus was betrayed by Judas for 30 pieces of silver.

Joseph maintained his moral integrity under severe trial, in the house of Potiphar in Egypt. Jesus, the Son of God, was tempted in all things as we are, yet without sin. In all Joseph's suffering at the hands of the Gentiles, God was with him. This was also true, and more so, of Jesus.

On Joseph's promotion to a position of power, he was given another name, Zaphenath-Paneah, meaning 'Saviour of the World' (Egyptian) or 'Revealer of Secrets' (Hebrew). Similarly, God has given His Son, in His high exaltation, the Name above every name, Jesus, the Saviour, in Whom are hidden all the treasures of wisdom and knowledge. Joseph received a Gentile bride, Asenath, before receiving his brethren on their repentance. The Lord will receive His Bride, the Church, before He re-instates His 'brethren', Israel, at their acceptance of Him as Messiah.

Both Joseph and Jesus were characterised by tears. The exhortation to 'go to Joseph' can easily be rendered 'go to Jesus; whatever He says to you, do.' (Jn. 2. 5.).

In coming to Jesus, are you doing His bidding?

April 12

'But put on the Lord Jesus Christ, and make no provision for the flesh to fulfil its lusts.' (Rom. 13. 14.).

The believer's responsibility to his neighbour is being stressed in this chapter of Romans. Five simple exhortations are given, in the context of demonstrating God's love to our neighbour.

Firstly, we must waken up out of spiritual sleep, in view of the soon return of Christ. The dawn of His advent is approaching; so, secondly, we must put aside the deeds of darkness. These are catalogued in the next verse (v.13) as orgies and drunkenness, sexual promiscuity and sensuality, strife and jealousy. Thirdly, having cast aside the old garments, we must put on the full armour of light, the new attire. This armour is supplied by God and is described in Ephesians 6. 13-18. It must be appropriated by faith. Fourthly, we must walk honourably and decently, as in the open light of day. Fifthly, we must clothe ourselves with the Lord Jesus Christ.

When we were baptised (by the Spirit) into Christ, at conversion, we clothed ourselves with Christ. (Gal. 3. 27.). He became for us our Garment of Salvation, our Robe of Righteousness. Positionally, God saw us in Christ, a new creation and clothed in His righteousness. But practically, by faith, we must reckon it to be real in our experience, day by day. We must be constantly renewed in the spirit of our mind and put on the new nature, created in God's likeness, in true righteousness and holiness. (Eph. 4. 23, 24.).

Clothing ourselves with Christ means that His characteristics and attributes will be seen in us, as delineated in Colossians 3. 12 - 14. We shall have hearts of compassion, kindness, humility, gentleness and patience, and beyond all these things put on love which is the perfect bond of unity.

What kind of clothes are you wearing?

April 13

'Who has believed our report, and to whom has the Arm of Jehovah been revealed. ..... He is despised and rejected of men; a Man of Sorrows and acquainted with grief; and we hid, as it were, our faces from Him; He was despised and we esteemed Him not.' (Isa. 53. 1, 3.).

There are 5 stanzas in this Song of the Suffering Servant, each containing 3 verses. This division into five corresponds with the Pentateuch, the five Books of Moses. The verses quoted above are the first and last of the three verses, corresponding to the Book of Exodus. Here, we have Messiah taking His place with the nation, which rejects Him. The prophetic message regarding the 'Arm of Jehovah' was not acceptable to the people. They expected 'His Arm' to put on strength and shatter their foes. (Isa. 51. 9; 52. 10.). Can the 'Arm of Jehovah' be the Son of a carpenter (as was supposed), living in a lowly home in despised Nazareth (Jn. 1. 46.), despised and rejected by the respectable, reputable, religious rulers of the land?

The Paschal lamb (Ex. 12.) was scrutinised by Jehovah alone for the first 10 days of the year. So it was with God's Lamb for 30 years; He grew up before HIM! From the stump of the fallen tree of the royal house of David came a shoot, a sapling, a root from dry ground, infinitely pleasing to the Father; in contrast, the chief men of the nation esteemed Him not.

He was a Man of Sorrows; He suffered the indignity of being rejected by His own. They even accused Him of being demon-possessed (Jn. 8. 48.) and insane (10. 20.)! There was the sorrow of the unbelief of His own half-brothers (7. 5.). Then the sorrow of being betrayed by Judas, forsaken by His other disciples, and denied by Peter. All this, and more, was surely a grief to Him. But He bore it all, willingly.

What is your estimation of the Arm of Jehovah, the Man of Sorrows ?

April 14
Horn of salvation

' "Blessed be the Lord God of Israel, for He has visited and redeemed His people, and has raised up a Horn of Salvation for us in the house of His servant David." '
(Lk. 1. 68, 69.).

The word of the Lord to Zacharias, through the angel Gabriel, had been fulfilled; Elizabeth, his wife, had given birth to a son. Now, on the eighth day, the child must be named. Zacharias wrote on a tablet, "His name is John." At once, his mouth was opened and his tongue loosed, and he began to praise God. What a contrast between these words and the last ones he uttered in the temple, in unbelief at the angel's message.

His praise to God followed the so-called eighteen Benedictions. These were spoken by the priests, before the lot was cast to choose the one who would burn incense, or by the people at the time of incense-burning. He referred particularly to the fifteenth Eulogy. "Speedily make to shoot forth the Branch of David. Thy servant, and exalt His Horn by Thy salvation; for in Thy salvation we trust all the day long. Blessed art Thou, Jehovah, Who causeth to branch forth the Horn of Salvation".

The horn is a symbol of power in conquest. Joseph is described as having the horns of a buffalo. With them, he will push the peoples together to the end of the earth. (Deu. 33. 17.). Then the psalmist writes, "Through Thee (his King and God), we will push back our adversaries." (Ps. 44. 5.).

The horn is also an emblem of majesty and supremacy. Kings are likened to horns. (Dan. 8. 21; Rev. 17. 12.). At the commencement of his rise to power, Antichrist is described as 'a little horn'. (Dan. 7. 8.).

Our Lord Jesus is the 'Horn of Salvation'. He is God's power in salvation for all who trust in Him.

Do we let the 'Horn of Salvation' push back all our adversaries?

April 15
The bequeather

' *"Peace I leave with you; My peace I give to you; not as the world gives, do I give to you. Let not your heart be troubled, neither let it be fearful"* ' *(John 14. 27.).*

Our Lord is giving to His disciples His final instructions, before going to Gethsemane, and eventually Golgotha via Gabbatha. This final part of His instruction, in the privacy of the upper room, had to do with His last Will and Testament.

Our Lord's clothing was appropriated by the four soldiers on duty at the Cross; His mother was entrusted to the care of John by Him, while hanging on the Cross. At the point of death, He committed His spirit into the Father's hands. Then His body was taken by Joseph of Arimathea and laid in his new tomb.

But what legacy did the disciples receive? There was certainly no gold nor silver bequeathed to them, for there was none. But our Lord's bequest to them was infinitely more precious - His peace.

What is this peace? It is peace with God, through sins blotted out by the Blood of Jesus. It is the peace of God's Presence in the heart and mind of the believer. It is wholeness of spirit, soul and body. It is harmony with God and men; and much, much more!

Who are the beneficiaries of the bequest? Only those who believe on the Lord Jesus for salvation. Those who could find no soul-satisfaction in the world but who have found it in Christ alone.

The distinctiveness of this bequest is apparent. Our Lord Jesus has given His peace to us; that which can protect us even in the greatest storms of life: A peace transcending all that the world can offer, which is only physical, temporal and often superficial. This peace frees us from heart-trouble and fear.

Have you claimed your legacy of peace from the Bequeather?

April 16

'My friends and companions stand aloof from my wounds; and my kinsmen stand afar off.' (Ps. 38. 11.).

The historical occasion of the writing of this psalm is uncertain.   Probably it was composed by David during the rebellion of his son Absalom.   If that is so, then the sin mentioned in the psalm would be that of indulging his children and the awful outcome for himself, his family and the whole nation.

His sins affected him spiritually;   they were a heavy burden to him (v. 4).   They affected him emotionally;   he went mourning all day long (v.6.).   His sin also affected him physically;   there was no soundness in his flesh because of Jehovah's indignation, no health in his bones because of his sin (v.3).   His sorrow was compounded by the attitude and actions of his friends and foes.   His friends stood aloof from his 'plague', or 'stroke', as if he was a leper.   His foes encircled him to ensnare and accuse him. But the psalm ends with a note of hope, as the psalmist cries to the Lord, his Salvation, to come quickly and help him.

Contrary to king David, Jesus, his illustrious son never suffered for His own sins, for He had none.   No, He suffered for the sins of others.   Isaiah wrote 'For the transgression of my people was He stricken.' (Isa. 53. 8.).   This is the same word used by David in Psalm 38. 11.

During those awful hours of our Lord's intense sorrow and suffering on the Cross, where were His disciples?   They had all forsaken Him and fled when He was arrested.   Only John was standing by the Cross with Mary, the mother of Jesus, Mary the wife of Clopas and Mary Magdalene.   'And all his acquaintances, and the women who followed Him from Galilee, stood afar off, beholding these things.' (Lk.23.49.).   All this our Lord endured in order that we might never need to be afar off from Him, but that we might be with Him for ever in Glory.

How near are you to Jesus?

April 17

'And when He had called unto Him His twelve disciples, he gave them authority over unclean spirits, to cast them out, and to heal every kind of disease and every kind of sickness.' (Mat. 10. 1.)

The choosing and the making of disciples was of paramount importance in our Lord's ministry. (Jn. 6. 70.).   He appointed twelve that they might be with Him and that He might send them to preach and to heal.   The number 12 in Scripture signifies governmental completeness.   For example, there were 12 patriarchs from Shem to Jacob and 12 sons of Israel.   There were 12 judges raised up as saviours for Israel, as recorded in the Book of Judges.   Also, the heavenly Jerusalem, described in Revelation 21 and 22, is characterised by the number 12.   It was 12 foundations, 12 gates which are 12 pearls, 12 angels, as well as the names of the 12 apostles of the Lamb.

Our Lord's method of making disciples is instructive.   He appointed the Twelve to be with Him, to learn by observing how He lived, as well as hearing what He taught and seeing His wonderful deeds.   At least four of them were fishermen and Matthew was a tax-collector.   Philip seemed to show some skill in arithmetic. (Jn. 6. 7.).   Luke records (Acts 4. 13.) that the Jewish rulers realised that Peter and John were uneducated and untrained men, and they took note that these men had been with Jesus.   That made all the difference.

As the disciples (i.e. learning ones) became apostles (i.e. sent ones), they were given authority by the Lord to do His work.   What they had seen their Teacher do, they were now able to do, with His power working through them.   But, like their Discipler, they had to make the ultimate sacrifice.   If early tradition is true, ten of them were martyred, one committed suicide and only John died a natural death.

Are you a disciple of Jesus?   How do you show this to be true?

April 18

The angel who redeemed Israel

' *"The Angel Who redeemed me from all evil, bless the lads; and let my name be named upon them, and the name of my fathers Abraham and Isaac; and let them grow into a multitude in the midst of the earth." ' (Gen. 48. 16.).*

Jacob was nearing the end of his earthly pilgrimage.   He had spent the last 17 of his 147 years in Egypt. When Joseph heard that his father was ill, he went to him with his sons Manasseh and Ephraim.   Joseph placed his elder boy, Manasseh, on Jacob's right and the younger, Ephraim, on Jacob's left to receive the patriarch's blessing.   But Jacob stretched out his right hand and laid it on the head of Ephraim, and, crossing his arms, he laid his left hand on Manasseh's head.   Joseph objected in vain; his father was acting under Divine constraint.   So the younger was blessed before the elder. Scripture is full of such instances.   Jacob himself was an example of this, although he sought the blessing by craft.   Now Joseph received the blessing of the double portion (Ezek. 47. 13.); he had earned it.

In his blessing, Jacob speaks of the 'Elohim' before Whom his father walked, the 'Elohim' Who had been his Shepherd all his life long and the Angel Who redeemed him from all evil or harm, as a Kinsman would, Who was willing to pay the price of redemption.   The work of the Holy Trinity may be discerned here.   God, the Son, is that Angel-Messenger Who came to redeem us from all evil.   In order to accomplish that, He must not just 'assume' human form, as He did when He wrestled with Jacob at Peniel.   He Who is verily God must become truly human, to be our Kinsman-Redeemer.   Then the price was paid in precious Blood, poured out on the Cross.

Has the Angel, Who redeemed Israel, redeemed you from all evil?   Then thank Him !

April 19
The servant of the Jews

'For I say that Christ has become a Servant to the circumcision (i.e. the Jews) on behalf of the truth of God, to confirm the promises made to the father.' (Rom. 15. 8.).

The Apostle Paul is emphasising the unity of all believers, both Jews and Gentiles, 'that you may with one mind and one mouth glorify God, even the Father of our Lord Jesus Christ.' (v.6.). They are exhorted to receive one another as Christ had received them. The apostle now demonstrates that although the coming of Christ was initially for the Jews, it was also for the blessing of the Gentiles.

His consistent testimony, here, is in line with that of the Lord Jesus, Who said to the Canaanite woman, "I was sent only to the lost sheep of the house of Israel." (Mat. 15. 24.). Our Lord entered the sheepfold of Israel by the door. (Jn. 10. 2.). Also, when He sent out the twelve apostles, Jesus said to them, "Do not go in the way of the Gentiles, and do not enter any city of the Samaritans, but rather go to the lost sheep of the house of Israel." (Mat. 10. 5, 6.).

So our Lord came as a ministering Servant to the circumcision. He came, not to be ministered to, but to minister, and to give His life a ransom for many. (Mk. 10. 45.). This was the ultimate goal of His service, to pay the awful price of redemption by the out-pouring of His precious Blood.

In all this, the truth of God's word was maintained. Also the promises made by God to the patriarchs were fulfilled. For what purpose? In order that the Gentiles might glorify God for His mercy. Quotes from the writings of Moses, David and Isaiah are then given by Paul to prove this premise.

What helps you to accept a fellow-believer with whom you are at variance?

April 20

The servant who suffered deaths

'And they appointed His grave with the wicked men, but with the rich man in His death, because He had done no violence, neither was any deceit in His mouth.'
(Isa. 53. 9.).

This section of the Servant's Song (vs. 7 - 9) corresponds to the Book of Numbers, or 'Book of the Desert' in the Pentateuch.   It was named thus by the Jews because it described the desert trials of God's pilgrim people, fraught with failure.   In contrast, with all His trials, Jehovah's Servant never failed, being faithful unto death.

The intention of the Jewish rulers would have been to dishonour the body of Jesus by dumping it in a common grave with those of the two robbers crucified with Him.   But God had planned otherwise.   He put it into the heart of   Joseph of Arimathea, a secret disciple of our Lord, to approach the Roman governor, and beg the body of Jesus. Permission was granted, and the sacred body was taken down from the Cross by loving hands, and reverently laid in Joseph's new tomb.   Thus the ancient prophesy was fulfilled. (Isaiah 53. 9).

W. E. Vine, in his commentary on the Book of Isaiah, writes,   "The Hebrew word rendered 'death' is in the plural;   this is expressive of the violent character, not to say the comprehensive nature of His death."   Physical death results in the separation of soul from body;   this certainly was the experience of our Lord Jesus.   But, in His orphan-cry,   "My God, my God, why hast Thou forsaken Me!", there is evidence of another dimension of separation, of Christ from God, as He became Sin-offering.   This, for Him, was death.

The plurality of our Lord's death is also seen in the fact that He died for all.   But it must be understood that not all escape spiritual death   -   only those who believe in Jesus for salvation.

Can you say, "I am a guilty sinner, but Jesus died for me"?

April 21

' "And thou, child, shall be called the prophet of the Highest; for thou shalt go before the face of the Lord to prepare His ways; to give knowledge of salvation unto His people by the remission of their sins, through the tender mercy of our God; whereby the Dayspring from on high hath visited us, to give light to them that sit in darkness and in the shadow of death, to guide our feet into the way of peace." ' (Lk. 1. 76-79.)

Zacharias' hymn of praise is also a prophecy. The more general terms of the first part lead into more specific details, as he reveals his son's career. John the Baptist, as he would be known would be a prophet and a forerunner, preparing the way for Jehovah-Jesus. This was surely fulfilled in the ministry of John. Zacharias traced the source of all these events back to the heart of God, full of tender mercy and loving kindness.

It was this tender mercy of God that planned for the visit of the Dayspring from on high. The Greek word, 'anatole' translated here as Dayspring, is elsewhere translated 'Sunrise' or 'east', in the Scripture (e.g. Mat. 2. 1, 9.). Its other meaning, 'a shoot' or 'branch' is found in the Septuagint. (e.g. Jer. 23. 5.).

Our Lord Jesus is that Light Who came into the world. (Jn. 8. 12.). He was the Rising Sun Who visited us from heaven. For what purposes? To shine upon us who sat in sin's darkness and death's shadow; to show us the way of peace, and guide our feet into that way.

'I heard the voice of Jesus say, I am this dark world's light.
Look unto Me, thy morn shall rise, and all thy days be bright.
I looked to Jesus and I found in Him, my Star, my Sun;
And in that light of life I'll walk, till travelling days are done.'

Has the Heavenly Dayspring brought the dawn of a new day into your heart?

April 22
The vine

' "I am the true Vine, and My Father is the Gardener ... I am the vine, you are the branches. He who abides in Me, and I in him, he bears much fruit, for apart from Me, you can do nothing." ' (Jn. 15. 1, 5.).

Israel, in the past, was described as a vine: But the vine was cut down and burned with fire because of Israel's sin and rebellion against God. (Ps. 80. 16.). Our Lord Jesus describes Himself as the true Vine, genuine and trustworthy, fulfilling the type of Israel. He was planted in the soil of this world, in His incarnation, and was always perfectly dependent upon His Father, the Gardener. Men cried, "Destroy this Vine!", but they could not.

Now the undying life of this true Vine is shared by all who are joined to Him, that is, the branches. Just as the vine and its branches are one, so it is with Christ and His own. We who were like worthless twigs, have been grafted into the Vine, by faith in Him. We are in Christ and His life flows through us.

The Father, as Gardener, tenderly lifts up fruitless branches that have fallen, and cleans fruitful branches to make them more fruitful. Our indissoluble link with our Lord has a permanent purpose, the production of fruit, more fruit and much fruit; and what is this fruit? It is Christ-likeness: It is the manifestation of the fruit of the Holy Spirit which is the love of Christ, in all its dimensions (Gal. 5. 22, 23.); so
that joy is love rejoicing;
> peace is love resting;
> patience is love enduring;
> kindness is love touching;
> goodness is love giving;
> faithfulness is love trusting;
> gentleness is love stooping,
> self-control is love controlling.

The criterion for fruit-bearing is stated by our Lord, again and again, "Abide in Me," for without Him we can do nothing.

What must we do, as branches, to let the food flow and the fruit grow?

April 23

'Sacrifice and offering Thou didst not desire; mine ears hast Thou opened: Burnt offering and sin offering hast Thou not required. Then said I, Lo, I come; in the volume of the book it is written of Me. I delight to do Thy will, O my God; yea, Thy law is within my heart.' (Ps. 40. 6 - 8.).

Messiah is addressing Jehovah His God on the subject of animal and other sacrifices. He catalogues the major offerings as follows:

'Sacrifice' (Hebrew 'Zebach'), which embraces all the offerings;

'Offering' (Hebrew 'Minchah'), is the meal offering;

'Burnt Offering' (Hebrew 'Olah');

'Sin or Trespass Offering' (Hebrew 'Chattath'.).

Then He comments that such offerings Jehovah did not desire nor did He require. These were but pointers to the infinitely greater offering of Messiah, God's perfect Son. Indeed, the writer to the Hebrews states, with hind-sight, that 'It is impossible for the blood of bulls and of goats to take away sins.' (Heb. 10. 4.).

Then the writer quotes from the Septuagint (Greek translation of the Old Testament), which gives Christ's saying at His coming into the world, "A body hast Thou prepared Me." The Lord Jesus, in His prepared body, was willing to have His ears pierced or digged. He became the anti-type of the Hebrew slave of old, who, in the seventh year of his service, would not go out free, because of his love for his master, wife and children. So his master took him to the door-post and pierced his ear (singular) with an awl. Then he was his bondman for ever.

Not only were our Saviour's ears (plural) pierced (metaphorically) but His head, hands, feet and side also (physically), as He offered His body to God, once for all.

Does our desire to do God's will include ear-piercing?

April 24
The friend of tax-collectors and sinners

'The Son of Man came eating and drinking, and they say, "Behold a man, gluttonous and a wine-drinker, a friend of tax-collectors and sinners." But wisdom is proved right by her children.' (Mat. 11. 19.).*

Here is a most fitting description given to our Lord - a Friend of tax-collectors and sinners. It was given to Him in a derisory way by His detractors. They observed the contrasting life-styles of John Baptist and Jesus, and arrived at conflicting conclusions.

John had embraced an austere life-style. He dined on locusts and wild honey, and dressed in a garment made from camel hair. They concluded that he had a demon; they could not have been farther from the truth. Our Lord described John as being more than a prophet. He also said of John that there had arisen no one greater, born of women. He was the final witness to Messiah, in line with the prophets and the law of the Old Testament.

The people went out to John in the desert. In contrast, our Lord Jesus went into the hamlets and homes of the people, and ate and drank with them. But He displayed grace upon grace by accepting invitations from tax-collectors and sinners like Zacchaeus. (Lk. 19. 7.). What His enemies said of Him in a derogatory manner was completely true in a spiritual sense. The tax-collector was considered to be a traitor, in league with the occupying power of Rome. He was classed with other law-breakers as a sinner. Such people needed a friend and they found One in Jesus.

But Jesus, the sinner's Friend, not only came to where we were in His incarnation; He also took our place in death on a Cross of shame. Such was His humility and humiliation. He is still the Friend of outcasts and sinners.

Can you, as a sinner, claim Jesus as your Friend?

April 25

'The sceptre shall not depart from Judah, nor a law-giver from between his feet, until Shiloh come; and unto Him shall the obedience of the people be.' (Gen. 49. 10.).

Old Jacob had gathered his sons together to hear his last words. These would describe what would befall them at the end of days, at the coming of Messiah. It is the judgment seat of Jacob, which is but a faint picture of the Bema of Christ.

Judah is given the sceptre and the crown, forfeited by Reuben because of his incest, and by Simeon and Levi, because of their merciless slaughter of the Shechemite men. Jacob predicts that Judah will become the dominant tribe, from whom the royal line of Messiah will spring. This was commenced in David and culminated in our Lord Jesus, the Lion of the tribe of Judah. This line was preserved right through the Babylonian captivity and right on to the birth of Jesus, Son of David.

He was the promised Shiloh, the One whose right it is to reign, as some interpret the meaning of the title. Another source suggests that 'Shiloh' means 'tranquil', 'secure', 'successful', 'prosperous'. It is noteworthy that, at the time of our Lord's death, the Jews said, "We have no king but Caesar." They were crucifying their rightful King, the 'Shiloh' Who had come to them.

But this is not the end of the oracle. Jacob predicts that people will obey Shiloh. At His return, there will be ushered in a time of unprecedented peace and prosperity, a time of 'wine' and 'milk', a time of absolute law and order.

Have we applied to 'Shiloh' for the 'milk' and 'wine'. He alone can supply, without money and without price. (Isa. 55. 1.)

April 26

'But we preach Christ crucified, unto the Jews a stumbling block and unto the Greeks foolishness; but unto those who are called both Jews and Greeks, Christ the power of God, and the wisdom of God.' (1 Cor. 1. 23, 24.).

Christ crucified is the great central theme of the Bible.   In the Old Testament, the Cross is portrayed symbolically in many instances.   For example, it is seen in the offering up of Isaac by his father, Abraham, on Mount Moriah.   It is portrayed typically in the Levitical sacrifices, and prophetically in such scriptures as Isaiah chapter 53.

In the New Testament, the Cross is described historically in the Gospel records, then used doctrinally and practically in the Epistles;   but in Revelation chapter 5, the freshly slain Lamb in the midst of the Throne in heaven will be a reminder of the Cross externally.

The concept of a crucified Christ was a stumbling block to Jews, who expected and demanded the signs and wonders of a conquering Christ.   Gentiles, on the other hand, considered the concept of a Christ dying as a felon on a Cross as sheer unmitigated folly.

In contrast, those who are called of God, and are being saved, have a completely different view of the crucified Christ.   In Him, they discern the power and wisdom of God.   It is because they see the Cross as the means by which God can righteously reckon righteous guilty sinners who believe on Jesus: They see the Cross from God's stand-point.   Here is God's wisdom.

God's power is also released through Christ crucified and risen from the dead: Power through the indwelling Christ, to save sinners from the penalty, power and ultimately, the presence of sin.

Whose power and wisdom do we acknowledge?   Man's or God's in Christ crucified ?

April 27

'Ho, everyone that thirsteth, come ye to the waters, and he that hath no money; come ye, buy and eat; yea, come, buy wine and milk without money and without price.' (Isa. 55. 1.).

The Holy One of Israel (v. 5.), our Lord Jesus is depicted as the Divine Water-Carrier. He gives a great invitation to Israel to come to a spiritual feast, provided by Him.

The guest list for this feast extends beyond Israel to everyone who is spiritually thirsty and bankrupt. Indeed, all who are spiritually hungry and soul-dead are invited.

The menu is very attractive. On offer are waters of life and wine of gladness. (Ps. 104. 15.). There is also milk to nourish the young spiritually. The apostle Peter exhorts the saints to desire earnestly, as new-born babes, the pure spiritual milk of the word, so that they may grow up in their salvation. (1 Pet. 2. 2.). There is also bread to strengthen the inner man. This Bread came down from heaven, that one may eat of It and not die. (Jn. 6. 50.). The richest of fare is offered, so that the soul may delight itself in fatness. (Isa. 55. 2.). All is to be found in the Lord Jesus Christ, Who paid for them at infinite cost on the Cross.

The words of welcome on the invitation cards to this feast are very simple and self-explanatory. The invitation to come is given four times. The exhortation to hear the Lord's call is repeated again and again.

With the call, there is the faithful promise to Israel of an everlasting covenant, the holy and sure blessings promised to king David, ratified by the resurrection of our Lord Jesus Christ. (Acts. 13. 34.). He is God's Witness, Prince and Commander to the peoples. (Isa. 55. 5.).

How thirsty are you for the waters, wine and milk offered by the Divine Dispenser ?

April 28

' "For unto you is born this day in the city of David a Saviour, Who is Christ the Lord."
' (Luke 2. 11.)

The stupendous fact of the birth of Emmanuel, 'God with us', was revealed initially to humble shepherds. As they kept watch over their flocks, which were probably destined for sacrifice in the Temple at Jerusalem, the glory of the Lord shone around them. As the darkness of the night was dispelled by heavenly light, an angel of the Lord spoke to them. He said, "Fear not, for behold, I announce to you glad tidings of great joy, which shall be to all the people." (v.10.). What was the content of these glad tidings? A Baby had been born, none other than a Saviour, Who is Messiah-Jehovah.

Where was this Baby to be found? In Bethlehem, David's city, in accordance with the prophecy of Micah 5. 2. Under what circumstances? The humblest that could ever be imagined. He would be wrapped in swaddling bands and laying in a manger. Such an august Person in such humble surroundings! It was to be a sign for the shepherds and for all. That the One, Who created and controls the universe, would accept the restrictions and limitations of humanity, is a great wonder and mystery.

Then, it was as if the hosts of heaven could no longer keep silent. The shepherds heard them praising God for One Who would bring glory to Him, and peace to men on whom His favour rests: Peace which this One would make through the blood of His Cross.

The shepherds came in haste to Bethlehem, to see this Divine sign. They found the Babe lying in the manger.

'Veiled in flesh the Godhead see: Hail, the incarnate Deity;
Pleased as Man with Man to dwell; Jesus our Emmanuel.'

Why were humble shepherds so greatly honoured?

April 29

The omniscient one

'His disciples said unto Him, "Lo, now speakest Thou plainly, and speakest no proverb. Now are we sure that Thou knowest all things and needest now that any man should question thee; this we believe that thou camest forth from God ".
(Jn. 16. 29, 30.).

This witness of the disciples, "Thou knowest all things", is set in the final discourse of our Lord. On the following day He would die. But He had told them plainly, without proverb, that He was leaving the world and going to the Father. Hence the response from the disciples; they glimpsed in our Lord the attribute of omniscience. This, of course, is only possessed by God.

This fact is found elsewhere in the Gospel of John. Almost at the outset of the Gospel, it is recorded that our Lord Jesus understood perfectly, all (men) and what was in man. (Jn. 2. 24, 25.).

Before the feet-washing on that final Passover night, it is stated that Jesus knew that the Father had given all things into His hands. (13. 3.). Also, as He left Gethsemane later that night, it is written that Jesus knew all the things that were coming upon Him (18. 4.). He was perfectly aware of all the suffering He must endure, at the hands of wicked men and also a righteous God.

At the end of His ordeal on the Cross, Jesus knew that all things were now finished; having received a drink, in fulfilment of Scripture (Ps. 69. 21.), He said, "It is finished," then bowed His head and delivered up His spirit (Jn. 19. 28-30.).

Finally, Peter confessed to the Risen Christ, by the lake-side, that He knew all things and that He understood perfectly Peter's affection for Him (21. 17.). Jesus said to him, "Feed My sheep."

What practical effect should our Lord's omniscience have on us?

April30

'Yea, mine own familiar friend, in whom I trusted, who did eat of my bread, hath lifted up his heel against me.'   (Ps. 41. 9.).

This psalm was probably written by David at the time of his son Absalom's rebellion. It seemed to coincide with an illness overtaking David, so that he could not attend to his official duties. (2 Sam. 15. 3).   This would explain David's flight from Jerusalem, which otherwise would be completely out of character for him to do such a thing.

In that case, his familiar friend (literally 'the man of his peace') is identified as Ahithophel, who sided with Absalom against the king.   In the over-ruling providence of God, the counsel of Ahithophel was rejected by Absalom.   When that happened, Ahithophel went home, put his household in order, and hanged himself.

About one thousand years later, our Lord Jesus, the Son of David was in somewhat similar circumstances.   He too was betrayed by a close associate, Judas, and passed over the torrent Kidron. (2 Sam. 15. 23;   Jn. 18. 1.).   But, in His case, the determinate counsel and foreknowledge of God allowed lawless men to crucify and slay His Son. (Acts 2. 23.).

When our Lord quoted Psalm 41. 9, on the eve of His betrayal by Judas Iscariot, He omitted an important clause, "in whom I trusted". (Jn. 13. 18.).   Just before, Jesus had said ' "Ye are clean, but not all. For He knew who should betray Him." '
(Jn. 13. 10, 11.).

Then the Lord Jesus gave the sop to Judas (v. 26.) in fulfilment of the psalm, "he who eats bread with Me".   Earlier, our Lord had appealed to Judas' conscience
(v. 21.);   now, He appeals to his heart which remained hard and ready for Satan's entry
(v. 27.).   Eventually, like Ahithophel, he hanged himself.

How can we gain the confidence of our Lord Jesus Christ ?

May 1

' *"Come unto Me, all ye that labour and are heavy laden, and I will give you rest. Take My yoke upon you, and learn of Me; for I am meek and lowly in heart; and ye shall find rest unto your souls. For My yoke is easy, and My burden is light."* ' *(Mat. 11. 28-30.).*

God had visited His people, Israel, in the Person of His Son, our Lord Jesus Christ. He had performed many mighty miracles among them, especially in the lakeside cities, but they had not repented. Now the Saviour pronounces judgment on them.

Then, as Priest, He praises the Father. As Prince, He reminds us that all things have been delivered to Him by the Father. As Prophet, He knows the Father and is pleased to impart that knowledge to those of His choice.

Again, as Priest, He incites all who labour and are burdened to come to Him. He promises to such the gift of rest, present, perfect and eternal, bought by His own Blood at the Cross. As Prince He invites us to don His yoke, easy and light, made by Himself, the Master Craftsman, unlike those of kings Solomon and Rehoboam. (1 Kings 12. 13, 14.). He invites us to learn from Him, the great Prophet of God, by listening to the words of His lips and looking at the works of His life and death.

His was a life of meekness and humility. He chose the poverty of a peasant home in Nazareth. On one occasion, He said, "The Son of Man has not where He may lay His head." (Mat. 8. 20.). Again, He said, "I am among you as the One who serves" (Lk. 22. 27.) and proved it by washing his disciples feet. (Jn. 13. 5, 14.).

But His greatest act of meekness and humility was His Passion and Crucifixion. He surrendered Himself to sinful men, to vent their hatred against Him, without a word of retaliation from Him. He humbles Himself even unto death on a Cross. Now He is exalted.

Have you found soul-rest under the yoke of the meek and lowly One ?

122

May 2

' *"Joseph is a fruitful bough, even a fruitful bough by a well; whose branches run over the wall. The archers have provoked him, and shot at, and hated him: But his bow abode in strength, and the arms of his hands were made strong by the hands of the mighty One of Jacob; from thence (is) the Shepherd, the Stone of Israel." '*
(Gen. 49. 22 - 24.).

The Son of God is indeed both Shepherd and Stone. He said, "I am the good Shepherd." He also said, "The Stone which the builders rejected has become the head of the corner;" but He became these to Israel as an individual. The Shepherd-Stone of Israel was the Mighty One of Jacob. He was the One who strengthened Jacob's son, Joseph, in his resolve not to retaliate when evil was done to him, His bow abode in strength - it was never bent in anger.

The Lord was a Shepherd to Jacob, leading and feeding him, despite his waywardness. "He was with me in the way that I went," Jacob testified.
(Gen. 35. 3.). He was also a Stone to Israel, giving him sure and certain promises, upon which he could build his faith (vs. 9-12), just as he rested on the stone at Luz (28. 11.). He changed the name of the place to Bethel, the House of God, which has a sure foundation, the Rock of Ages, the Living Stone.

Israel, as a nation, rejected the Shepherd-Stone when He came; they set Him at nought, and crucified Him; but the time will come, at the end of their afflictions, when the Shepherd will regather Israel to their land. Then the nation will acknowledge their Shepherd as their tried and trusted Stone of Destiny.

Meanwhile, this same Jesus offers Himself to us as our loving Shepherd and living Stone.

Is Israel's Shepherd-Stone ours ?

May 3

'But we speak the wisdom of God in a mystery, even the hidden wisdom, which God ordained before the ages for our glory; which none of the princes of this age knew; for had they known it, they would not have crucified the Lord of glory'.
(1 Cor. 2. 7, 8.).

The Apostle Paul is describing here God's wisdom, namely, a crucified Christ, which was a mystery hidden before the ages began, but now revealed by God to those who love Him.

Who was this Christ? He was the Lord of the Glory. That is to say, He was and is Jehovah-God, the Inhabiter of the Eternal Glory, the Heaven of Heavens. That same One, whose glory filled the Tabernacle in the wilderness, and the Temple in Jerusalem; the One who appeared to Abram in Ur of the Chaldees; the One whom Stephen saw as he was being stoned to death, when he gazed at the glory of God and Jesus standing at God's right hand; the One whose glory blinded Saul of Tarsus on the Damascus road; the One whom our Lord's half-brother James described as our Lord Jesus Christ of the Glory. (Js. 2. 1.).

What happened to this Lord of Glory ? He was crucified as a common criminal and left to die: But it was not a great mistake. It was done in accordance with the pre-determined counsel of God.

Who did this awful deed? The princes of this age. The saints in Jerusalem, in their prayer to God, disclosed the identity of some of these princes, as they quoted from Psalm 2. 1, 2. They mentioned Herod, tetrarch of Galilee, Pontius Pilate, the Roman governor, with the nations, and peoples of Israel. (Acts 4. 27.). They had acted in ignorance: "But this is how God fulfilled what He had foretold through all the prophets, saying that His Christ would suffer." (3. 17, 18.). Then the preacher, the apostle Peter, urged upon them to repent and be converted.

What have you done with the crucified and risen Lord of Glory? Have you turned to Him from your wicked ways ? (v. 26.).

May 4

'And the Redeemer shall come to Zion, and unto them that turn from transgression in Jacob, saith the Lord.' (Isa. 59. 20.).

This Redeemer, mentioned on many occasions by the prophet Isaiah, had to be a near kinsman; and this is exactly what happened. God became Man; He had to be made like His brethren in every way. (Heb. 2. 17.).

The Redeemer came to Zion, as a Babe of eight days cradled in His mother's arms, to undergo the rite of circumcision and fulfil the law. When He was twelve years old, the Redeemer was found by His parents in the Temple at Jerusalem, in His Father's house. They discovered that He was missing on the way home after the Feast of Passover, and returned to look for Him.

At the outset of His public ministry, the devil led the Redeemer to Jerusalem, to the pinnacle of the Temple, and tempted Him to throw Himself down from there; but the Redeemer overcame the test by using the Word of God. He said, "It is said, thou shalt not tempt the Lord, thy God." (Deu. 6. 16.).

At the end of His public ministry, the Redeemer came to Zion, meek and mounted upon a donkey. As He approached Jerusalem, and saw the city, He wept over it, because they did not recognise the time of God's coming to them, and the city would be destroyed. They rejected the One Who came to them in peace and crucified Him. The Redeemer had come to Zion to pay the price for our forgiveness, in His own blood. Now, in Him, we have redemption through His blood, the forgiveness of sins.

The Redeemer will return to Zion at the end of the Great Tribulation. He will judge the nations and save His people Israel. He will come to those in Jacob who repent of their sins. Then all Israel will be saved (Rom. 11. 26.) to enjoy the millennial reign of Christ, the Kinsman-Redeemer.

Have we truly turned from our transgressions, and welcomed the Redeemer into the citadel of our heart ?

May 5

'And they came with haste and found Mary, and Joseph, and the Babe lying in a manger; and when they had seen Him, they spread the word concerning what had been told them about this Child'. (Lk. 2. 16, 17.).

All famous men enter the world as babies! It is a very humbling thought; birth is also a very humbling process.

The first child ever to be born must be special, but Cain turned out to be a murderer. He murdered his own brother. Although he was Eve's son, he belonged to the Evil One (1 Jn. 3. 12.); but 'this Child' was from the Father.

When Noah was born, his father Lamech gave him this name, which means 'rest'. The eyes of Jehovah 'rested' on Noah with favour. He was a righteous man because he believed God. He was God's instrument for the preservation of life beyond the Flood, but he failed subsequently because of his weakness for wine. There was no weakness caused by sin in 'this Child', our Lord Jesus.

Isaac was a child of promise, born when his mother was beyond the age of child-bearing, humanly speaking. In the full prime of his manhood, Isaac allowed his father Abraham to bind him to the altar on Mount Moriah. The father's hand was stayed by the Voice from heaven and a substitute was sacrificed in Isaac's place: But there was no substitute for 'this Child' when the time came for Him to be bound to the Cross.

The shepherds didn't keep these things they had heard and seen to themselves. They made known about the country the thing which had been said to them concerning 'this Child'.

Is our evangelistic zeal equal to that of the shepherds ?

May 6
The intercessor

' *"My prayer is not for them alone. I pray also for those who will believe in Me through their message, that all of them may be one, as Thou, Father, are in Me, and I in Thee, that they also may be one in us, that the world may believe that Thou has sent Me."* '
(John 17. 20, 21.)

The Lord now leads us into the Holy of Holies, as He allows us to listen to Him, communing with the Father.

His first intercession concerns Himself, that the Father should glorify the Son (vs. 1, 5.). This is the hinge-pin for all else in our Lord's prayer, which may be considered as a model of our Great High Priest's present intercessory work in heaven.

Our Lord then makes requests for those whom the Father has given Him, namely His true disciples,   He asks that they should be protected, by the power of the Father's name, from the evil one. (vs. 11, 15.). Also, He requests that the Father   will   set them   apart   by   the truth of   His word. (vs. 17, 19.).

Then our Lord prays for the unity of all believers, just as there is absolute unity between the Father and the Son. (vs. 21-23.). His desire is that we should all be with Him, to see His glory. (v. 24.).   Also, He has made the Father known to us and will continue to do so, in order that the Father's love for Him may be in us, and, wonder of wonders, that the Son Himself   may be in us !   (v. 26.).

These eight petitions will certainly be answered eventually because they are made by the great Intercessor,   the Son of   God Himself.   The Father cannot resist such pleas from One who always pleases Him.

How can we make the world believe that the Father has sent the Son ?

May 7

'O my God, my soul is cast down within me; therefore will I remember Thee from the land of Jordan, and of the Hermonites, from the hill Mizar. Deep calleth unto deep at the noise of Thy waterspouts; all Thy waves and Thy billows are gone over me.' (Ps. 42. 6, 7.).

The experiences outlined in those verses may be applied to those of our Lord Jesus Christ. On one occasion, as He contemplated the Cross with all its agony, He said, "Now is my soul troubled, and what shall I say? Father , save Me from this hour ? But for this cause came I unto this hour." (Jn. 12. 27.).

In the hour of His greatest trial, He remembered His God from the land of Jordan (the Descender). He Who had descended from Heaven to Humanity would ultimately descend into death itself, to gain life for others.

Then He remembered God from the land of the Hermonites (Sacred Peaks). The devil took Him up an exceedingly high mountain and tempted Him with the gift of all the world's kingdoms, if He would only worship him. Our Lord replied, "Thou shalt worship the Lord thy God, and Him only shalt thou serve."

There was also the Mount on which our Lord taught His disciples. Then there was the Mount of Transfiguration, which gave our Lord's three closest disciples a glimpse of Kingdom glory. Again, the 'little' hill ('Mizar' means 'little') is associated with great grief and anguish in the experience of the writer. The Saviour's experience at the place of a skull far transcends that of the psalmist. Deep called to deep when He cried, "My God, my God, why hast Thou forsaken Me?" All the breakers and billows of God's wrath against sin rolled over His holy soul, there, on the Cross.

'See the waves and billows roll o'er His sinless spotless soul.
Oh, my soul, it was for thee; praise Him, praise Him cheerfully'.

How can we ever praise Him enough for going down into the depths for us ?

May 8

' "But I say unto you, that in this place is One greater than the Temple." '
(Mat. 12. 6.).

In the reckoning of the legalistic Pharisees, the disciples of Jesus had just committed a heinous crime!   They had done work on the Sabbath day.   In their hunger, they had plucked some heads of grain, rubbed them between their hands, and eaten.   They were guilty of reaping and threshing on the Sabbath !

When the Pharisees challenged our Lord about His followers' behaviour, He referred them to two Scriptural precedents.   The first was from an incident in David's life when he entered the house of God, and ate the priests' consecrated bread, both he and his companions, because they were hungry (1 Sam. 21. 6.);   and it was on the Sabbath day. (Lev. 24. 8, 9.).   The second instance had to do with the practice of the priests in the temple service.   They had to do work on the Sabbath. (Num. 28. 9, 10.).   In both cases, the parties concerned were blameless, since both were engaged in the service of God.

Then the Lord used three devastating arguments.   Whom and what these Pharisees were witnessing were greater than the temple at Jerusalem - there in that cornfield !   Jesus was that Jehovah Whom the Jews sought to serve in the temple;   but they rejected Him, and their house would be desolated in 70 A.D.   So the service of Christ by His disciples was of paramount importance.   Therefore they had every right to fit themselves for His service, even on the Sabbath day.   Secondly, God would have mercy, not sacrifice (Hos. 6. 6.);   in this instance, it was for men's physical well-being. On a previous occasion, our Lord quoted this Scripture in connection with men's spiritual health. (Mat. 9. 13.).   Finally, the Son of Man pointed out to His scrutineers that He is Lord of the Sabbath.   It is His to dispose of, as He pleases.   Indeed, His resurrection replaced it by the first day of the week.

What is your part of the present temple of God ?

May9

'Now Moses kept the flock of Jethro his father-in-law the priest of Midian; and he led the flock to the far side of the desert, and came to the mountain of God - to Horeb. And the Angel of Jehovah appeared to him in a flame of fire out of the midst of a bush; and he looked, and, behold, the bush burned with fire, and the bush was not consumed.' (Ex. 3. 1, 2.).

Moses was intrigued by this 'great sight' of a thorn bush burning yet not being consumed. When he turned aside to observe it, God spoke to him from it. So the Angel of Jehovah was none other than God, the Son.

That burning bush was a picture of the people of Israel. Their sighing and their crying seemed to be insignificant, yet God heard them. He was with His people in the midst of their fiery trial and was preparing for their deliverance. Moses, now eighty years old, was His chosen instrument. His forty years of experience looking after his father-in-law's sheep, would enable him to look after God's people for the next forty years in the desert.

That 'great sight' of the indestructible burning bush presents us with another picture; that of our Saviour's passion. The humble thorn bush is a reminder of His lowly manhood, while the flame reminds us of His Saviourhood and suffering for sin on the Cross. His Godhead is seen in His resurrection from death, which could never destroy Him, no more than the flame could destroy the bush.

Moses never forgot that 'great sight' of Him Who dwelt in the bush. At the end of his life on earth, he referred to it, in his blessing of Joseph. (Deu. 33. 16.).

How did Moses react to the challenge from the God of the burning bush ? How do we react when God challenges us ?

May 10
Christ, our passover

'Purge out therefore the old leaven, that ye may be a new lump, as ye are unleavened. For even Christ our Passover is sacrificed for us.' (1 Cor. 5, 7.).

The picture of the Jewish Passover, followed by the feast of unleavened bread is in Paul's mind here, as he rebukes the brethren in the assembly at Corinth.

God gave instruction to Israel that the Passover lamb had to be sacrificed on the fourteenth day of the first month of the year. At that time, all leaven had to be purged out of each house, in order that the feast of unleavened bread should be kept for seven days.

The apostle refers to this practice here, to drive home a spiritual lesson. Our Lord Jesus Christ, the Lamb of God, has already been sacrificed. This is an historical fact. Now, in a spiritual sense, believers in Him should purge out the old leaven of carnality and rid themselves of this evil, in order to become a new batch of dough.

Leaven in Scripture always presents a picture of evil. Our Lord warned His disciples against the leaven of the Pharisees and the Sadducees i.e. hypocrisy and materialistic humanism. (Mat. 16. 6; Lk. 12. 1.). He also warned against worldliness, the leaven of Herod. (Mk. 8. 15.). Beware of these doctrines today also, the apostle Paul gives an additional warning against the leaven of legalism. (Gal. 5. 7-9.). The Galatian believers were being taught to mix law with grace. It was and is a great error.

Christ has fulfilled His part as the slain Passover Lamb. Now we must do our part to fulfil the feast of unleavened bread, spiritually.

Is there any leaven in our lives which needs to be purged ?

May11
The anointed one

' *"The Spirit of the Lord Jehovah is upon Me, because Jehovah has anointed Me to preach good tidings unto the meek; He has sent Me to bind up the broken-hearted, to proclaim liberty to the captives, and the opening of prison to those who are bound; to proclaim the acceptable year of Jehovah, and the day of vengeance of our God." '* (Isa. 61. 1, 2.).

Our Lord Jesus read from the passage of Scripture in the synagogue at Nazareth, at the commencement of His public ministry. (Lk. 4. 16 - 21.). It is significant that He finished His quote after 'the acceptable year of Jehovah', leaving the next phrase about 'the day of vengeance of our God' unsaid.

The preaching of 'the acceptable year of the Lord' has continued for almost two millennia with all the attendant blessings. Even during our Lord's public ministry it was so. When John Baptist sent his disciples to enquire about our Lord's identity, He told them to report to John what they had heard and seen. 'Blind men see and lame walk; lepers are cleansed and deaf hear; and dead are raised, and the poor are evangelised.' (Mat. 11. 5.).

It is still the year of the Lord's favour, when all who repent and believe in Jesus as Saviour and Lord are accepted by God in Him, the Beloved. (Eph. 1. 6.). God's day of vengeance will not begin until His programme for this present era of grace is completed, and the saints are removed to be forever with Christ at His coming to the air. (1 Thes. 4. 17.).

"Today, this Scripture is fulfilled in your ears", the Saviour said to them that day. (Luke 4. 21). The rest of the prophecy awaits fulfilment at His coming as King.

Which facet of the emancipating message has attracted you to the Saviour?

May 12

'And behold, there was a man in Jerusalem whose name was Simeon; and this man was just and devout, waiting for the consolation of Israel; and the Holy Spirit was upon him; and it was revealed to him by the Holy Spirit that he should not see death before he had seen the Lord's Christ.'   (Lk. 2. 25, 26.).

Mary and Joseph had a solemn and sacred duty to perform . They had to bring Mary's first-born son Jesus to the temple in Jerusalem on the appointed day to present Him to the Lord.   They also had to offer a sacrifice, in accordance with the law of the Lord. They could only afford the least expensive offering, that of two turtle doves or two young pigeons.

As they brought the Child into the temple, a dramatic event took place.   A man named Simeon met them.   This man was waiting for the 'Consolation of Israel', Who was none other than the Lord's Christ.   The Holy Spirit had revealed to him that He would see the Messiah before he saw death.

Israel needed consolation;   the nation was suffering under the yoke of bondage, imposed upon it by the all-pervasive power of Rome.   There was also a self-inflicted bondage of rules and regulations imposed upon the people by their leaders.   Comfort and consolation were much needed.

Simeon was waiting for the 'Consolation of Israel', and had found Him - a young Child in His mother's arms.   But others, at that time, with access to the book of the prophet Daniel, could have arrived at the conclusion from chapter 9, verse 25, that Messiah the Prince, Israel's Consolation, was at hand.

What consolation have you obtained from the 'Consolation of Israel'?

May 13
The king with a kingdom

'Jesus answered, "My kingdom is not of this world; if My kingdom were of this world, then would My servants fight that I should not be delivered to the Jews: but now is My Kingdom not from hence." ' (Jn. 18. 36.).

Pontius Pilate, the Roman governor had never been faced with a prisoner like Jesus of Nazareth. The dignity of His demeanour was impressive. His behaviour was that of a king, for He was and is a King. He had offered Himself to Israel as the nation's rightful Sovereign, but the Jewish leaders had rejected Him out of hand. Now He was to be crucified.

Because of this, all had changed. The Jews had rejected their King and His kingdom. So our Lord explained to Pilate that, yes, certainly He was a King with a Kingdom, but its character was spiritual and not material. Otherwise, His servants would have fought, in order that He might not be delivered up to the Jews.

Our Saviour used a special word to describe His servants. It came originally from the nautical world and denominated His disciples as 'under-rowers'. The men in a Roman galley would row exactly at their chief's command. The word had come to mean an 'attendant officer.' Those of this present era who have become the King's 'attendant officers' should be ready to run at His command.

The compelling power in His Kingdom is love; a love which was demonstrated by Him in His death for us. Those who trust Him become the recipients of His love, and can then, in measure, return that love by serving Him.

How obedient are we to the King's commands? (Jn. 14. 15.).

May14

'My heart is indicting a good matter: I speak of the things which I have made touching the King ... "Thy throne, O God, is for ever and ever; the sceptre of Thy kingdom is a right sceptre" ' (Ps. 45. 1, 6.).

The glories attributed to the King, in this psalm, far exceed those of king Solomon, even at the zenith of his career. This most mighty King (v. 3.), is none other than our Lord Jesus Christ. (Heb. 1. 8.).

His moral glory as perfect Man is first mentioned by the psalmist. He is fairer than the sons of men; grace is poured into His lips (v. 2.).

Verses 3 to 5 speak of His national glory, when He comes to reign over the earth. No longer is He viewed as the meek and lowly Nazarene, but as the Smiter of the nations.

Because the King is God, His throne is for ever and ever, and His glory is therefore eternal. His rule is characterised by righteousness.

Because of His love for righteousness and His hatred of wickedness, His God gave Him an added glory. He anointed Him with the oil of gladness above His companions. The apostle Peter spoke of this in the house of the centurion, Cornelius, when he described how God anointed Jesus of Nazareth with the Holy Spirit and with power. (Acts 10. 38.). His pre-eminent glory is also noted here, with His promotion above His companions.

Next to be mentioned is our Lord's resurrection glory. He arose from the burial chamber (the ivory palaces) with garments full of fragrance.

His bride, the church, has an acquired glory. Her clothing is of wrought gold. Also, the King's glory will be acknowledged by the peoples who will praise Him for ever and ever.

Have you already acknowledged the glory of the mighty King, Jesus ?

May 15
The sower

'And He spoke many things to them in parables, saying, "Behold, the sower went out to sow --- He Who sows the good seed is the Son of Man." ' (Mat. 13. 3, 37.).

There is no difficulty in identifying the Sower - our Lord Jesus tells us that He is the Son of Man, namely, Himself.

He went out from the Father's House in Heaven, and into the world, to sow the good seed, that the Kingdom of the Heavens had drawn near. This message was rejected by the Jews, and the Sower Himself became the Seed, the grain of wheat which fell into the ground and died, to bear much fruit.

Now, He continues to sow the seed through His servants. They take the good seed of God's word (Lk. 8. 11.) and broadcast it across the world - the field is the world. (Mat. 13. 38.). The soil is the human heart.

The seed falls into four kinds of heart. First, there is the hard heart. The word is heard but not understood and Satan snatches away the seed. Second, the shallow fleshly heart; the word is received quickly with joy but doesn't take root. When the word brings trouble there is a falling away. Third, the divided heart; the word-seed is choked by the influence of the world, so there is no fruit. Fourth, the honest and good heart: the word is heard and understood, received (Mk. 4. 20.) and kept (Lk. 8. 15.). This heart is transformed by the operation of God's word, and fruit is produced.

The Sower expects us to go, sow and see the seed grow.

Do we let the word of the Sower dwell in us richly, to produce fruit for His glory? (Col. 3. 16.).

May16

'And Jehovah spoke to Moses and Aaron in the land of Egypt, saying,   "----- On the tenth of this month, they shall take to themselves each a lamb, for a father's house, a lamb for a house. -----   And the blood shall be to you for a sign upon the houses where you are; and when I see the blood, I will pass over you; and the plague shall not be among you for destruction, when I smite the land of Egypt." '
(Exod. 12. 1, 3, 13.).

Israel was enslaved in the land of Egypt. The first-born was under God's sentence of death.   Their release from this sentence and their passport to freedom was the passover lamb.   This yearling lamb or goat kid is a beautiful picture of our Lord Jesus Christ.

The first instruction that God gave was that each family must select a lamb. The Lord Jesus is God's choice, God's lamb.   Is He our choice?

Then the lamb had to be scrutinised from the tenth to the fourteenth day of the first month of the year, to ensure that it was without blemish or spot.   The flawlessness of the Lamb of God was declared by the Father, demons and men.
(Mat. 3. 17;   27. 24;   Mk. 1. 24;   Lk. 23. 47.).

But on the fourteenth day, the lamb must be slain, and its blood applied to the door posts and lintel. This gave complete protection to all within that house.   For God said, "When I see the blood, I will pass over you."   By faith, we can find a sure shelter from God's wrath against sin, under the Blood of the slain Lamb of God.

The lamb had to be roasted with fire (a picture of God's judgment) then eaten by the people, ready for departure.

Are you receiving nourishment from God's Passover Lamb ?

May 17
The last Adam

'And so it is written, the first man Adam became a living soul; the last Adam, a life-giving Spirit.' (1 Cor. 15. 45.).

The question had been asked by someone in the Corinthian assembly, "How are the dead raised, and with what body do they come?" (v. 35.). The apostle Paul answers this question by using three analogies from nature namely, the sowing of seed, the different kinds of flesh and the different glories of bodies, heavenly, earthly and heavenly orbs.

He refers again to the analogy of the seed (vs. 42 - 44) and teaches that although the body of a dead saint is sown in corruption, dishonour and weakness, it will be raised in incorruptibility, glory and power. A natural body is sown, but a spiritual body will be raised. Then Paul quotes from the book of Genesis, in connection with the creation of the first man, Adam, who became a living soul, after Jehovah Elohim breathed into him the breath of life. (Gen. 2. 7.). But the last Adam, the Lord Jesus Christ, is a completely different order of Man from the first Adam: He has become a life-giving Spirit, through His death, resurrection and ascension back to Heaven. He is now willing and able to impart spiritual, eternal life to all who believe on Him.

Our Saviour is the Second Man, the Lord out of Heaven, Who made Adam out of the dust of the ground. So we, who bear the image of Adam, the one made of dust, shall, in resurrection, bear the image of our risen Lord Jesus, the Heavenly One. He will transform our body of humiliation into conformity to His body of glory (Phil. 3. 21.), at His return.

Have you applied for spiritual life from the last Adam ?

May 18
Zion's daughter's salvation

'Behold, Jehovah hath proclaimed unto the end of the earth: Say to the daughter of Zion;   Behold thy salvation cometh;   behold, His reward is with Him, and His work before Him.   And they shall call them, the holy people, the redeemed of Jehovah;   and thou shalt be called, the sought out, the city not forsaken.' (Isa. 62. 11, 12.).

This prophecy awaits a final fulfilment in the end time, after the Great Tribulation.   The proclamation of Jehovah will be made by the 144,000 Israeli witnesses (Rev. 7. 4.) that the daughter of Zion's Salvation is coming.   The gates will be opened wide and the highway prepared for a final exodus of God's earthly people, the Jews, to return to Jerusalem.

When our Lord Jesus entered Jerusalem as the Prince of Peace, He was lauded by the common people.   (Jn. 12. 15.).   But ultimately, He was rejected, crucified and slain.   At His return all will be different.   He will come as Zion's Salvation, to reward His followers' faithfulness and wreak retribution upon His enemies.

Then Jerusalem will be endowed with a new name.   She who was once called 'Forsaken' and 'Desolate',   will be called   'Holy People',   'Redeemed of   Jehovah', 'Sought Out',   and 'Not Forsaken'.   The question asked of the daughter of   Zion   by the prophet Jeremiah,   "Who will heal thee?"   (Lam. 2. 13.) will be fully and finally answered at the return of   her Salvation, our Lord Jesus Christ.   Then   Zion's daughter will exult and rejoice because Jehovah   God   will   be   in   the   midst,   mighty   to save.   (Zeph.   3. 14 - 17.).

Can we say that the daughter of Zion's Salvation,   the Lord Jesus Christ, is our Salvation too ?

May 19

'Then he took Him up in his arms and blessed God, and said, "Lord, now let Thy servant depart in peace, according to Thy word; for mine eyes have seen Thy Salvation, which Thou hast prepared before the face of all peoples; a light to lighten the Gentiles and the Glory of Thy people Israel." ' (Lk. 2. 28 - 32.).

There, in the temple court in Jerusalem, Mary, the mother of Jesus entrusted her precious babe to aged Simeon, who received Him into his arms and blessed God.

In his prayer, Simeon assumed the place of a bond-slave addressing his Master. The word he used of God is that from which the English word 'despot' derives. The Divine Despot was engaged in a benign act, that of sending His Salvation into the world, that Child Whom Simeon cradled in his arms. Now that God's word to Simeon was accomplished, he was ready to depart this life in peace.

Simeon had no parochial view of the Lord's Salvation. God had prepared it before the face of all peoples, not just the people of Israel. Simeon then described prophetically the nature and sequence of the Lord's Salvation, this Babe in his arms. First of all, He would be a Light bringing light to the Gentiles. This word has been fulfilled during the last two millennia. Many millions from the nations have entered into the light of the Lord's Salvation.

Secondly, Simeon predicted that the Child would be the Glory of the Lord's people, Israel. This word will be fulfilled at our Lord's return to earth to set up His millennial kingdom.

How many names and titles of our Lord Jesus are to be found in the 'Simeon' episode? (Lk. 2. 25 - 35.).

May 20
The faultless one

'Pilate therefore went forth again, and saith unto them, "Behold I bring him forth to you, that ye may know that I find no fault in Him." ' (Jn. 19. 4.).

Pilate, the Roman governor, could find no basis for a charge to be brought against Jesus, the prisoner. On three separate occasions during the mock trial, he said so publicly.

On his first admission of the prisoner's guiltlessness, Pilate should have released Him (18. 38.). Instead, he compromised: He allowed the Jews to choose whom he should release, according to the custom at the Passover, hoping that they would ask for Jesus. They chose Barabbas, a robber, whose name means 'Son of the Father'. So they rejected Jesus, the true Son of the Father, and selected a murderer (Lk. 23. 19.), a son of Satan, to be released instead. Pilate countenanced this, despite the strong warning received from his wife to have nothing to do with 'that righteous Man' (Mat. 27. 19.).

Then Pilate had Jesus scourged, thus fulfilling the prophetic word in the Psalms, 'The ploughers ploughed upon my back; they made long their furrows' (Ps. 129. 3.); also Isa. 50. 6. After the soldiers had performed their mock coronation, Pilate brought out Jesus, wearing the crown of thorns and the purple robe again declaring that he could find no basis of guilt.

When the chief priests and the Jewish officers saw Him, they cried out for His crucifixion. Pilate said to them, "Take Him yourselves and crucify Him for I find no guilt in Him" (Jn. 19. 6.).

Pilate stood condemned that day, as he passed unjust sentence upon the Judge of all the earth to be crucified.

Why did Pilate condemn a faultless Man to die that day?

May21

'Our God shall come, and shall not keep silence; a fire shall devour before Him, and it shall be very tempestuous round about Him.' (Ps. 50. 3.).

God has intervened already in the history of humanity: He became a Man. God spoke in and through His Son. It was a word of mercy and truth, righteousness and peace which was uttered in all its fulness at Calvary, on Mount Zion, for the whole earth to hear. It is the word of the Cross to those who are perishing, folly; but to those who are being saved, the power of God.

Since the ascent of the Son to heaven and the advent of the Spirit to form the 'ekklesia', more than nineteen centuries ago, God has not intervened overtly in human affairs. He has lengthened out the day of grace, not wishing for any to perish but for all to come to repentance. (2 Pet. 3. 9.).

However, our God will come, in the Person of the Son of Man, crucified yet resurrected, exalted and glorified. He shall come with a word of mighty power and awful judgment. He shall annihilate all opposition with the breath of His mouth; He shall destroy the lawless one by the splendour of His presence. (2 Thes. 2. 8.).

The whole of creation (the heavens and the earth) will participate in and be witness to the reign of Messiah, as Judge over His peoples on earth, both Jews and Gentiles, during the millennium.

What steps can you take to prepare yourself to participate in the glory of the Coming One ?

May22
The planter

'He presented another parable to them, saying, "The kingdom of heaven is like a grain of mustard seed, which a man took and planted in his field. Though it is smaller than all your seeds, yet when it is full-grown is greater than herbs, and becomes a tree, so that the birds of the air come and nest in its branches." '
(Mat. 13. 31, 32.).

In the parable of the mustard seed, our Lord describes the visible extension of the kingdom of heaven during this present era.

Firstly, there was the planting of the seed by a Man in His own field. The field is the world (v. 38), which belongs to the Lord. The tiny seed of the gospel was planted by Him, outside Jerusalem's walls.

Secondly, from such a small beginning, there was a great growth in the gospel's influence. The little mustard seed became the largest of garden plants. During the first three centuries of this age, the kingdom of heaven spread throughout the known world, as the gospel triumphed over paganism.

Then something unnatural took place; the herb became a tree in contravention of Genesis 1. 12. This corresponds with the influence of the Roman Emperor Constantine who made Christianity the state religion. Thus, as this age progressed, there was abnormal growth of the professing Church. Also, just as the tree became a shelter for the birds, so the professing Church will become a shelter for all kinds of evil (Mat. 13. 4, 19.). In its final form, after the rapture of the true Church, it will dominate the world. Babylon will be at the hub of this one-world religion; it will be destroyed by the Beast, the penultimate world ruler, (Rev. 17. 16.), who will then be destroyed by the Lamb, our Lord and Saviour.

Which church growth are you promoting - the true or the false ?

May23
The wood in the waters

'And he cried to Jehovah; and Jehovah showed him wood, and he threw it into the waters and the waters became sweet. There He made for them a statute and an ordinance, and there He tested them.' (Ex. 15. 25.).

The children of Israel had been rescued from slavery in the land of Egypt by the blood of the lamb. Then they were rescued from the might of Pharaoh's army by the power of the Lord. The waters of the Red Sea were divided, and the sons of Israel went through the midst of the sea on the dry land. Then the waters returned and covered the chariots and horsemen of all the host of Pharaoh.

Now, another test awaited Israel. For three days the people travelled in the deserts of Shur, without finding water. When they discovered it, the waters were bitter and they could not drink it. So they called the place 'Marah', which means 'bitterness'. In answer to Moses' plea, Jehovah showed him a piece of wood, evidently from a tree nearby, which, when thrown into the waters, made them sweet.

Just as water is needed to sustain physical life, so the water of God's word is required to maintain spiritual life. The bitter, unpalatable waters of Marah are a reminder of the law, which pronounces death and judgment upon all. On the other hand, the wood, cast into the waters, is a reminder of the coming of God's grace into humanity, in the Person of His son, bringing life and sweetness to all who receive Him.

It was completely contrary to the natural order of things. Water normally brings life to the trees; whereas here, the 'Tree' brings 'life' to the 'waters'. So it is in the Divine order of things.

Have the bitter waters in your life become sweet by the presence of Christ?

May24
Christ became poor

'For you know the grace of our Lord Jesus Christ, that, though He was rich, yet for your sakes He became poor, that you through His poverty might become rich.'
(2 Cor. 8. 9.).

The Christians in Corinth were being exhorted by the apostle Paul to send material help to the needy saints in Jerusalem and Judea. He strengthens his exhortation by reminding his readers of the example of our Lord Jesus.

Firstly, he reminds us of what we know and have learned of our Saviour; that, in grace, He became a Man called Jesus, although He was, and is, Lord Jehovah. He was the unique Son of the Father, full of grace and truth. He was fairer than the sons of men; grace was poured into His lips. Therefore God has blessed Him for ever. (Ps. 45. 2.). As a child, the grace of God was upon Him. (Lk. 2. 40.). At the outset of His public ministry in Nazareth, all were amazed at the words of grace which were proceeding out of His mouth. (Lk. 4. 22.).

Secondly, the text tells us what He was: He was rich. When was He rich? Certainly not here in this world. This statement can only refer to His pre-existence as Lord and Maker of all creation. (Ps. 50. 10.) Such riches in glory were His, beyond our wildest dreams.

Yet, thirdly, our Lord willingly became poor for our sakes. He took the form of a bond-servant, being made in the likeness of men. (Phil. 2. 7.). He said on one occasion, "The Son of Man has nowhere to lay His head," (Lk. 9. 58.). In death on the Cross, His head found rest on His own breast (Jn. 19. 30.), after redemption's work was done.

Finally, we are reminded of what all true believers have become. They are possessed of eternal riches in Christ. (Eph. 1.11; 1 Pet. 1. 4.).

Can I say, by God's grace, that the wealth of all heaven is mine ?

May25
The treader of the winepress

' "I have trodden the winepress alone;   and of the peoples there was none with Me. I also trod them in My anger, and trampled them in My fury;   and their life-blood is sprinkled on My garments, and I stained all My clothing." '   (Isa. 63. 3).

The question has already been asked at the beginning of this particular prophecy, "Who is this ...... ?" (v. 1.).   "It is I, speaking in righteousness, mighty to save" comes the reply.   The identity of this One is clearly given in Revelation 19. 11-16.   His name is the Word of God, King of kings and Lord of lords.   He is none other than our Saviour, Jesus.

The next question to be asked is, when will this take place?   The context gives the answer: During the day of vengeance and the year of the Lord's redemption (v. 4.). When will that be ?   At the end of the period known as the Great Tribulation (Rev. 7. 14; Mat. 24. 21) when our Lord Jesus returns with His church to earth according to the prophetic word. (Acts 1. 11.).

In that day, His feet will stand again on the mount of Olives (Zech. 14. 4.), thus partly answering the next question as to where these things will take place.   The wine trough will be very large, filled with the life-blood of hundreds of millions of soldiers. (Rev. 14. 20.).   The armies of the nations will be destroyed there.

What will happen then ?   Our Lord will vanquish personally the armies of the Antichrist and the eastern kings, none helping Him.   He will accomplish this with 'the sword of His mouth'. (Rev. 19. 15.).   He will rescue the remnant of His people, the Jews, bringing many from their hide-outs in Edom.   He will return in triumph to Jerusalem to set up His earthly kingdom.

Does our Lord Jesus reign supreme in your heart now ?

May 26
The boy Jesus

'And when He was twelve years old, they went up to Jerusalem after the custom of the feast; and when they had fulfilled the days, as they returned, the boy Jesus stayed behind in Jerusalem. And His parents did not know this.' (Lk. 2. 42, 43.).

This unique insight into the boyhood of our Lord Jesus is recorded only by Luke. No doubt much of the detail was given to him by Mary, the mother of our Lord.

Joseph, his wife Mary and her son Jesus had travelled from Nazareth to Jerusalem, to celebrate the Feast of Passover there. They became part of a great crowd of more than a million people visiting the city on such an occasion.

On their return after the feast, Mary and Joseph supposed that Jesus was with their company. It was only when they stopped for the night they made the alarming discovery that their boy was not with them. It was, and still is, a very serious discovery to realise when Jesus is not present, either in the company or in the life (Rev. 3. 20.). But the situation can be remedied.

Next day, they hurried back to Jerusalem with hearts full of apprehension for their boy. Their search for Him in the city probably began in earnest on the third day. Eventually, they found Him in the temple courts, sitting among the teachers, listening to them and asking them questions, in all modesty and humility. All who heard Him were astonished at His understanding and answers.

When Mary remonstrated with her son, He replied; "Did you not know that I must be in the things (or, the house) of the Father of Me." (Literal translation). Our Lord, even at the age of twelve, was gently reminding His mother of His heavenly origin. Mary had said to Him, "Your father and I ------." He said to her, " ----- the affairs of My Father."

Have you the assurance of the presence of Christ ?

May27

'Jesus said to her, "Woman, why are you weeping? Whom are you seeking ?" Supposing Him to be the gardener, she said to Him, "Sir, if you have carried Him away, tell me where you have laid Him, and I will take Him away." ' (John 20. 15.).

It was a perfectly natural mistake that Mary made, early on that first resurrection morning. After all, the new tomb was in a garden which would need the skills of a gardener. So, when confronted with the risen Christ, Mary supposed that He was the gardener.

She had already seen the empty tomb with the great stone rolled away from the entrance. When she returned, and looked for a second time into the tomb, she saw two angels sitting where the body of Jesus had been. But even this did not stop her tears from flowing.

The cause of her crying was very clear. They were due to ignorance. Mary, and the others, did not understand the Scripture concerning our Lord's resurrection. The sight of the empty tomb should have produced joy and not sorrow.

However, when Mary turned around and saw, as she supposed, the gardener, the Lord Jesus spoke to her. These were His first words after His resurrection: "Woman, why do you weep, whom do you seek ?"

These words could have come from a caring gardener, but, in fact, they were spoken by the Gardener of Mary's soul. She never answered His gentle, compassionate questions. She was intent on finding a corpse and returning it to a tomb!

Then the supposed gardener became Mary's shepherd, calling her name. She recognised Him immediately and cried out "Rabboni !" (Jn. 10. 3, 37.).

Do we recognise the call of the Risen Christ and obey Him ?

May 28
The green olive tree

'But I am like a green olive tree in the house of God: I trust in the loving-kindness of God for ever and ever.'   (Ps. 52. 8.).

David wrote this psalm when he was in great distress.   He admitted responsibility for the death of the family of Ahimelech the priest (1 Sam. 22. 22.).   In his flight from king Saul, he went to Nob, to Ahimelech, who helped him.   David led him to think that he (David) was on secret business for the king.   But Doeg the Edomite, Saul's chief herdsman, was there and reported the matter to Saul.

King Saul summoned the priestly family to come to him.   He ordered his guard to kill them, but they were unwilling.   Then he told Doeg the Edomite to strike. down the priests, which he did (1 Sam. 22. 18, 19.).   But Abiathar, the son of Ahitub escaped and told David.

Now, in this psalm, David confronts Doeg with his evil.   Its source was his tongue;   he told lies to the king about Ahimelech the priest.   Then David predicts God's judgment upon him.   This 'mighty man' will be broken down, snatched up, torn away and uprooted.   The Anti-Christ, whose mouth speaks boastfully, will suffer the same fate at the return of our Saviour.

In contrast, David likens himself to an olive tree, flourishing in the house of God.   The olive tree reminds us of our Lord Jesus.   It is an emblem of peace, after the storm of God's wrath (Gen. 8. 11.).   Our Saviour brings us peace after enduring God's judgment upon sin.   (Jn. 20. 19, 20.).   It is also an emblem of fruitfulness since it produces berries which yield nutritious oil.   The life-giving Holy Spirit was sent by the ascended Son of God, to bring eternal life to each believer.

How can we become like 'the Green Olive Tree', our Lord Jesus Christ?   Read again Psalm 52. 8, 9.

May 29

' "The kingdom of heaven is like a treasure, hidden in the field, which a man found and hid, and for the joy of it he goes and sells everything he has and buys that field." ' (Mat. 13. 44.).

This parable, the first of the final four in the series of eight, was told by our Lord to his disciples privately in the house (v. 36.).   He was revealing to them the inner secrets of the kingdom of heaven, relating to this present era.

To be consistent with the other parables, the following deductions may be made;   the field is the world   (v. 38.) and the Man who is in the field is the Son of Man (v. 37.). Other Scriptures help us towards the conclusion that the treasure is the nation of Israel. (Ex. 19. 5;   Deu. 7. 6;   Ps. 135. 4.).

Just as the treasure was hidden in the field, so Israel, as a complete nation, was hidden among the other nations in the world. (Jn. 7. 35;   Jas. 1. 1;   1 Pet. 1. 1.).

This had been the lot of the nation for centuries before the coming of our Lord Jesus: But when He came into the world, He found the treasure in those of His own who received Him. (Jn. 1. 11, 12.).   His mission was directed towards the lost sheep of the house of Israel. (Mat. 10. 6;   15. 24.).

The Man hid the treasure again, after finding it.   After Messiah's rejection by His own, Israel was set aside by God. The bulk of the nation is still hidden in the world.   Then, in the parable, the Man, for the joy of it, sells everything and buys the field.   Jesus endured the Cross for the joy set before Him (Heb. 12. 2.) 'He is the atoning Sacrifice for our sins, and not only for ours but also for the sins of the whole world.'   (1 Jn. 2. 2.). Sadly, not all who are in the world wish to have their sins removed.   Only those who believe on the Lord Jesus are redeemed by His precious Blood.

What contrasts and comparisons do you find between this parable, and the previous one in the series, given in v. 33 ?

May 30

'And the house of Israel named it manna; and it was like coriander seed, white; and the taste of it was like wafers made with honey.' (Ex. 16. 31.).

One month after their exodus from Egypt the people of Israel faced another crisis. They were hungry, and the whole community grumbled against Moses and Aaron. Their need was very great; to fill more than two million mouths with food every day, in a barren wilderness, was no small task.

But God was faithful and rained bread from heaven every day, except the seventh, for forty years; and on the sixth day the people gathered twice as much bread to supply the need of the rest day, or Sabbath.

This 'manna', as the people named it, is a beautiful picture of our Lord Jesus, as He Himself taught. (Jn. 6. 32, 33.). He is the living Bread sent down from heaven, enabling the partaker to live for ever (v. 51.). The Saviour offers Himself freely to all, just as the manna was God's gift to all the people.

When the Israelites first saw this 'bread of angels', they said to each other, "What is it?" This is the meaning of the Hebrew word 'manna'. When our Lord entered Jerusalem as Messiah the Prince, all the city was stirred, saying, "Who is this?" (Mat. 21. 10.). Like the manna, many could only see His humility and humanity and were blind to His deity. He was despised and rejected, as also was the manna, when the people spoke against God and Moses, and said, "We detest this miserable food!" (Num. 21. 5.).

The Manna contained all that was needed for the health of the people; the sweetness of honey and the strength of olive oil. (Num. 11. 8.). The preparatory grinding or crushing of the manna is a reminder of our Lord's sufferings on the Cross. He was 'sore broken' there for us. (Prov. 11.15.).

Are we diligent in our daily appropriation of the heavenly Manna, our Lord Jesus Christ ?

May 31
God's unspeakable gift

'Thanks be unto God for His unspeakable Gift.' (2 Cor. 9. 15.)

God's indescribable gift, our Lord Jesus Christ, is the supreme illustration of all the principles of giving which Paul teaches in the previous part of the chapter, leading up to this final verse.

Firstly, the principle of sowing and reaping is mentioned (v. 6.). The amount of reaping depends upon the amount of sowing, whether small or large. God's inestimable Gift of His Son was sown in death on the Cross in order to yield a rich harvest. (Jn. 12. 24.).

Secondly, giving must be on a voluntary basis from a cheerful heart (v. 7.). Our Lord gave Himself freely, without reservation to do the Father's will and die. All reluctance on His part was overcome in Gethsemane. He was willing to drink, to its dregs, the bitter cup of God's wrath against sin.

Thirdly, God's abundant grace in His saints produces abundant work on their part (v. 8.); God's overflowing grace in His Son has completed a work of infinite and eternal worth, the work of redemption.

Fourthly, God promises to increase our store of seed and harvest of righteousness (v. 10). Concerning God and His Son, it is written, "He has scattered, He has given to the poor; His righteousness abides forever. His horn will be exalted in honour". (Ps. 112. 9.).

Also, thanks are given to God because of His saints', and above all, His Son's generosity (v. 11.). He, and they through Him, supply the needs of God's people who glorify God as a result. Praise God for His surpassing grace and for the inexpressible Gift of His Son, our Saviour! (vs. 11-15.).

Shall we thank God, right now, for His unspeakable Gift ?

June 1
The one with outstretched hands

' *"I have stretched out My hands all the day unto a rebellious people, who walk in the way which is not good, after their own thoughts."* ' *(Isa, 65. 2).*

In the beginning, the Son of God stretched out His hands to create the heavens. (Ps. 102. 25.).

That same One, as He entered into perfect manhood, took the tools of a carpenter into His hands, in the lowly workshop in Nazareth.   But as He entered into public service, the people said,   "What wisdom is this which is given unto Him, that even such mighty works are wrought by His hands?" (Mk. 6. 2.).   He laid His hands upon the eyes of a blind man, and he saw all things clearly   (8. 25.).

He reached out His hands in love to embrace the children and bless them   (10. 16.).

When the appointed time came, God's Holy Son let men stretch out His hands on a Cross of wood, and pierce them with iron spikes, transfixing Him to the beam.   Thus the ancient prophecy was fulfilled (Ps. 22. 16.).   When the work of redemption was done and He surrendered His spirit in death, loving hands laid His body in the tomb. But He broke the bonds of death and rose in triumph to show Himself to His own.

After forty days, when the witness of His resurrection was completed, He ascended into heaven.   As He did so, He lifted up His hands and blessed His disciples. (Lk. 24. 50.).   They worshipped Him.

Meantime, many Gentiles are finding a safe refuge in the arms of Jesus, while Israel, as a people, spurn His outstretched pierced hands as patiently He waits to bless them too. (Rom. 10. 21.).   This long day will end soon with Israel's judgment and regeneration. (Mat. 19. 28.).

Have you humbled yourself under the mighty hand of God ?   (1 Pe. 5. 6.).

153

June 2

"John answered all, saying "I indeed baptise you with water; but One mightier than I is coming, the thong of whose sandals I am not worthy to unloose; He shall baptise you with the Holy Spirit and with fire" ' (Lk. 3. 16.).

The fiery ministry of John the Baptiser had kindled in the hearts of his hearers an expectation of Messiah. Could it be that John was He ? John's reply was clear and unequivocal. "I am not the Christ," he said, "I am the voice of one crying in the wilderness, 'make straight the path of the Lord (Jehovah)' " (Jn. 1. 20, 23.).

Our Lord Jesus was mightier than John in every respect. He was none other than Jehovah-God, for Whom John was preparing a path. John was just the herald, announcing the approach of the King of kings. John did not consider himself worthy to do the task of our Lord's humblest servant, and unloose His sandal-thong. Yet our Lord said of him, that, among those born of women, there had not risen a greater. (Mat. 11. 11.).

John was a lamp, albeit a burning and a shining one, but Jesus, the Son of God, is the Light of the world. (Jn. 5. 35, 36.). John did no sign (Jn. 10. 41.), but Jesus even raised the dead because He is the Resurrection and the Life.

Then John made two prophetic announcements. Firstly, the coming Christ would baptise with the Holy Spirit. This was fulfilled at the commencement of the Church age. (Acts 1, 5; 2.1; 11.16.). This took place when the ascended Son of God sent the promised Holy Spirit on the day of Pentecost. Secondly, our Lord will baptise with judgmental fire at His return to set up His earthly millennial kingdom. (2 Thess. 1. 8.).

Are we willing to use John's words, when he said concerning the Saviour, "He must increase but I must decrease"? (Jn. 3. 30.)

June 3

'Then came Jesus, the doors being shut, and stood in the midst, and said, "Peace be to you." Then He says to Thomas, "Reach hither thy finger and behold My hands; and reach hither thy hand and thrust it into My side, and be not faithless but believing." And Thomas answered and said to Him, "My Lord and my God." ' (Jn. 20. 26 -28.).

The name 'Thomas' is derived from an Aramaic word, meaning 'Twin'. The Greek equivalent, Didymus, is also given in the above context (v. 24.).

There are many 'twins' or 'doubles' in this account of how the risen Lord Jesus met Thomas. It was a twin event with that which had taken place eight days previously, when our Lord rose from the dead. Thomas had not been present then. It was on the first day of the week.

The circumstances were duplicated. The door was shut, but Jesus came and stood in the midst of those gathered in the room. Walls and doors constituted no barrier for Him. Jesus gave again the same greetings, "Peace be to you".

The same evidence was offered to Thomas as to the disciples; His wounded hands and side. He encouraged Thomas to see His hands and thrust his hand into the great spear-wound in His side. This was exactly the evidence Thomas had demanded (v. 25.). Then our Lord gave him the twin exhortation, not to be unbelieving but believing.

Thomas uttered the twin response, "My Lord and my God!" He was completely convinced that Jesus is Jehovah-God. Our Lord then drew attention to twin characteristics. seeing and believing, and the blessing which is promised to those who have not seen and have believed.

Have you confessed Jesus to be your Lord and your God ?

June4
The judge and guide

'Let the nations be glad and sing for joy; for Thou shalt judge the peoples righteously, and guide the nations upon earth.   Selah.'   (Ps. 67. 4.).

This short psalm, which is also a song, comes to a crescendo right in the middle at verse 4.   Before and after this verse there is an identical exhortation.   "Let the peoples praise Thee, O God, let all the peoples praise Thee".

The psalm looks forward to the future when God's face will again shine on the nation of Israel.   The Apostates will be removed and a remnant will turn to the Lord at His return to earth.   Then all the peoples will praise God.

He will judge   'the habitable earth in righteousness by the Man Whom He has appointed, giving the proof of it to all, in having raised Him from the dead'.
(Acts 17. 31.).   So God's King on earth will be none other than our Lord Jesus Christ in that day.   At the end of the seven years of tribulation, He will appear.   The surviving nations will rejoice and sing for joy.

Our Lord will come as Shepherd-King, not only to judge, but also to lead and guide the nations like a shepherd leading his flock.   Then His way shall be known on earth and His saving health among the nations (v. 2.).

There will be ample cause for all the peoples of the nations to rejoice.   There will be peace and plenty for all during the millennial reign of the righteous Judge (v. 6.). 'All the ends of the earth shall fear Him' (v. 7.).

Is Jesus your Shepherd-King, judging and guiding your life ?

June 5
The merchant

' "Again, the kingdom of heaven is like a merchant seeking beautiful pearls; and having found one pearl of great value he went and sold all that he had and bought it." ' (Mat. 13. 45.).

The pearl of this parable is a lovely picture of the church of God. This is evident, first of all, in the way that the pearl was formed. A tiny particle of grit entered the oyster, who built 'mother-of-pearl' around this irritation. As a result, the oyster weakened and died. The offender, causing the oyster's death, became a gem of great worth. Similarly, the sinner, causing Christ's death, becomes a saint of great worth. (Rom. 5. 8.).

Another precious picture of Christ and His church is seen in the way that the pearl was found. A diver, at great risk, went down into the depths of the sea to find the pearl. He then brought it from darkness up into the light. The Son of God entered into the depths and darkness of the waters of God's wrath against sin, to bring His church into the light of His love.

The pearl was also found by the trader who evidently knew its great value. He assessed its beauty, unity, symmetry and integrity, and was prepared to sell all that he had to secure that pearl. Similarly, 'Christ loved the church and gave Himself for it, so that He might sanctify it, purifying it by the washing of water by the word that He might present the church to Himself, glorious, having no spot or wrinkle or any such thing' (Eph. 5. 25 - 27.).

Our Saviour gave His back to the smiters, His cheek to those who plucked out the hair, His body to be transfixed on a Cross and His blood to be poured out thereon. He paid the ultimate price for the church.

The Saviour now says,
"All this I gave for thee,
  What hast thou given to me ?"

June 6
The smitten rock

' "Behold, I will stand before thee there upon the rock in Horeb; and thou shalt smite the rock, and there shall come water out of it, that the people may drink." And Moses did so in the sight of the elders of Israel.' (Ex. 17. 6.).

Israel had arrived at Rephidim under God's guidance; but there was no water for them to drink. The people murmured against Moses who cried to Jehovah. He instructed Moses to go to Horeb, the mountain of God (3. 1.). He had to take with him representatives of the elders, as witnesses, and also his staff. It had to be the same staff with which he smote the river in Egypt before the eyes of Pharaoh and all the waters turned into blood.(7. 20.).

Moses did as the Lord had commanded. With Jehovah standing before him and the elders observing him, he smote the rock and water came out from it; enough to supply the need of the whole nation throughout their wilderness journey. Moses named the place 'Massah' or 'Testing', and 'Meribah', or 'Quarrelling', because the people had tested God and had quarrelled with Moses.

Now the Rock was Christ. (1 Cor. 10. 4.). It was on another mountain, namely Moriah, the mount of Jehovah, (Gen. 22. 14.), that our great spiritual need was met, many years later. With the elders of Israel watching (Mat. 27. 41; Lk. 23, 35.), the Roman soldier plunged his spear into the side of the Son of God, and immediately there came out blood and water (Jn. 19. 34.). John, the elder (2 Jn. 1.), witnessed it and reported it truly. The Blood brings complete cleansing to all who apply it and the Water brings eternal life to all who receive it.

Have you come to the Rock and received living water to quench your soul-thirst? (Jn. 7. 37 - 39.).

June 7

'For I am jealous over you with godly jealousy; for I have espoused you to one Husband, that I may present you as a chaste virgin to Christ.' (2 Cor. 11. 2.).

The Corinthian church was at risk from visiting Judaising teachers. They claimed to be apostles (v. 13.), but were not. They had brought letters of recommendation (3. 1.); they also commended themselves (10. 18.), and linked themselves with self-styled 'super-apostles' (11. 5.).

Eden had come to Corinth, Christ, the heavenly Adam (Rom. 5. 14; 1 Cor. 15. 21, 22, 45.) had become Bridegroom to a spiritual Eve, the church at Corinth. God had used His servant Paul to do the work of bringing the two parties together. No wonder the apostle was jealous over the saints at Corinth with a jealousy which was from God. But Satan, that old serpent, was using his emissaries, these false apostles, to turn the saints away from single-minded devotion to Christ.

Just as the servant of Abraham had brought Rebecca to his master's son, Isaac (Gen. 24, 65.), so Paul, as the Father's servant, had presented the assembly of saints at Corinth to Christ, the Father's unique Son.

Paul describes the assembly as a 'chaste virgin'. This description demonstrates God's grace and power. In an earlier letter to the saints at Corinth, the apostle had to remind them of what they had been. 'And such were some of you; but you have been washed ----- sanctified -----justified in the name of the Lord Jesus and by the Spirit of our God,' he wrote. (1 Cor. 6. 11.).

In listening to these false teachers, the saints were leaving themselves wide-open to another 'gospel' which mixed grace with law, and another 'spirit' which was not of Christ (2 Cor. 11. 4.). Hence the need for the apostles strong warning. We need this same kind of warning today.

How highly do we rate our devotion to Christ as our espoused Husband ?

June8

"For by fire and by His sword will Jehovah enter into judgment with all flesh; and the slain of Jehovah shall be many." (Isa. 66. 16.).

Jehovah will bring Israel to the birth again.   Our Lord Jesus described it as the 'regeneration'.(Mat. 19. 28.).   It will coincide with the Son of Man returning and sitting down on His throne of glory.   The experience for Israel will be like a woman giving birth even before her labour pains are upon her;   it will happen so suddenly.   The nation will be reborn in a day   (v. 8.);   it will be the work of Jehovah-Jesus (v. 9.).

Those who love and mourn for Jerusalem will then be delighted in her, as a baby delights in his mother's milk (vs. 10. 11.);   they shall be satisfied.

Jehovah will give Jerusalem peace like a river (v. 12.), and she shall be comforted as a child by her mother (v. 13.).   This event will take place at the end of the seven years of tribulation and the beginning of the millennium.

In stark contrast to this scene, our Lord will avenge Himself of His enemies (vs. 14 - 18.).   He will descend with flames of fire (2 Thes. 1. 7-9.) and His chariots will be like a whirlwind (v. 15.).   All flesh will be judged by the fire of His presence and by the sword of His mouth (Rev. 19. 15.).   He is called   'Faithful' and 'True', and His name is called 'The Word of   God'.   He is 'King of kings and Lord of   Lords'.   He is none other than Jesus of Nazareth, returning to reign.

His judgment will be righteous because of all the abominable practices of men in that day.   The slain of the Lord, and also the saved of the Lord, shall be many.

Do we always remember that our God is a consuming fire?   (Heb. 12. 29.)

June9

'And Jesus Himself, when He began (His ministry) was about thirty years of age, being, as was supposed, the son of Joseph, who was (the son) of Heli.' (Lk. 3. 23.).

Our Lord Jesus was about to embark on His public service for God. He had reached the age of about thirty years. Priests began their public ministry at that age. (Num. 4. 3.). The patriarch Joseph was thirty years old when he entered the service of Pharaoh, king of Egypt (Gen. 41. 46.). David was thirty years old when he became king of Israel (2 Sam. 5. 4.). When Jewish scribes reached the age of thirty years, they were allowed to teach. So it was a most significant time in the life of our Lord, the One Who is Priest, Saviour, Sovereign and true Scribe.

It was assumed by the people that Jesus was the son of Joseph. This was certainly the reckoning according to law. The Jews said on a later occasion, "Is not this Jesus, the son of Joseph, whose father and mother we know? How can He now say, I came down from heaven?" (Jn.6. 42.). At another time they asked, "Is not this the carpenter's Son? Is not His mother called Mary, and His brothers, James and Joseph and Simon and Judas? And His sisters, are they not all with us? Where then did this man get all these things?" (Mat. 13. 55. 56.).

It is at this point that Luke gives the genealogy of Jesus. He traces it back in time to Adam, the son of God, as is fitting for the ideal Man. On the other hand, the genealogy of a king is traced from the source of his dynasty and ends with himself. Matthew gives that in his Gospel.

People were wrong in what they thought of our Lord's sonship. His true Father was God and His mother was a virgin.

What lessons can we learn from what we know of Joseph, the supposed father of our Lord?

June 10

'Jesus therefore says to them, "Little children, have you any food?" They answered Him, "No". And He said to them, "Cast the net on the right side of the ship and you will find." They cast therefore, and they were not able to draw it for the multitude of fishes.' (Jn. 21. 5, 6.).

The Lord had promised His disciples, prior to His death, that after His resurrection He would go before them into Galilee. (Mk. 14. 28.). When He rose from the dead, He repeated His promise that His disciples would see Him in Galilee. (Mat. 28. 10.). John records one instance when this promise was fulfilled.

It took place after a night of fruitless fishing. Seven disciples, led by Peter, went out to fish on the Sea of Tiberias, and now they were heading for home with nothing to show for their night of toil.

Just as dawn began to break, and they were about 90 metres from the shore, they heard the voice of the Son of God, who was standing there. The Master Fisherman had come to help them. He instructed them where to cast the net, and they obeyed instinctively, not realising yet that it was the Lord.

When the net was filled even beyond its capacity with fish, sent there by the Son of God, John said to Peter, "It is the Lord!" Maybe he remembered the other catch of fish, three years previously, when Simon Peter had obeyed the Lord's command. (Lk. 5. 4 - 7.).

When the net was safely on the shore, they counted the catch and were astonished at the number of fish - 153 !

There was another wonder; despite the great catch, the net was not torn!

What is the practical lesson in the catch of 153 fish ?

June 11

'Thou hast ascended on high,   Thou hast led captivity captive: Thou hast received gifts for men, and even for the   rebellious,   that   Jah   Elohim   might   dwell   there.'   (Ps. 68. 18.).

The verse is the climax of a stirring song of victory.   God   had vanquished   all His foes;   He had led out the prisoners (v. 6.);   kings and armies were routed (v. 12.);   the Almighty   had   scattered   kings   in   the   land. (v. 14.).

This ascending King is none other than our Lord Jesus Christ, as explained by the apostle Paul.   He quotes v. 18 of the Psalm in Eph. 4. 8,   and uses it to refer to our Lord's return to heaven, after vanquishing all our foes by His death and resurrection.

The apostle also explains that, before our Lord ascended, He descended into the lower parts   of   the   earth.   It is clear that, when Jesus died, His soul descended into Sheol (Hebrew) or Hades (Greek).   There, He proclaimed His victory   over   Satan   to   the spirits in prison. (1 Pet. 3. 19.).

He ascended from Hades (Ps. 16. 10;   Acts 2. 27.) with the keys of death and Hades (Rev. 1. 18.), 'leading captivity captive'.   The Old Testament saints in the upper part of Sheol-Hades were transferred by our Lord to the upper Paradise at His resurrection and return to heaven.   They are 'the spirits of righteous men made perfect' in the heavenly Jerusalem (Heb. 12. 23.), who have been removed from Paradise below.

The gifts which Christ received for men have been given to men by the advent of the Holy Spirit.   Present-day saints are permanently indwelt by Him, and are the recipients of the gifts which He brings.

What is your spiritual gift from the Ascended One ?

June 12

'And He said to them, "For this reason every scribe discipled into the kingdom of heaven is like a house-owner who brings forth out of his treasure things new and old." ' (Mat. 13. 52.).

The Lord Jesus has just asked His disciples if they had understood the content of the previous seven parables: "Yes," they said, but in reality, their understanding was meagre, as is ours. This was revealed in the disciples' question, just before our Lord was taken up to heaven. "Lord, are you at this time going to restore the kingdom to Israel?" (Acts 1. 6.).

However, our Lord graciously takes the disciples at their word and presses home their responsibility to teach others what He had taught them. At first glance, they appeared to be an unlikely source for scribes, but, in the Lord's providence, Peter and John and Matthew had the high honour conferred upon them.

The disciple must be like his Master, who is described here as the House-owner. Our Lord Jesus describes Himself as such in other Scriptures (Mat. 10. 25; 20. 11; Lk. 13. 25; 14. 21.). Presently, God's house is the church of Christ (1 Tim. 3. 15.), having Him as its Lord and Owner. He has purchased and is building it (Mat.16. 18; 1 Cor, 6. 20.). He is also the Possessor of all the treasures of wisdom and knowledge (Col. 2. 3.). The resources in His storeroom are inexhaustible.

Our Lord has revealed these truths concerning the kingdom of heaven to us in these eight parables.

Which of the previous seven parables contain new treasures and which contain old ?

164

June13

' *"Behold, I send an Angel before thee, to keep thee in the way, and to bring thee into the place which I have prepared."* ' *(Ex. 23. 20.).*

In their journey through the desert, Israel had arrived in front of Mount Sinai. Moses, as representative of the people, approached the thick darkness where God was. (20. 21.). As well as the Ten Commandments, God had given to Moses a variety of other laws regulating life in the community of Israel.

Now God gives a promise; He is sending an Angel, indeed His Angel (23. 23.), Who will guide the people of Israel to the Promised Land. The Angel's identity is revealed in the statement by God, that if the people provoke His Angel, He (i.e. the Angel) will not pardon their transgressions, "For My Name is in Him." (v. 21.). Later, when the people did rebel, Moses pleaded with God and said, "Lord, let the Lord, I pray Thee, go in our midst; for it is a stiff-necked people; and pardon our iniquity and sin and take us for an inheritance" (Ex. 34. 9.). During Jesus' first advent, the Jews were right when they said, "Who can forgive sins, but God only?" (Mk. 2. 7.). They had just heard our Lord say to a man, "Your sins are forgiven." The incarnate Son is God, and so is the pre-incarnate Son, in the form of God's Angel.

The work of the Angel was manifold. He would guard, and guide the people to their divinely - appointed destination (Ex. 23. 20.). He would instruct them as God's Representative. He would not forgive their rebellion, if provoked (v. 21.). He would go ahead of them and bring them into the land (v. 23.).

Are we careful in the presence of God's Angel, our Lord Jesus, and listen to His voice? (v. 21.).

June 14
The one seed

'Now to Abraham and his Seed were the promises made. He saith not, "And to seeds," as of many; but as of One, "And to thy Seed," Who is Christ.' (Gal. 3. 16.).

The Old Testament reference which the apostle Paul has in mind should embrace Abraham and his seed in them. Hence, there are two, which read as follows:-

"All the land which thou seest, to thee will I give it, and to thy Seed forever." (Gen. 13. 15.).

"I will establish My covenant between Me and thee and thy seed after thee in their generations for an everlasting covenant, to be a God unto thee, and to thy Seed after thee; and I will give unto thee, and to thy Seed after thee, the land wherein thou art a stranger ------." (17. 7, 8.).

There is another text which, in a general way, Paul is referring to, namely, "And through thy Seed shall all the nations of the earth be blessed; -----." (22. 18.).

The apostle stresses the singularity of the word 'Seed' in these promises, as referring to One Person, namely Christ. While the plural form 'seeds' is not a normal word to use (either in Hebrew or Greek) of human offspring. God could have used another word, such as children, to stress plurality of persons. But He didn't, in order that the singularity of the word 'Seed' would describe Messiah, the 'One Seed'.

God's promises will be fulfilled in that 'One Seed' of Abraham, the anti-type of Isaac, our Resurrected Lord Jesus Christ. As Abraham's Seed and Son, he will possess the land of Palestine at His return to earth. He, as David's Son, will institute His millennial kingdom, in conjunction with Abraham's seed, Israel. Then, all the nations of the earth will be truly blessed.

What blessings and promises come to us, who are also Abraham's seed, through faith in Christ Jesus, the 'One Seed'. (Gal. 3. 26 - 29.)

June 15
A righteous branch

' "Behold the days come," saith Jehovah, "that I will raise unto David a Righteous Branch, and a King shall reign and prosper, and shall execute judgment and justice in the earth. In His days, Judah shall be saved, and Israel shall dwell safely, and this is His name whereby He shall be called Jehovah - our Righteousness." ' (Jer. 23. 5, 6.).

Jeremiah, the prophet, has just recorded a message of judgment upon the royal house of Judah (ch. 22.), ending with a woe upon false shepherds (23. 1, 2.). Then Jehovah makes a gracious promise; He will gather the remnant of His flock and bring them back to their own land. So hope is held out to the Jewish people, which will be realised in the future. The phrase, "Behold the days come" (v. 5.), found 16 times in the book, introduces an additional message of hope.

Jehovah will raise up a Righteous Branch to King David. This Branch or Shoot will spring out from the fallen tree of David's descendants. The concept is found elsewhere in the Old Testament Prophets. (Isa. 4. 2; Jer. 33. 15; Zech. 3. 8: 6. 12.).

This Branch, Who shall reign as King in a future day, at His return to earth, has already presented His credentials to the Jewish people. He suffered rejection and crucifixion at their hands. (Acts 2. 23.).

The characteristics of this Branch-King are described. He is righteous; indeed His name will be called 'Jehovah-Tsidkenu' (Jehovah - our Righteousness). Thus, being a Man, a descendant of David, He is also God of very God. He is also therefore wise and will do what is just and right in the land. Not only will Judah be blessed by the Millennial reign of the Righteous Branch, but also Israel.

How can we participate in the kingdom of the Righteous Branch now in our day and age?

June 16
The spirit-filled man

'And Jesus being full of the Holy Spirit, returned from Jordan, and was led by the Spirit in the wilderness.' (Lk. 4. 1.).

Our Lord's baptism in Jordan was behind Him, with that word of approbation from His Father in heaven, and the descent of the Holy Spirit like a dove upon Him. Now His Spirit-filled Manhood must be tested in the wilderness, where that same Spirit was leading Him.

Between Jericho and Jerusalem, there is a mountain called Quarantania. The place of our Lord's temptation is reputed to be in this part of the wilderness of Judea. The period of His temptation was forty days, a standard probationary period (Ex. 24. 18; 1 Kings 19. 8; Jonah 3. 4.). The personage who administered the temptation was the devil himself.

The Saviour's temptation reached a climax at the end of these forty days, during which he had not eaten. It was then that the 'accuser' hurled his three flaming missiles at the Man, Christ Jesus. These were crafted to test the perfect Manhood, Messiahship and Deity of Jesus. But the Spirit-filled Man seized the Spirit's sword, the Word of God, and used it with devastating effect. The devil had challenged Him to satisfy His physical hunger by telling a stone to become bread. But Jesus said, "It is written: 'Man shall not live by bread alone.' " (Deu. 8. 3.).

The other two attacks were repulsed in an identical manner. "Worship me," the devil said, "and all the world's kingdoms shall be Thine." The Christ replied, "Thou shalt worship the Lord thy God and serve Him only." (Deu. 6. 13.). Finally, replying to the devil's challenge to prove His deity by a sensational act - supposedly based on Scripture! (Ps. 91. 11, 12.) - God, the Son said to him, "Thou shalt not tempt the Lord, thy God." (Deu. 6. 16.).

What lessons can we learn from the way that Jesus handled temptation ?

June 17

'As soon then as they had come to land, they saw a fire of coals there and fish laid thereon, and bread.'   Jesus says to them, "Come, have breakfast".   None of the disciples dared to ask Him, "Who art Thou ?" knowing that it was the Lord.'   (John 21. 9, 12.).

The same Lord, Who had made all the fish in the sea, sent 153 of them into the disciples' net.   He had also made a meal for these seven weary fishermen.   There was the charcoal fire burning brightly in the dawn with the barbecued fish placed on it, together with freshly-baked bread.   Jesus asked them to bring some of their great catch to augment the morning meal.   There was more than enough provision for eight people.

Then Jesus invited them to come and break their fast by partaking of the   Master Chef's meal.   The table which the Lord had prepared for His disciples was designed to teach them at least two things.   Firstly, they would be aware of the Master's concern and compassion for them, hungry and tired after a night of futile fishing.   Secondly, they would realise that, although He was risen from the dead, His loving relationship with them was just the same as before.

The disciples, on their part, were full of awe at His presence.   For them, it was an eerie experience to be in the company of One Who could disappear and re-appear at will.   No wonder they refrained from asking Him questions.

Jesus acted as Host and Waiter at the meal, as well as Chef.   He came to them with the bread and gave to them, and then also with the fish.   They must have recalled a previous occasion when He fed many thousands with bread and fish. (Jn. 6. 9, 10.). The place must have been quite near.

What menu has the Master Chef planned for you today ?

June 18

'For the zeal of Thine house hath eaten Me up, and the reproaches of them that reproached Thee have fallen upon Me.' (Psalm 69. 9.).

The disciples of the Lord Jesus had cause to remember this Scripture, as they watched Him doing a strange work. It happened at the beginning of our Lord's public ministry. They had come up with Him to Jerusalem for the Passover. They must have watched with astonishment, as the Son of God made a scourge of cords, and drove out the money changers and animals from the court of the temple. (Jn. 2. 17.).

Three years later, our Lord's zeal for God's house, spiritual, not material, brought Him to Golgotha and consumed Him, as He hung on the Cross. His zeal was just as strong then, as ever, despite all the opposition arrayed against Him. The psalm lists these opposing influences.

His many enemies wished to destroy Him (v. 4): Even His brothers disowned Him (v. 8). The local pundits spoke against Him (v. 12.): Even the drunkards mocked Him in their songs (v. 12): He looked for sympathy and comforters, but found none (v.20): The soldiers, before they crucified Him, gave our Lord wine vinegar mingled with gall, but He refused its pain-deadening effect (v. 21; Mat. 27. 34.). Above and beyond all that suffering, God smote and wounded Him (v. 26). Such was our Lord's zeal for God and His work, that He willingly endured all the agony.

Because of our Lord's zeal for God's house, the situation has changed completely. Now, the poor and the prisoners call upon Him, and He hears and answers them. One day soon, the heavens, the earth and the seas will praise Him, Who is the Zealous One.

Taking, as our example, the Zealous One, how could we increase our zeal for the House of God ? (1 Tim. 3. 15.)

June19
The carpenter's son

'And it came to pass, when Jesus had finished these parables, he departed thence; and having come into His own country, He taught them in their synagogue, so that they were astonished, and said, "Whence has this (Man) this wisdom and these works of power? Is not this the carpenter's Son? Is not His mother called Mary, and His brothers James and Joseph and Simon and Judas? And His sisters, are they not all with us? Whence then has this (Man) all these things?" (Mat. 13. 53 - 56.).

The inhabitants of Nazareth and the surrounding region were faced with a dilemma. They were confronted with two conflicting sets of evidence in the person of Jesus. On the one hand, they were impressed by His words of wisdom in the synagogue and His works of power. On the other hand, they were aware of our Lord's humble background and upbringing as the Son of the village carpenter as was supposed. So what was the reaction of these people? They were offended in Him.

If Jesus had been the son of the local land-owner or merchant or teacher, the citizens of Nazareth might have understood the situation better. But, in their eyes, Jesus was just the carpenter's Son. Apparently, there was little opportunity of formal education for Jesus (Jn. 7. 15.), as the eldest in a large family. He would have had to take His place at the carpenter's bench from an early age.

But, in one significant aspect, our Lord's situation was unique from all others. Being God, He could pre-arrange the occupation of His supposed father. So why did He choose to be the Son of a carpenter? To be reminded of His mission here on earth. The wooden beams and iron nails would be a daily reminder of the Cross which inexorably lay ahead of Him, upon which He must die for the sin of the universe.

What is your estimation of Jesus? Is He more than a carpenter's Son? What difference does your assessment of Christ make in your life?

June20

' *"And they shall make an Ark of acacia wood; two cubits and a half, the length thereof; and a cubit and a half, the breadth thereof; and a cubit and a half, the height thereof: And thou shalt overlay it with pure gold; inside and outside shalt thou overlay it; and shalt make upon it a crown of gold round about." ' (Ex. 25. 10, 11.).*

The Hebrew epistle gives us liberty to see in the Tabernacle and its furniture and furnishings, pictures of heavenly and eternal things. This can certainly be said of the most important article in the Tabernacle, the Ark of God, or the Ark of the Covenant. It is a significant type of our Lord Jesus Christ.

Firstly, this is seen in the materials used in its construction. The chest was made of acacia wood (a symbol of our Lord's perfect humanity) overlaid with pure gold (a symbol of our Lord's absolute deity).

Secondly, it is suggested that its dimensions have a significance. The perimeter length of its front, back and base was 8 cubits, which is the number of resurrection and new life. Its two sides had a perimeter length of 6 cubits, denoting the true humanity of our Lord.

Thirdly, its contents speak of the Saviour. The two stone tablets remind us that God's law was written in our Lord's heart. The pot with manna reminds us that He is the Bread of God sent down from heaven. Aaron's rod that budded reminds us that He is the Resurrection and the Life.

Fourthly, its function speaks of our Lord's atoning work. The Ark was the meeting place between God and Man. The atoning blood was sprinkled on its covering, called The Mercy Seat, on the Day of Atonement. But God displayed Christ as a Mercy Seat to justify those who have faith in His blood. (Rom. 3. 25, 26.).

Can you find practical lessons from the Ark as a type of Christ in the following passages? Num. 10. 33; Josh. 3. 13-17; 4. 17, 18; 6. 9.

June 21

'Brothers, the grace of our Lord Jesus Christ be with your spirit: Amen.'
(Gal. 6. 18.).

God's grace is His love in action, as He bestows His favour upon mankind, the object of His grace. That grace is seen in all its fulness in His Son, our Lord Jesus Christ. We observe His grace as He, the rich one, became so poor, in order that we, through His poverty, might become rich. (2 Cor. 8. 9.)

When our Lord became a Man, there were those who contemplated His glory, as of an Only-Begotten from alongside the Father, full of grace and truth. (John 1. 14.). The law was given by Moses, but grace and truth came into being through Jesus Christ (v. 17.). In His Manhood, our Lord had a special anointing of grace. The Psalmist writes of Him, "Thou art fairer than the sons of men; grace is poured into Thy lips." (Ps. 45. 2.).

Men marvelled at the gracious words that He spoke. He said to the women taken in adultery and brought to Him, "Neither do I condemn thee; go, and sin no more." (Jn. 8. 11.). He said to the thief, crucified next to Him, "Verily, I say to thee, today shalt thou be with me in Paradise." (Lk. 23. 43.).

Then, there was the gracious work that He did. He touched the unclean, to cleanse the leper and to raise the dead. He anointed the eyes of the blind man, to make him see. He embraced and blessed the children who came to Him. He took the place of a bond-servant, and washed His disciples' feet. But, grace upon grace, He took the sinner's place on the Cross, and wrought redemption there-on. Truly, He is the Gracious One.

What gracious words and works has the Gracious One spoken to, and done for you?

June22

' "Is it nothing to you, all ye that pass by?   Behold and see if there be any sorrow like unto my sorrow which is done unto me, wherewith Jehovah hath afflicted me in the day of His fierce anger." ' (Lam. 1. 12.).

The city of Jerusalem was in mourning.   Nebuchadnezzar's army had sacked it and carried its nobility back to Babylon.   The walls were levelled and the temple was destroyed.   The famine in the city was so sore that women boiled their babies and ate them (4. 10.).   Why had Jehovah's judgment come upon the city?   Because of its sin: The people, together with prophets and priests, had sinned against God.   So Jehovah's fierce anger had descended upon the city.

Although the city's sorrow was great, that of the Saviour was infinitely greater.   As He hung on the Cross outside the walls of that same city of Jerusalem, He could well use these words, "Is it nothing to you, all ye that pass by?"   To many of them, it was just a spectacle, with the crucified Son of God as the object of their ridicule.   'And those who passed by reviled Him wagging their heads and saying,   "Aha, Thou that destroyed the temple and buildest it in three days, save Thyself and come down from the Cross." ' (Mk. 15. 29.).   The chief priests and the scribes also mocked Him.

But the sorrow which transcended all other was that inflicted upon the Saviour by God. It was during the three hours of darkness when Jehovah laid on Jesus the iniquity of us all.   His sorrow culminated in His cry "My God, my God, why hast Thou forsaken Me?"   God's fierce anger against sin was poured out on His Sinless Son in that day, and was exhausted.   Now blessings draught for me, and for all who believe in Jesus.

In what ways does the anguish of the Sorrowing One affect me?

June 23

'The Spirit of the Lord is upon Me, because He has anointed Me to preach good news to the poor; He has sent Me to heal the broken hearted, to proclaim deliverance to the captives, and recovering of sight to the blind; to set at liberty those who are bound; to proclaim the acceptable year of the Lord.' (Lk. 4. 18, 19.)

The place was Shiloh in the conquered land of Canaan. It was the place where the tabernacle had been erected when Israel entered the promised land. The year was an extremely special one, the year of Jubilee, the fiftieth year since the law was given at Sinai. The day also was very special, the tenth day of the seventh month, the day of atonement. Only on this day, could the high priest of Israel enter the holy of holies in the tabernacle with the blood of the sacrificed animals. He sprinkled that blood before and on the mercy seat to cover his sins and those of the people. Then he laid his hands on the scapegoat which was sent away into the wilderness. Only then could the trumpet sound, and the year of Jubilee begin (Lev. 25. 9.). The trumpet proclaimed liberty throughout the land to all its inhabitants.

Many centuries later, another and greater year of Jubilee was proclaimed by Messiah-Jesus, in the synagogue in Nazareth. But in order that the spiritually poor may be enriched, the broken-hearted healed, Satan's captives delivered from his power, the spiritually blind made to see, and the crushed liberated, the atonement must be made. The precious blood of Jesus must be shed.

With great joy, we can proclaim that the atoning work is done. Now we wait for the Lord to call us to meet Him in the air, with the archangel's voice and the trump of God.

How can we best proclaim this year of jubilee?

June 24
Our forerunner

'This hope we have as an anchor of the soul, both sure and steadfast, and which enters into that within the veil, where the Forerunner has for us entered, even Jesus ......'. (Heb. 6. 19, 20.)

Through the presence of the indwelling Christ, we, as saints, have the hope of glory. (Col. 1. 27.). This hope is not dependent upon us, but on God. All that we had to do was to receive Christ by faith, in order to lay hold of the hope set before us. Now, our hope rests on God's promise contained in His word and confirmed by His oath. As it was with Abraham, so it is with us. (Gen. 22. 16.). As a result of these two unchangeable things, God's promise and God's oath, we have strong encouragement.

In our frail barque, we were tossed to and fro on the stormy seas of sin. We despaired of ever reaching the heavenly shore. But all was transformed when we welcomed the Saviour on board. He has guided us through the hidden reefs and rugged rocks of adversity into a safe haven.

Now He has taken the ship's cable, leapt into the sea and swum to the shore. He has secured the rope to a solid anchorage, Himself, as He has entered within the veil into the Holiest Place in the Heavenly Tabernacle. This was the task of the Forerunner: He was the one who came to a place where the rest of his company would follow. Our Lord Jesus is described as such only here, in this Scripture in Hebrews.

Having such a secure and firm anchorage, what kind of people should we be?
See 1 John 3. 3; Romans 12. 12; 2 Corinthians 3. 12; 1 Peter 3. 15.

June 25

'His name shall endure for ever: His name shall be continued as long as the sun, and men shall be blessed in Him: All nations shall call Him blessed.' (Ps. 72. 17.)

This Psalm concludes the Second Book of Psalms which begins at Psalm 42. This Book corresponds to the Book of Exodus which is called, in Hebrew, the Book of 'the Names'. This is because the book begins with the names of the sons of Israel who came with their father Jacob into Egypt. The Second Book of Psalms also has to do with the nation Israel, its ruin, Redeemer and redemption.

Ps. 72 was probably written after Solomon's second investiture. (1 Chron. 29. 22, 23; 23. 1.). It contains David's final prayer for his son. But, without doubt, the content of the psalm is Messianic. It describes the Redeemer's righteous reign, during which all nations shall call Him 'Blessed'.

There will be many reasons for calling our Lord Jesus such a Name, during His thousand-year reign. The psalmist mentions some of these:-
He will judge God's people with righteousness (v. 2.).
He will save the children of the needy (v.4.).
He will crush the oppressor (v.4.).
He will cause the righteous to flourish (vs. 6, 7.).
He will cause prosperity to abound (vs. 7, 16.)
He will have universal dominion (vs. 8 - 11.).
He will deliver, have compassion on and save the poor and needy (vs. 12 - 14.).
He will bless all nations (v. 17); therefore all nations will call Him 'Blessed'.

How many of the items noted above apply to you, now, in a spiritual sense, so that you too can call King Jesus 'Blessed' ?

June 26
A prophet

'And they were offended in Him.   But Jesus said unto them.   "A prophet is not without honour except in his own country, and in his own house."   And He did not many mighty works there because of their unbelief.'   (Mat. 13. 57, 58.).

There is no doubt that our Lord Jesus Christ was a prophet.   He says so in the text quoted above.

All the marks of a prophet are therefore found in Him.   For example, the prophet must be commissioned and sent by God, as Moses was.   This was undoubtedly true of the Saviour.   The Father sent the Son: Men had to acknowledge this fact.   The rabbi Nicodemus confessed this when he said to Jesus, "We know Thou art a teacher come from God; for no one can do these miraculous signs that Thou doest unless God is with him."   (Jn. 3. 2.)

Another mark of a prophet was that he did the work of God.   This was abundantly true of our Lord Jesus.   The Gospels record at least 35 works of power, performed by Jesus.   These included healings, exorcisms, controlling Nature and raising the dead. These demonstrated that Christ is the Power of God. (1 Cor. 1. 24.).

Again, a true prophet was noted for proclaiming the Word of God.   This was evident in our Lord's teaching, whether it was forth-telling (Mat. 5 - 7) or fore-telling
(Mat. 24 - 25.)

Here was proof that Christ is the Wisdom of God.   When the risen Christ met Cleopas and his companion on the Emmaus road, they described Him as, "A Prophet mighty in deed and word ------".   (Luke 24. 19.)

But Jesus, as God's true Prophet, was rejected and slain by His own kinsmen and countrymen, at Jerusalem, fulfilling His own prophetic word. (Lk. 13. 32, 33.).

Do you know Jesus, the anointed Prophet of God, in your life? See John 4. 19, 29.

June 27

' *"If his offering be a burnt offering of the herd, let him offer a male without blemish; he shall offer it at the door of the tabernacle of the congregation that he may be accepted before Jehovah.' "* (Lev. 1. 3.).
' *"It is a burnt sacrifice, an offering made by fire, of a sweet savour unto Jehovah"* ' (v. 17.).

This offering, together with the others, is a picture of the suffering and sacrifice of Christ, offering Himself without spot to God. It is the first of a series of five, the order describing man's approach to God from His standpoint. Hence the series begins with the burnt offering which was wholly for God, and ends with the guilt or trespass offering, which stresses the guilt of man.

In the 'burnt' or 'ascending offering' we see God, the Son fulfilling, through God the Spirit, the will of God, the Father (Heb. 9. 14.); and this He did, in all the strength of His deity and all the perfection of His humanity. The offering had to be a male yearling (Lev. 9. 3.), without defect.

The offerer brought his offering into the court of the tabernacle. There, on the northern side of the altar of burnt offering, he laid his hand on the head of the offering. He then slew it and its blood was sprinkled by a priest around the altar. We are reminded by this that we are 'accepted in the Beloved' having 'redemption through His Blood, even the forgiveness of sins'. (Eph. 1. 6, 7.).

The fact that the offerer had to slay the offering reminds us of our responsibility in causing the death of Christ. For, had we not sinned, He had not died.

All the animal, in its various parts, excluding the hide (which was the priest's portion), was laid on the altar and 'converted by fire into incense'. This symbolises the perfection of Christ's obedience to the will of God causing to rise to Him a 'savour of rest'. (Eph. 5. 2.).

How can we emulate Christ as our Burnt Offering ? See Romans 12. 1.

June 28

The beloved

'Having predestinated us to adoption as sons through Jesus Christ to Himself, according to the good pleasure of His will, to the praise of the glory of His grace, which He freely bestowed on us in the Beloved.' (Eph. 1. 5, 6.)

The apostle Paul reminds the readers of this letter of all the spiritual blessings that are theirs in Christ. The source of these blessings is the Tri-une God. The apostle shows us our spiritual possessions in Christ, firstly from God the Father (1. 4 - 6.), secondly, from God, the Son (vs. 7 -12,), and thirdly, from God, the Holy Spirit (vs. 13, 14.).

Before the space-matter-time universe was created, God, the Father, chose us, in Christ, not in ourselves. But the privilege of election carries with it a responsibility. It is that we should be holy and blameless before Him.

Also, through Jesus Christ, the Father has adopted us as His sons. It was a loving act of predestination on His part. As the Father's adopted sons, we can begin to enjoy our inheritance now. It was secured for us when Christ died, and given to us who believe when the Holy Spirit entered our lives. So we have good reason to praise the glory of God's grace.

Again, it is in the Beloved that the Father accepts us, and puts us into a position of grace and favour. The Father has freely given to us His glorious grace, in His Son, the Beloved One.

In eternity past, the Son was the Father's Beloved. At our Lord's baptism, having glorified God in His perfect humanity for thirty years, the Voice from heaven declared Him to be His Son, the Beloved, in Whom He was well pleased.
(Mat. 3. 17.). On the mount of our Lord's transfiguration, the same declaration was made, and heard by the favoured few who were there. (Mat. 17. 5.). But God's grace is so great, that we who are accepted in the Beloved are also beloved of God, the Lord. (1 Thes. 1. 4; 2 Thes. 2. 13.).

Is the Father's Beloved your Beloved? If so, what difference does it make in your life?

June 29

'And above the platform over their heads was the likeness of a throne as the appearance of a sapphire stone;   and upon the likeness of the throne was the likeness as the appearance of a Man.' (Ezek. 1. 26.)

Ezekiel was an exile   in a strange land when God gave him these visions recorded by him.   He was a priest without a temple, but   God   made   him   a   prophet   with a testimony.

True to the meaning of his name, Ezekiel was 'strengthened by God' at the outset of his ministry.   God gave him a vision of His throne and His person.   Then He strengthened him and commissioned him for service.

For Ezekiel, the event was unforgettable.   He noted the time and the place.   God graciously gave His servant a glimpse of   His glory.

First, Ezekiel saw what looked like a fiery storm approaching from the north.   Then he saw the four living beings with their human form, having faces, legs, feet but also wings. But these cherubim were associated with the chariot-throne of Jehovah, having great wheels within wheels, with the rims full of   eyes.

As Ezekiel lifted his gaze higher, he saw above the living beings a crystal-like platform with the likeness of a throne above that.   Then he saw God in human form upon the throne.   The reader is forced to the conclusion that here is a Christophany, namely, a pre-incarnate appearance of the Son of God.   The awesome majesty of this One overwhelmed the prophet.   He fell on his face before Him.

What is the significance of the reference to the rainbow in v.28 ?

June 30
The holy one of God

'And in the synagogue there was a man who had a spirit of an unclean demon and he cried out with a loud voice saying "Let us alone; what have we to do with Thee; Jesus of Nazareth ? Art Thou come to destroy us ? I know who Thou art; the Holy One of God." ' (Lk. 4. 33, 34.).

The Saviour was now in Capernaum. He was teaching in the synagogue on the Sabbath. Then a man began to shout at the top of his voice. The man was demon possessed.

From the Gospel record, this condition was not uncommon at that time. On at least eight distinct occasions, including this one, our Lord healed individuals who were demon possessed. But these instances were only part of a pattern in the ministry of our Lord Jesus (Mk. 1. 34, 39; Lk. 4. 41.), and of His disciples (Mk. 6. 13; Lk. 10. 17.).

When Satan sinned at the beginning he evidently took with him many angels who are called 'his'. (Mat. 25. 41; Rev. 12. 9.). Demons are included in that number of 'fallen' angels. They are described as unclean spirits. They have power to cause dumbness (Mat. 9. 32.), blindness (12. 22.), insanity (Lk. 8. 27.), and deformity (13. 11.) to humans whom they possess.

The demon in the man in the synagogue in Capernaum revealed certain things in the man's cries. It was terrified in the presence of the Nazarene; it was one of many ("us"); it was afraid that its judgment was imminent ('Hast Thou come to destroy us?') ; it knew the identity of Jesus, the Holy One of God.

"Be muzzled!" Jesus said sternly, "Come out of him!" The demon obeyed and came out of the man without injuring him.

Have you believed and have you come to know that Jesus is the Holy One of God ? (John 6. 68, 69.).

July 1

'Now of the things which we have spoken this is the sum: We have such an High Priest who sat down at the right hand of the throne of the majesty in the heavens; a Minister of the Sanctuary, and of the true Tabernacle, which the Lord pitched and not man.' (Heb. 8. 1, 2.).

The writer of this letter to the Hebrew Christians stresses repeatedly the excellencies of God's Son, our Saviour. Already, he has shown that our Lord's ministry as a High Priest is superior to the Aaronic order, because He will never again die. (7. 23, 24.). Consequently, His ministry of intercession is completely competent, being able to save those who come to God through Him. (v. 25.). Also, our Lord's ministry is untainted by sin, Godward, manward and selfward (v. 26.), unlike all earthly priests. Again, His ministry does not entail further sacrifice of Himself; this work has been done already at Golgotha, and never needs to be repeated. (v. 27.).

So now the Son is a Minister of the Sanctuary, by eternal appointment. This is the heavenly Sanctuary, the dwelling place of God, of which the earthly sanctuary was but a shadow. God's dwelling place in heaven is described as a Tabernacle both here and elsewhere in Scripture. (Heb. 9. 11; Rev. 13. 6.).

There is another marked difference between the ministry of the Aaronic priests and that of our great High Priest. They had to stand in the earthly sanctuary, but He sat down in the heavenly sanctuary, at the right hand of God. (Heb. 10. 11, 12.). That place of majesty is also a place of ministry, as our High Priest ministers in the true Tabernacle which the Lord pitched, and not man.

What practical difference does it make, for us to have such a Minister of the Sanctuary ?

July 2

' *"Let Thy hand be upon the Man of Thy right hand, upon the Son of Man Whom Thou madest strong for Thyself." ' (Ps. 80. 17.).*

In this psalm, the writer is lamenting because of the destruction of Israel as a nation. The northern kingdom had been invaded by Assyria, and the people taken into exile. Only the southern kingdom of Judah was left. Then it too was taken into captivity by Babylon.

In his prayer, the psalmist reminds God that He is the Shepherd of Israel and that the nation is His flock, whom He led out of Egypt.

Then the writer recalls that God, as a Gardener, planted Israel, as a vine in the land of Canaan. But, after much labour, He had abandoned it, to the mercy of the passers-by and the wild beasts.

Last of all, the poet appeals to God, as a Father, Who raised up Israel as a son (v. 15. N.I.V.). He reminds God that they are His vine and His people who are perishing.

Joseph and Benjamin, the sons of Rachel, beloved of Jacob, are in the mind of the psalmist. Joseph's sons were Ephraim and Manasseh, mentioned at the start of the psalm. When Rachel was giving birth to her second son, she called him 'Benoni' meaning 'Son of my Sorrow', but his father called him 'Benjamin, Son of the Right Hand.' These two names were fulfilled in Jesus, the Son of Man, in His Cross and in His Crown. He is truly the Man of God's right hand. This unique place of honour is His by right and by redemption. At His return to heaven, God said to Him, "Sit at My right hand until I make Thine enemies a footstool for Thy feet." (Ps. 110. 1.).

Do we honour and reverence the Man of God's right hand, Whom He delights to honour?

July3

'And Jesus went forth and saw a great multitude, and was moved with compassion toward them, and He healed their sick.' (Mat. 14. 14.).

Compassion is defined as having sorrow for the suffering of another, or pity, inclining one to spare or to succour.   It was a divine attribute.   The psalmist David wrote, ' ' "But Thou, O Lord, art a God full of compassion" '. (Ps. 86. 15.).
Again, 'Jehovah is gracious, and   full of   compassion, slow to anger, and of   great mercy'.   (Ps. 145. 8.).

It is therefore no surprise that Jesus, God incarnate, is described as having compassion. 'When He saw the multitudes, He was moved with compassion on them, because they fainted and were scattered abroad, as sheep having no shepherd.'   (Mat. 9. 36.).
Our Lord's compassion caused Him to challenge His disciples to ask Him   for   workers to   be   sent   into   His   harvest   field.

The sight of a great multitude moved Jesus with compassion for them, so that He healed their sick (14. 14.). On a similar occasion, because of His compassion for the people, our Lord provided food for four thousand men, besides women and children, from seven loaves and a few small fish (15. 32.).

The compassion of the Christ was also directed towards individuals, such as two blind men on the outskirts of Jericho, who received their sight when Jesus touched their eyes (20. 34.).   Again, in compassion, He touched a leper and he was cleansed (Mk. 1. 41.).   His compassion caused Him to raise and restore to life a dead son to his widowed mother at a town called Nain. (Luke 7. 13).

Christ's compassion was the compulsion which drove Him to the Cross, there to die for lost, sick, perishing, blind, unclean, dead sinners such as we.

In what ways does Christ's compassion constrain us to serve Him ?

July4
The meal offering

'And when any will offer a meal offering unto Jehovah, his offering will be of fine flour, and he shall pour oil upon it, and put frankincense thereon; and he shall bring it to Aaron's sons the priests; and he shall take from it his handful of its fine flour and of its oil with all of its frankincense; and the priest shall burn the memorial of it upon the altar, to be an offering made by fire of a sweet savour unto Jehovah.'
(Lev. 2. 1, 2.)

While the burnt offering depicts Christ in death, the meal offering represents Christ in life; hence there is no mention of the shedding of blood.

Firstly, let us consider the composition of the meal offering. The main ingredient was fine flour, which is the chief constituent of ordinary bread. Since our Lord described Himself as the Bread of Life (Jn. 6. 35), we can deduce that the fine flour is a picture of His perfect humanity. The offerer poured oil on the flour, the oil being a symbol of the Holy Spirit. (Ps. 45. 7; Acts 10. 38.). Then the offerer added frankincense, all of which was burned on the altar by the priest. While the power of our Lord's earthly ministry is depicted by the oil, the purity of that ministry, and the pleasure it brought to the Father, is depicted by the frankincense. Salt, which is a type of the incorruptible Word of God (Col. 4. 6.), had to season every meal offering. (Lev. 2. 13.). No leaven, (typifying evil), nor honey (typifying natural sweetness), had to be used.

Secondly, consider its preparation: It was baked either in an oven, or a plate or a pan. These are a reminder of our Lord's life-time sufferings, for righteousness sake, sympathetically, and in anticipation of the Cross.

Thirdly, consider its partaker. It was an aroma pleasing to Jehovah. There was also a portion for the priests to be eaten in the court of the tabernacle.

Are we living in the sanctuary and feeding on Christ, the Anti-type of the meal offering?

July5

'For He is our peace, Who has made both one, and has broken down the middle wall of partition between us.' (Eph. 2. 14.).

Our Lord Jesus, the Prince of Peace, is also the very embodiment of peace. He alone could pay the price of peace. His own precious blood (v. 15; Col. 1. 20.). Now, through His servants, He proclaims peace to those both far and near. (Eph. 2. 17.).

These three truths are beautifully illustrated in the Gospel record. On the evening of our Lord's resurrection from the dead, He appeared to His disciples. It was the first day of the week. Bolted doors were no barrier to the risen Christ. As He stood in their midst, He said, "Peace be to you." (Jn. 20. 19.). It was a common greeting, but now with a deeper meaning. The Living Lord Jesus alone can bring peace to His disciples' troubled hearts and minds, both then and now. For He is our Peace. The realisation of His presence guarantees peace to the weakest saint. In the Person and Presence of the Prince of Peace we have peace.

Then He showed to them His hands and His side (v. 20.). His hands, with their spike wounds, and His side with its spear wound would remind them of the price of peace. It was paid in full by His precious holy blood. His hands which worked for them, and His side which bled for them, on the Cross.

After another greeting, our Lord said, "As the Father sent Me forth, I also send you." (v. 21.). He would proclaim this peace, through His servants, whom He would empower by the Presence of the Holy Spirit on the Day of Pentecost. (Jn. 7. 39.).

If we have the abiding Presence of the Prince of Peace, do we allow Him to preach His peace through us to others?

July6

'Thus says the Lord Jehovah.   "Remove the diadem and take off the crown; what is shall be no more. Exalt him who is low, and abuse him who is high.   I will overturn, overturn, overturn it; and it shall be no more, until He come Whose right it is, and I will give it Him." ' (Ezek. 21. 26, 27.).

God's decree was being issued by His servant Ezekiel to the city of Jerusalem, its holy places and the land of Israel (v. 2.).

Firstly, royalty was to be removed;   there were to be no more diadem and crown;   and it was so.   When our Lord Jesus came, an Idumean called Herod was ruler of Judea, under the Romans, of course!   This condition of things will continue to the end.

Also, the usual order of things will be reversed.   The humble shall be exalted and the proud shall be abased, the usurper, the profane wicked prince of Israel will be humbled, and the lowly despised Nazarene will be exalted on His royal Throne.

Before that can happen, there will be three overturnings. The city of Jerusalem and the land will suffer ruin.   Already this has happened twice;   first, by the Babylonians under Nebuchadnezzar in 587 B.C. then by the Romans under Titus in 70 A.D.   Now Israel is back in the city and the land which awaits a third and final devastation at the hands of the Beast and his cohorts.

Then God will give it to His Son at His return to rout His enemies and reign supreme. He alone is the rightful and righteous Owner of the city of Jerusalem and the land of Israel.

What overturning needs to be done in our lives before the Lord comes ?

July 7

'Now when He ceased speaking, He said to Simon, "Launch out into the deep and let down your nets for a haul"; and Simon answering said to Him, "Master, we have toiled all the night and have taken nothing; nevertheless at Thy word I will let down the net." ' (Lk. 5. 4, 5.).

The word 'Master' means 'One who is over others' in the Greek of the New Testament. It is used only of the Lord Jesus, and it is found only in the Gospel of Luke.

The Lord had used Simon's fishing boat as a pulpit, from which to teach the people. When He had finished, He instructed Peter to take the boat further out and lower the nets for a catch. Peter immediately acknowledged the Lord's superiority and authority, and obeyed, except for one detail. Jesus told Simon to let down the nets, but he only used one net. The strain on the net because of the great multitude of fishes in it was too great, and it broke. Both his and his partners' ship was filled with fishes. Then Peter was forced to acknowledge his sinnership and Jesus' lordship.

On another occasion, the Lord had fallen asleep as they were sailing across the lake. A storm arose and the ship was filled with water. His disciples woke Him up with the words, "Master, Master, we perish !" (8. 24.). Of course, this could never have happened, since our Lord's mission on earth still had to be fulfilled; to die on a Cross. So He rose and rebuked the wind and the waves, and there was a calm. The disciples were right to call Him Master, but the circumstances showed Him to be Lord.

The same lesson can be learned from the 'Mount of Transfiguration' (9. 33.). Peter had to learn that the One Whom he called 'Master' was none other than God's Son.

Have we acknowledged Jesus, not only as our Master, but also as our Lord ?

July 8
The spotless offering

'For if the blood of bulls and of goats, and the ashes of an heifer sprinkling the unclean, sanctifies to the purifying of the flesh: How much more shall the blood of Christ, Who through the eternal Spirit offered himself without spot to God, purge your conscience from dead works to serve the living God.' (Heb. 9. 13, 14.).

The phrase 'how much more' directs us to the contrasts which are presented here by the writer of this epistle.

There is the contrast between the blood of the sacrificial animals and that of the Christ. His was the precious, perfect, holy blood of the Lamb of God. The blood of bulls and goats could never be compared with that.

Then, in the days of the ceremonial law, only the flesh was purified by the ritualistic process, but now the conscience is purified by the application of the blood of Christ.

In contrast to the animals, our Lord Jesus offered Himself as a once-for-all sacrifice. Note that the God-head was involved here. It was by the eternal Spirit, the Christ offered Himself to God.

Again, the animals had to be unblemished physically. But our Lord was unblemished and without spot morally and spiritually. He said to the Jews on one occasion, "Which of you convinces Me of sin ?" (Jn. 8. 46.). The challenge was never taken up by them.

The Levites were set apart for service by the sprinkling of the water of purification. (Num. 8. 7.). We are released from dead works to serve the living God, through the cleansing power of the blood of Christ.

Has your conscience been purified ?

July 9
The reconciler

'Loving-kindness and truth are met together; righteousness and peace have kissed each other.' (Ps. 85. 10.).

In the first half of this Psalm, the author is speaking directly to Jehovah God. He reminds God of what He has done. He has brought His people back to His land, and covered all their sin. But the psalmist asks Him to revive His people again and grant them His salvation.

The writer then waits for God to speak; and He did speak, and He has spoken fully and finally, at the end of these days, in the person of His Son. God spoke peace to His people in sending to them His only Son. God's Salvation came near to those who feared Him, and Glory dwelt in the land. The disciples of Jesus beheld that Glory, as of an only-begotten from alongside the Father, full of grace and truth.

But, in coming to what was His own, His own people rejected Him and consigned Him to a Cross. It was then that God was in Christ reconciling the world to Himself, not reckoning to them their offences. (2 Cor. 5. 19.). It was there that loving-kindness and truth met together, and righteousness and peace kissed each other.

> 'Mercy and truth unite; Oh, 'tis a wondrous sight,
> All sights above.
> Jesus the curse sustains; guilt's bitter cup He drains,
> Nothing for us remains;
> Nothing but love !'

Then Truth sprang out of the earth when Jesus rose from the dead. Now Righteousness on God's throne looks down from heaven. When He returns, the land will yield its increase.

What do you do with this Word of Reconciliation ?

July 10
The feeder of the multitudes

'And He commanded the multitudes to sit down on the grass, and took the five loaves and the two fishes, and looking up to heaven, He blessed and broke and gave the loaves to His disciples, and the disciples gave to the multitudes. And all ate and were filled.' (Mat. 14. 19, 20.).

The importance of this miracle is seen by the fact that an account of it is found in each of the four Gospels. (Mk. 6; Lk. 9; Jn. 6.).

The evening was approaching and the people were still surrounding the Saviour. His disciples counselled Him to dismiss them, so that they could buy food and find lodgings in the villages nearby.

But our Lord said to His disciples, "They have no need to go. Give them to eat." Philip calculated that it would take the equivalent of eight months wages to buy a little food for such a large crowd of people. After all, there were 5,000 men, besides women and children.

Then our Lord commanded the men to sit down. They did so in groups of 100 or 50. He took the five barley loaves and two small fishes which a little boy had offered to Him. When He had given thanks, He broke the loaves and divided the fishes, and gave to His disciples for distribution: All were satisfied. Not only so, but the disciples gathered up twelve hand baskets full of fragments afterwards.

It was obviously an act of creation on the part of our Lord Jesus Christ, God incarnate. Not from nothing, as was the case with the creation of the heavens and the earth, but from the little lad's gift. The Creator-God had visited His people, and was well able to meet their need. He did this ultimately through His sacrificial death at Golgotha.

How can we help in the Lord's present work of feeding the multitudes ?

July 11
The peace offering

'And if his offering be a sacrifice of peace-offering, if he present it of the herd, whether it be a male or female, he shall present it without blemish before Jehovah'.
(Lev. 3. 1.).

The peace offering reminds us that our Lord Jesus has made peace by the blood of His Cross. (Col. 1. 20.).   So we have peace with God through the sacrifice of His Son. The blood of the peace offering was sprinkled on the altar, thus speaking of atonement. This resulted in fellowship, with thanksgiving. (Lev. 7. 12.).   In this, we are reminded that the basis of our peace and fellowship with God is the sacrificial work of our Lord Jesus Christ on the Cross.   (1 Cor. 1. 9.).

The idea of fellowship is very prominent in the peace offering.   The fat of the animal was offered by fire to God.   It was an odour of a sweet fragrance to Jehovah.   This was called the 'food' or the 'bread' of the offering. (Lev. 3. 11.).   So God had His portion from the sacrifice of His Son.   The priest also shared in the sacrifice: He was given its breast and right shoulder   (7. 31-34.), after the breast was waved as a wave-offering before Jehovah, and the shoulder was presented as a heave offering. The flesh of the sacrifice of his peace offering was the portion of the offerer.   It was the only sacrifice of which the offerer partook.   So God, the anointed priests, the offerer with his family all partook of the same sacrifice of the peace offering.

In the same way, and particularly at the Lord's Supper, the believers enjoy such fellowship with God spiritually.   He delights in the death and resurrection of His Son, and so do they.   They hear Him say, "My body given for you," and "My blood shed for you."

What were the duties of the offerer of the peace offering, and what are the present-day lessons ?   See   Leviticus 3. 2;   7. 16, 19.).

July 12
The head

'But, speaking the truth in love, we may grow up into Him in all things, Who is the Head, the Christ; from Whom the whole body fitly joined together and compacted by that which every joint supplies, according to the effectual working in measure of every part, makes increase of the body unto the edifying of itself in love.'
(Eph. 4. 15, 16.).

Our Lord Jesus Christ is Head over all things to the assembly (Eph. 1. 23.), which is His body. On His ascension above all the heavens, the Head initiated the assembly by sending the Holy Spirit on the Day of Pentecost. As He indwelt those who believed and received the Word, He brought spiritual gifts for the building up of the body of Christ.

Just as the head controls the physical body, so the assembly, the body of Christ, is controlled by its Head in the heavens. What the body says is subject to the control of the Head. What the body sees is controlled by the Head. What it hears and does is under the control of the Head.

The Head makes the body fit together and hold together, so that there is unity in the body. Of course, we are considering the ideal and the ultimate condition of the assembly, the body of Christ. Presently, there are many divisions and schisms. But in the plan and purpose of God, there is and will be one body in the Lord.

It is also a comfort to remember that when any member of the body suffers, the Head also suffers. Saul of Tarsus learned that in His first encounter with Jesus, the Risen Head. (Acts 9. 4.). Saul was not only causing the saints to suffer, but also the Saviour. The Lord said to him, "Why are you persecuting Me? "

Do we always speak the truth in love, and thus acknowledge the Head ?

July 13

'Then he brought me back the way of the outer gate of the sanctuary which faces the east; and it was shut. And Jehovah said to me; "This gate shall be shut; it shall not be opened, and no man shall enter in by it; because Jehovah, the God of Israel, has entered in by it, therefore it shall be shut." ' (Ezek. 44. 1, 2.).

Ezekiel was given a vision of the temple which will be built at the beginning of our Lord's millennial reign. It is enclosed by a wall (40. 5.). The outer court is described, where the people gather (vs. 6 - 27.). Access to it is through three gates in the north, south and east walls.

Ezekiel had already seen a sad sight. He saw the glory of Jehovah departing from the threshold of Solomon's temple (10. 18.). Then he saw the glory of the God of Israel at the entrance of the east gate (v. 19.). Then it stood over the mount to the east of the city (11. 23.). This was the Mount of Olives. It was from this same spot that the glorious Son of God ascended back to heaven. (Acts 1. 9, 12.). He had already pronounced judgment on the city of Jerusalem and the sanctuary. (Mat. 23. 37, 38.).

But the Shekinah glory will return in the form of Jesus, Messiah. He will enter by the east gate and take up His residence in the millennial temple. (Ezek. 43. 4.). The east gate will then be closed to all others, except for the prince (46. 12.); it will be opened when the prince brings his burnt offerings and peace offerings. Since 'no man' is allowed to enter it, the prince must be David, resurrected (34. 23, 24; 37. 24, 25.). He is said to have sons (46. 16.). His most illustrious son is Jesus, Who is also his Lord.

Have you welcomed into the sanctuary of your heart, the One Who will enter the earthly sanctuary by the east gate ?

July14
A great prophet

'And there came a fear on all; and they glorified God saying, "A great Prophet has arisen among us," and "God has visited His people." ' (Lk. 7. 16.).

Our Lord had just performed a mighty miracle. He had raised a dead youth to life.

He had journeyed from Capernaum by the lake to the hill town of Nain, about 25 miles (40 km.) to the south-west. He arrived at the gate just as a funeral procession was emerging from it. The Lord comforted the widowed mother, now bereft of her only son. He touched the open coffin and commanded the young man to arise. The 'corpse' sat up and began to speak: Jesus gave him back to his mother.

The reaction of the people present was natural, and almost predictable, considering what they had just witnessed. The expectation of the return of Elijah was widely spread at that time (9. 8, 19.); and did not Elijah, by prayer and the power of God restore a dead son to his widowed mother? (1 Kings 17. 23) This was also repeated by his successor, Elisha (2 Kings 4. 36.). The location of this notable miracle was at Shunem, which was only 2 miles (3km.) southwest of Nain.

The crowd was right to conclude that God had come to care for His people. But this great Prophet Who had arisen to accomplish this task was none other than God's Son. A prophet must prophesy; and one of our Lord's greatest prophecies was that He would suffer many things and be slain, and rise again the third day. (Lk. 9. 22.). This prophecy was fulfilled exactly as our Lord had predicted.

The Great Prophet has also foretold His return, first for His heavenly people, the church, and then for His earthly people, Israel. He will fulfil His faithful word.

Are you relying on the work and the word of the great Prophet?

July 15

'Looking to Jesus, the Author and Perfecter of faith; Who for the joy that was set before Him endured the Cross, despising the shame, and has sat down at the right hand of the throne of God.' (Heb. 12. 2.).

All believers in the Lord Jesus Christ are depicted here as running in a race. It is a long-distance race, which begins when we trust Jesus for salvation and ends when we are with Him in glory. There is therefore great need for endurance to continue running in faith's marathon. But there is also great encouragement from the witness of those who have run well in the past.

We are exhorted by the writer of the Epistle to do three things. Firstly, we should lay aside every weight. These weights would be like a runner wearing a heavy coat. They could be identified as love of family and home, love of comfort and ease, and so on.

Secondly, we should cease from besetting sin. This trips us up so that we stumble and fall. The chief sin is that of unbelief, for 'whatever is not of faith is sin'. (Rom. 14. 23.).

Thirdly, we must fix our eyes on Jesus. He is our Goal. He is the Author (Leader and Source) and Perfecter (Completer) of faith. We looked to Him for salvation (Isa. 45. 22.) and we are looking for Him to return (Heb. 9. 23.). Meanwhile, we must look away from all else and fix our gaze solely on Him. He is our great Exemplar. He is the One Who has gone before us, and now shows us the way. For, 'although He was Son, He learned obedience from the things which He suffered'. (Heb. 5. 8.). He will enable us to complete the race of faith.

What specific help do we have that was also used by the Pioneer and Perfecter of faith during His earthly sojourn?

July 16
The afflicted one

' *"From my youth I have been afflicted and close to death; I suffer Thy terrors, I am overcome. Thy fierce wrath goeth over me; Thy terrors have cut me off."* '
(Ps. 88. 15, 16.).

The composer of this psalm was an illustrious man. His name was Heman, meaning 'Faithful'. He was the grandson of Samuel the prophet. (1 Chr. 6. 33.). King David appointed him, with others, to be responsible for the singing and music in the sanctuary. He was well qualified for the work because he was called 'the singer'.

The psalm has been described as the saddest song in the Psalter. The writer was evidently in deep despair; the reason for his condition is not given. It may have been due to some kind of illness. But he traces the source of his affliction back to Jehovah-God. "Thou hast put me in the lowest pit, in dark places, in the depths. Thy wrath hath rested upon me, and Thou hast afflicted me with all Thy waves: Selah." (v. 7.). The proof is here, that the psalmist was a man of prayer as well as a man of sorrows.

But his experience is but a faint reflection of an infinitely deeper one; that of the Man of Sorrows on the Cross at Golgotha. Earlier, in Gethsemane, our Lord said, "My soul is exceedingly sorrowful unto death." (Mk. 14. 34; Ps. 88. 3.).

Now in the darkness, forsaken by friends, loved-ones and God Himself, the Saviour is alone in His affliction. God's fierce wrath against sin rolls over Him, the sinless One, like the waves of the sea. "He was cut off out of the land of the living. For the transgression of my people was He stricken." (Isa. 53. 8.). There, God's sword of anger was exhausted, and now God's Son is exalted.

Can we say and sing, "All for my sake, my peace to make; Now sleeps that sword for me." ?

July17

'And when He had sent the multitudes away, He went up into the mountain apart to pray; and when evening came, He was there alone.' *(Mat. 14. 23.).*

The day had been a very busy one for our Lord. He had healed the sick and fed the multitude: Now it was evening. Jesus constrained His disciples to embark and go on before Him to the other side of the lake Gennesaret.

It was then that another problem had to be precluded. The men who had seen the sign which Jesus had done, on feeding the multitude, had concluded that He was a prophet; not only a prophet but the Prophet, the coming One, the Messiah! So they were about to seize Him and make Him King. But He dismissed the crowds and sought solitude in the mountain. There He was alone with His Father, God.

Our Lord's life was characterised by prayer. He prayed at His baptism (Lk. 3. 21.): He prayed in the desert (5. 16.): He spent a night on the mountain in prayer before He called and chose the twelve disciples, the next day (6. 12, 13.): He prayed before asking His disciples to declare His identity (9. 18, 20.): On one occasion, as He was praying, His disciples asked Him to teach them to pray (11. 1.): He prayed for Peter that his faith would not fail (22. 32.): He agonised in prayer in the Garden of Gethsemane (vs. 41, 44.): While on the Cross, He prayed (23. 34, 46;
Mat. 27. 46.).

On the night of the Last Supper, our Lord Jesus concluded His final ministry to His disciples with prayer to His Father (Jn. 17.).

Sufficient has been said in this study to show that the Saviour was a Man of prayer. Indeed, His ministry of prayer continues, as He intercedes for us at God's right hand (Rom. 8. 34; Heb. 7. 25.).

What can we learn from the example of the Son of God, as One Who prays, to help us in our prayer life ?

July 18

' "If the priest that is anointed sins according to the sin of the people, then let him bring for his sin which he has sinned a young bullock without blemish to Jehovah for a sin offering." ' (Lev. 4. 3).

The sin offering had to do with the principle of sin. It was for sins committed unconsciously or unintentionally at the time (vs.1, 2). The apostle Paul was a good example of this, when he wrote, 'I obtained mercy, because I did it ignorantly in unbelief.' (I Tim.1.13). Also, when Jesus was crucified, He said, "Father, forgive them, for they know not what they do." (Lk.23.34). The whole human race, both Jew and Gentile, was represented there at the Cross, but the Son pleaded with the Father to forgive them. Later, the apostle Peter said to the men of Israel, "And now, brethren, I know that you did it in ignorance, as also your rulers; but God has thus fulfilled what he had announced beforehand by the mouth of all the prophets, that His Christ should suffer." (Acts 3. 17,18).

There had to be a righteous basis for forgiveness to be granted. That basis was found when the Saviour became Sin-Offering on the Tree. 'Him (Christ) who knew not sin He (God) has made sin (offering) for us, that we might become the righteousness of God in Him.' (2 Cor.5.21). Again, it is written, 'Once, in the consummation of the ages, He has been manifested for the putting away of sin by the sacrifice of Himself.' (Heb.9.26). Again, Peter wrote, 'Who His own self bore our sins in His own body on the tree.' (1 Peter 2.24).

The body of any sin offering, whose blood was taken into the holy place, was burned outside the camp. In fulfilment of this, our Lord entered into the heavenly sanctuary, once for all, through His own blood (Heb.9.12), after he had suffered outside the city of Jerusalem.

Have we obeyed the injunction to go forth to Him outside the camp? (Heb. 13.13).

July 19
Christ loved the church

'Husbands, love your wives, even as Christ also loved the Church and gave Himself for it: That he might sanctify and cleanse it with the washing of water by the word: That He might present it to Himself a glorious Church, not having spot or wrinkle or any such thing; but that it should be holy and without blemish.' (Eph.5.25-27).

Love is a personal attribute which esteems its object so highly as to be willing to give all for its benefit and well-being.   This attribute of God is described in the following Scriptures:-

'For God so loved the world that He gave His only-begotten Son.' (Jn.3.16)
'Christ also loved the Church and gave Himself for it.'   (Eph. 5. 25.)
'The Son of God Who loved me and gave Himself for me.' (Gal.2.20)

Thus true love is demonstrated by an act of the will. It is not an emotional feeling: It is unconditional - it doesn't say, "I will love you, if you will love me!"

The apostle uses Christ's love for the Church as a pattern for husbands to love their own wives. The figure of the Church as the Bride of Christ is clearly seen here.

Firstly, the Bride must be purchased at infinite cost, the precious blood of Christ. Just as Eve was fashioned from the side of Adam, so the Church was formed from the wounded side of the Saviour. He delivered Himself up even to death for it.

Secondly, Christ is now preparing the Bride for His presence. He is using the Word of God with its sanctifying and cleansing effect in the lives of the saints   (Jn. 15.3 ; 17.17).

Thirdly, at our Lord's return, He will present the Assembly to Himself, all glorious, without flaw or blemish.

Are you allowing the Word of God to do its cleansing work in your life day by day ?

July 20
The smiting stone

' "Forasmuch as thou sawest that the Stone was cut out of the mountain without hands, and that it broke in pieces the iron, the brass, the clay, the silver, and the gold; the great God hath made it known to the king what shall come to pass hereafter; and the dream is certain, and the interpretation thereof sure." ' (Dan. 2. 45)

Nebuchadnezzar, king of Babylon, had a dream of world empires. It was given to him by God, in the form of a great image.

Its head of gold was Babylon, which represents autocratic rule. Its breast and arms of silver was Medo-Persia, which represents aristocratic rule (5.28). Its belly and thighs of brass was Greece, which represents military rule. Its legs of iron was Rome which represents merciless rule. Its feet and toes of iron and clay is Rome revived, which represents democratic rule.

The Stone which smote the feet of the image is our Lord Jesus Christ and represents Divine rule. The Stone was cut out of the mountain without hands. Our Lord sprang from the tribe of Judah, chosen by God for that purpose, the mount Zion which He loved. (Ps. 78. 68). The shaping of the Stone was a work of God. The Holy Spirit came upon the Virgin Mary and the power of the Highest overshadowed her to produce the Holy One, Jesus.

The Stone will break in pieces and consume all these kingdoms at the end of the seven year tribulation period. (Dan. 9. 27). Then He will set up His universal and eternal Kingdom. The Stone became a great mountain and filled the whole earth (2.35).

Has the God of heaven revealed to you the secret of the Smiting Stone? If so, is your reaction that of Daniel? (v.19)

July 21

'Now when John had heard in the prison the works of the Christ, he sent two of his disciples, and said to Him, "Art Thou the Coming One , or do we wait for another?" ' (Mat.11. 2, 3).

John lay in the dungeon of Herod's palace at Machaerus, on the eastern shore of the Dead Sea, awaiting news that Messiah-Jesus had lifted up the axe (2.10). It would be wielded at the root of the trees. One such tree would be Herod Antipas, in whose dungeon John lay. But it didn't happen. Instead, his disciples brought him reports that Messiah was consorting with tax-collectors and sinners (9.11).

But John followed the proper course by sending his disciples with his questions to Jesus. His question, "Art Thou the Coming One?", might be paraphrased, "Art Thou He who shall establish the Messianic kingdom with outward power?" Our Lord could have answered that question by saying, "Yes, but not yet." But he didn't. Instead, He reminded John that the prophetic word was being fulfilled by the work which He was doing. In other words, Jesus was performing Messianic miracles and more.

At the same time as the Lord was doing mighty miracles of healing, He quoted to John's disciples from the book of Isaiah. 'The blind receive their sight, the lame walk, the deaf hear,' (Isa. 35. 5, 6); and more than that, the lepers are cleansed and the dead are raised up. Then Jesus added, "And the poor have the gospel preached to them; and blessed is he who shall not be offended in Me."

There was no need for John or his disciples to wait for another - Messiah had come!

Are we waiting for the Coming One to return?

July 22
The unchanging one

'Jesus Christ, the same, yesterday, and today, and for ever.' (Heb.13.8)

'Yesterday', Jesus died on a Cross, but God raised Him from the dead on the third day. This was the triumphant message given by the angel to the faithful women. They had come to the garden tomb to anoint the body of Jesus. The angel said to them, "You seek Jesus, Who was crucified? He is not here, for he is risen, as He said. Come, see the place where the Lord lay."

Also, 'yesterday', Jesus was exalted by the right hand of God, Who made Him both Lord and Christ. Moreover, 'yesterday', those who had become leaders of the Hebrew Christians had accepted Jesus as the Messiah (Christ) by faith. Even His half-brothers, James and Jude, had believed on Him. James had an important contribution to make in the life of the church in its early history, as one of its leaders. (Acts 15.13).

Now, Jesus Christ, Whom these Christian leaders trusted and looked to, is just the same today. He is the same physically; a real Man of flesh and bone in the excellent Glory. He is the same spiritually, the God-Man, with all the attributes of Deity. His love and compassion are the same as they ever were. His holiness and righteousness are the same. His power and might are the same. Also, in His pure and perfect Manhood, He bears the marks of His suffering for sin. John saw in the midst of the throne in heaven a Lamb with the marks of slaughter upon It. (Rev. 4. 6).

To the eternal ages, He is the unchanging One. All creation is subject to change and decay, but He changes not. Jesus is the same forever. (Heb. 1. 12).

How can the unchanging nature of Jesus Christ help you now ?

July 23
The seed of David

' "I have made a covenant with My chosen, I have sworn to David My servant. Thy Seed will I establish for ever, and build up thy throne to all generations." Selah.'
(Ps. 89. 3, 4)

The writer of the psalm was Ethan, or Jeduthun. (1 Chron. 25. 1, 6;   16, 41).   He was one of Solomon's wisest counsellors. (1 Kings   4. 31).   But Solomon's heart had turned away from God, and he had built idols for his wives.   So Jehovah said that he 7would tear the kingdom from him, leaving only one tribe for his son.
(1 Kings 11. 11-13).   In spite of that, God would keep His promise to Solomon's father, David, that his house, kingdom and throne would endure and be established forever.   (2 Sam. 7. 16).

Now, in this psalm, the promise is repeated.   The primary theme of the song is the loving-kindness and faithfulness of Jehovah.   Each of these words occurs seven times in the psalm.   The complementary theme is the promise of the Seed.   God's loving-kindness gave David the promise and His faithfulness will fulfil it.

The promised Seed is the Christ.   He was born of the Seed of David according to the flesh (Rom. 1. 3), but He was also the Son of God.   He was declared to be so by the resurrection from the dead.

Three times in the psalm, the promise is given that God will establish the Seed of David for ever (vs. 4, 29, 36): Also, His throne will be made firm through all generations, as long as the heavens endure.   This will take place after the Great Tribulation, the time of Jacob's trouble, when the Deliverer will come out of Zion.   He shall reign for ever and ever.

How do we know that God will keep His covenant with David, and with us?

July24
The walker on the sea

'And in the fourth watch of the night, Jesus went out to them, walking on the sea; and when the disciples saw Him walking on the sea, they were terrified, saying, "It is a ghost"; and they cried out for fear. But Jesus immediately spoke to them, saying, "Take courage; it is I; be not afraid." ' (Mat. 14. 25-27)

The weather had deteriorated since the disciples had set sail for the other side of the lake. The wind was against them and the ship was being tossed to and fro by the waves. They had resorted to rowing, but were making no headway. What made matters worse was the absence of their Master. Indeed, He had dispatched them to the other side, and had remained on His own.

Then they saw what they took to be an apparition, coming towards them. They were terror-stricken and cried out with fear. But it was Jesus, walking on the sea. He was creating a path for Himself on the surface of the water. As Creator, He could dispense with the first law of thermodynamics which states that matter cannot be created or destroyed. He was creating an anti-gravitational energy to sustain His body as he walked on the water.

In His reply to His disciples' cry of fear, our Lord revealed to them His true identity as the 'I Am'. He used the special Name which He had revealed to Moses at the burning bush on Horeb. God said to Moses to tell the children of Israel that 'I Am' had sent him to them. (Ex. 3. 14).

In effect, Jesus was saying to the disciples (and to us), " I am in control of every circumstance in life; there is no need to be afraid. "

With the Walker on the sea within the vessel of our lives, what reason have we to be afraid ?

July25
The trespass offering

' "And he shall bring a ram without blemish out of the flock, according to thy evaluation, for a trespass offering to the priest, and the priest shall make an atonement for him concerning his ignorance wherein he erred and knew it not, and it shall be forgiven him. It is a trespass offering; he has certainly trespassed against Jehovah." ' (Lev. 5. 18, 19)

There is a sharp contrast between the trespass offering and the sin offering. The sin offering reminds us of the sinful nature of humanity and of the root of evil within each one of us. (1 Jn. 1. 8). The trespass offering reminds us of the sinful deeds of humanity, and of the fruit of evil produced by each of us. (1 Jn. 1. 9.). The contrast is between sin as a principle demanding a sin offering, and sins as a practice demanding a trespass offering.

The trespass offering reminds us that 'we all stumble in many ways'. (Jas. 3. 2). We offend against God and in connection with His holy things. (Lev. 5. 14). We offend against our neighbour by deceiving him, robbing him, cheating him, lying to him, swearing falsely against him, or any other common sin (6. 2, 3.). The holiness of God demands that the offender must die.

It is therefore imperative that we find a Substitute, a perfect Trespass Offering; and this we have in the Son of God. On the Cross, Jehovah-God made His soul a 'trespass offering'. (Isa. 53. 10.). God's holy Son became the fulfilment of the ram without blemish, which was slain and whose blood was sprinkled against the altar, on all sides. (Lev. 7. 2).

But restitution must be made and a fifth part added. (5. 16; 6. 5). This our Saviour did for us when He restored that which He took not away. (Ps. 69. 4). Christ, by His sacrifice has paid all our debts and infinitely more. Thus the believer can say that God has forgiven all his trespasses. (Col. 2. 13).

What practical lesson can you find in the Trespass Offering?

July 26

'And masters, do the same things to them (your slaves), giving up threatening, knowing that both their Master and yours is in heaven, and there is no acceptance of persons with Him.' (Eph. 6. 9.)

The apostle is dealing with different relationships here. Firstly, relationships in the home, then those in the work place, between bondmen and masters. Of course, he is writing to believers.

He commands the slaves to be obedient and serve their masters wholeheartedly, as unto the Lord and not to men. He reminds them that whatever good they do will be rewarded by the Lord at the Bema of Christ.

The masters are then reminded to treat their employees righteously, honestly and respectfully. No threats should be used against them, because they (both masters and servants) are aware of their Master's presence in heaven. Because He is there, He can scrutinise all. He is the Lamb in the midst of the throne in heaven, having seven eyes which are the seven Spirits of God sent out into all the earth. (Rev. 5. 6). In a word, our Master is omniscient; He observes and notes every detail in the masters' treatment of their servants.

Moreover, our Master is returning soon, and His reward is with Him, to give everyone according to what he has done. (Rev.22. 12). He will be completely impartial in His judgment. He is God of gods and Lord of lords, the great God, mighty and awesome, Who shows no partiality and accepts no bribes. (Deut. 10. 17).

Let us avoid being like the evil bondman who said in his heart, "My master delays his coming." He then began to mistreat his fellow-servants and keep wrong company. (Mat. 24. 48, 49.). He had a sad end.

In our dealings with others, do we show the same impartiality as that of our Master?

July 27

'He answered and said, "Look, I see four men loose, walking in the midst of the fire, and they have no hurt; and the form of the fourth is like the Son of God." '
(Dan. 3. 25).

When Nebuchadnezzar, king of Babylon issued a decree, it had to be implemented. For, as Daniel said later to the king's grandson, "Whom he would he slew, and whom he would, he kept alive" (5.19.).

The king had decreed that anyone who did not fall down when the music played and worship the golden image which he had made, would be bound and cast into the midst of a burning fiery furnace.

Three young men had suffered the penalty. They were Jews - Daniel's companions in captivity. Their names had been changed from Hananiah ('Ja' is gracious), Mishael (Who is like God) and Azariah (Helped by 'Ja') to Shadrach (Slave of the Moon-god), Meshach (Who is like the Moon-god?) and Abed-nego (Slave of the god of Wisdom). But this could not change their resolve to serve God.

The king was astonished; as he looked into the lower entrance of the furnace he saw four men loose, walking in the midst of it. The appearance of The Fourth Man was like the Son of God (or, of the gods.).

In the furnace, the three had perfect liberty, Divine company, complete immunity, preserved dignity. As they emerged, they bore an outstanding testimony. God had not only delivered them from the furnace, but was with them in it.

The Fourth Man never came out with them; He went up through the flames! Just as our Lord endured the Holocaust of Calvary and subsequently went up to Glory.

Could the three have derived hope from Isa. 43. 2?

What kind of fire are we called to endure, but never without the company of The Fourth Man?

July 28

'He said to them, "But whom do you say that I am?"   Peter answering said,   "The Christ of God" '   (Lk. 9. 20).

The scene is undoubtedly set in the region of Caesarea Philippi, as recorded by Matthew (Mat. 16. 13) and Mark (Mk. 8. 27).   But Luke chooses to omit the name of the place.   Instead, he inserts the note that our Lord was praying alone, although his disciples were with Him.   We catch a glimpse here of the loneliness of the Son of Man.   The loneliness which He endured to the fullest extent on the cross, when He was even forsaken of God.

As He prays, He asks the question, "Whom do the crowds say that I am?"   They reply, "John the Baptist, Elias, or one of the old prophets risen again."   Then He becomes more personal, and asks them directly, "Whom do you say that I am?"   Peter replies for the rest of the disciples when he says, "The Christ of God".

Others had already come, claiming to be the Messiah, the Anointed of God, but they were impostors.   God had not sent them. They did not enter in by the door of the sheepfold. (Jn 10. 1, 2).   They were thieves and robbers: But the true Messiah must be born in Bethlehem Ephratah. (Mic. 5. 2).

It was divinely communicated to old Simeon by the Holy Spirit that he should not see death before he would see The Lord's Christ, that is to say, Jehovah's Christ, The Christ of God. (Lk. 2. 26.).   When Mary came into the temple with the Child Jesus, Simeon received Him into his arms.   He blessed God for His Salvation, for His Christ.

Then, as our Saviour was suffering on the Tree, in accordance with His own predictions (9.22), the rulers sneered and said, "He has saved others;   let Him save Himself, if this is The Christ, The Chosen One of God" (23. 35.).   But this was why He came into the world, to bear the sins of many.

Why did Jesus strictly warn His disciples not to tell others that He was the Christ of God?

July 29
Great shepherd of the sheep

'Now the God of peace, Who brought again from the dead   The great Shepherd of the sheep in virtue of the blood of the eternal covenant, our Lord Jesus, equip you in every good work to do His will, working in you that which is well pleasing in His sight through Jesus Christ; to Whom be glory for ever and ever. Amen.'
(Heb. 13. 20, 21)

The good Shepherd Who laid down His life for the sheep (Jn. 10. 11) is named here as the great Shepherd Who was brought up from the dead by the God of peace.   This is the only direct reference to our Lord's resurrection in the book of Hebrews, although it is implied elsewhere in the treatise.

Our Saviour is that great Shepherd of the sheep because of the greatness of His Person.   In the benediction, He is named as our Lord Jesus.   This is the same as saying that He is Jehovah-Jesus, both God and Man.   Also, He is referred to as Jesus Christ or Jesus-Messiah.   There is none greater than He.

He is the great Shepherd because of the greatness of His victory over even death.   He was brought back from the dead by the God of peace.

He is the great Shepherd - because of the greatness of His Sacrifice.   He has entered the Most Holy Place in heaven once for all by His own blood. (Heb. 9. 12).

He is the great Shepherd because of the greatness of His Promise.   The new and eternal covenant between God and His people was sealed by the blood of Jesus.

He is the great Shepherd because of the greatness of His power.   It is available to equip us to do God's work.

He is the great Shepherd because of the greatness of the number of His sheep.   He is bringing many sons to glory. (Heb. 2. 10.).

He is the great Shepherd because of the greatness of His glory.   It will be to eternal ages: Amen.

What agency does God use to work in us to do His will through Jesus Christ, The Great Shepherd?

211

July30

'For He shall give His angels charge over thee, to keep thee in all thy ways.   They shall bear thee up in their hands, lest thou dash thy foot against a stone.'(Ps.91.11,12) 'I will set him up on high, because he has known My name.'   (v.14b)

Satan knew that the psalm was Messianic.   He therefore used part of it during the temptation of our Lord Jesus. (Mat. 4. 6).

The Devil had taken the Son of God to Jerusalem, the holy city and had set Him on the pinnacle of the temple.   Challenging the Saviour, he said,   "If Thou be the Son of God, cast Thyself down, for it is written, 'He will give His angels charge concerning Thee, and on their hands they will bear Thee up, lest Thou dash Thy foot against a stone!' "

By comparing Satan's quote with the original Scripture, it can be seen that he omitted an important phrase, namely, 'to keep Thee in all Thy ways.'   God guaranteed His Son perfect protection, as He continued to walk in God's ways.   So the Lord defeated Satan's temptation by again quoting Scripture, 'Thou shalt not tempt the Lord thy God.' (Deut. 6. 16).

If Satan had continued to quote the next verse of Psalm 91, he would have been referring to his own defeat, accomplished at the Cross.   (Gen. 3. 15;   Heb. 2. 14.). 'Thou shalt tread upon the lion and the cobra; the great lion and the dragon shalt Thou trample under feet.' (Ps. 91. 13).   The Devil is depicted in Scripture as a lion (1 Pet. 5. 8),   a serpent and a dragon. (Rev. 12. 9.).

There was no angelic help for the woman's Seed at Golgotha.   But God delivered His Son from death and exalted Him, as predicted in the psalm. (Ps. 91. 14.).   Our High Priest lives for ever. (v.16;   Heb. 7. 25.).

Do these promises of protection and exaltation apply to present-day saints?   Give a Scriptural basis for your answer.

July 31

'He says to them, "But whom do you say that I am?"   And Simon Peter answered and said, "Thou art the Christ, the Son of the living God." '   (Mat.16. 15,16)

Peter's confession at Caesarea Philippi arrives at a climax when he witnesses to the truth that Jesus is the Son of the living God.

This description of God as the living God occurs around thirty times in the Bible, divided almost equally between Old and New Testaments.

In the Old Testament, the voice (Deut. 5. 26),   the armies (1 Sam. 17.   26, 36.) and the words (Jer. 23. 36) of the living God are referred to.   Also, a Persian king, Darius, addressed Daniel as servant of the living God. (Dan. 6. 20.).   Then he described the living God as enduring forever with a kingdom which will not be destroyed, and His dominion will be forever.   He delivers and rescues, and He works signs and wonders in heaven and on earth, Who has delivered Daniel from the power of the lions. (vs. 26, 27.)

Again, in the kingdom age, Israel will be regathered, and it shall be said to them, "You are the sons of the living God." (Hos. 1. 10).

But the living Father had revealed to Peter that Jesus is His unique Son.   Then came the new revelation of the church, to be built, not on Peter ('a Stone') but on 'the Rock', Christ Jesus. (1 Cor. 3. 11,12).   The apostle Paul describes it as the house of God, which is the church of the living God, the pillar and ground of the truth. (1 Tim. 3. 15).

Almost immediately after Peter's confession, our Lord disclosed how He, the Son of the living God, would be put to death by the leaders of the people and be raised up on the third day.

After Peter had made his confession of faith, what did Jesus give to him, and when did he use this gift?

August 1

' "This shall be the law of the leper in the day of his cleansing: He shall be brought to the priest, and the priest shall go forth out of the camp; and the priest shall look, and behold, if the plague of leprosy is healed in the leper, then shall the priest command to take for him who is to be cleansed two birds alive and clean, and cedar wood, and scarlet, and hyssop." ' (Lev. 14. 2-4)

The transaction between the leper and the priest took place outside the camp of Israel. The leper was there already, just as the sinner is at a distance from God. But the priest had to go there, just as the Saviour came from God to meet the sinner. 'God has sent His unique Son into the world so that we might live through Him. In this is love, not that we loved God, but that He loved us and sent His Son to be the propitiation for our sins' (1 Jn. 4. 9,10).

The shedding of blood was the true basis of the cleansing of the leper. One of two clean little birds (or sparrows) was killed in an earthen vessel over running (literally, 'living') water. Its blood mingled with the water in the pot. The other bird was dipped in the blood-dyed water, then released over the open field. Here is a beautiful picture of our Lord, Who through the eternal Spirit (depicted by the 'living water') offered Himself without spot to God (Heb. 9. 14). He was crucified in weakness, yet He lives by God's power (2 Cor. 13. 4). The double truth is displayed in the two birds, that our Lord Jesus was delivered for our offences and raised again for our justification (Rom. 4. 25).

A bunch of hyssop was bound with scarlet wool to a cedar staff. It was dipped into the pot and then used to sprinkle 'the leper' seven times with the blood of the dead bird. Then the priest could declare him to be clean. An infinitely more efficacious remedy is now found in the Gospel. The blood of Jesus, God's Son cleanses us from all sin (1 Jn. 1. 7).

As cleansed sinners, is our reaction like that of the leper whom the Lord Jesus cured? (Luke 17. 12 - 19).

August 2

'Wherefore God also has highly exalted Him, and given Him the Name which is above every name: That at the Name of Jesus every knee should bow, of things in heaven, and things in earth, and things under the earth; and that every tongue should confess that Jesus Christ is Lord, to the glory of God the Father.' (Phil. 2. 9,10)

The apostle Paul is exhorting the saints at Philippi (and us) to have the same mental attitude as that of Christ Jesus (v.5).

He begins his exhortation by reminding his readers that God the Son was equal, in every respect, to God the Father, before the Son's incarnation. Yet, in unsurpassed humility, He came from the eternal glory into time and space, to do the Father's will.

The sevenfold condescension of the Christ is then described, followed by a corresponding description of His exaltation by God. The Son laid aside His privileges, taking the form of a slave; God exalted Him and has given Him the Name above all others. Men wrote the Name 'Jesus' and put it above His Cross in mockery, but God has exalted that Name above every other name eternally.

The Name, 'Jesus', which is used as a curse by many to-day, has been acclaimed by God as the pre-eminent Name; and rightly so, since the Name of 'Jesus', which is derived from the Hebrew, 'Jehoshua', means 'Jehovah-Saviour'. It contains the special Name of God revealed to Moses (Ex. 3. 15; 6. 3), and the special work of salvation done by our Lord, through His death on the Cross. All humanity, sooner or later, will confess that Jesus is Jehovah (Isa. 45. 23).

Have you acknowledged the supremacy of the Saviour in your life and confessed Him as your Lord? With what result?

August 3

'I saw in the night visions, and behold, One like a son of man came with the clouds of heaven, and He came up to the Ancient of Days, and they brought Him near before Him: And there was given Him dominion, and glory, and a kingdom, that all peoples, nations and languages should serve Him. His dominion is an everlasting dominion, which shall not pass away, and His kingdom that which shall not be destroyed.'
(Dan. 7. 13,14)

Daniel had a dream, and in it he saw four great beasts. Later, in his vision, he is told what these beasts are. They represent "four kings who will arise from the earth" (v.17). They are seen in composite form in the book of Revelation as part of the one beast. It has seven heads and ten horns; it is like a leopard; it has feet like the feet of a bear; its mouth is like that of a lion (Rev. 13. 1, 2). This beast, in its final form, will be controlled by Satan through Antichrist, the 'Little Horn' (Dan.7. 8). The domination of the Beast will last for three and half years, during the Great Tribulation (7. 25; Rev. 13. 5).

This domination will be shattered when our Lord Jesus returns as 'One like a son of man'. He will keep His promise to His disciples, (Mat. 24. 30.), and to the high priest of Israel, when He said, "Hereafter you shall see the Son of Man sitting at the right hand of power, and coming on the clouds of heaven." (26. 64).

The 'One like a son of man' is God, the Son incarnate. The 'Ancient of Days' is God, the Father. The kingdom which the Son of Man receives is universal, eternal, immortal and indestructible.

Will you have a share in the kingdom of the 'One like a son of man' ? By what right?

August4

' " But a certain Samaritan, as he journeyed, came where he was; and when he saw him, he had compassion on him, and went to him, and bound up his wounds, pouring in oil and wine, and set him on his own beast, and brought him to an inn, and took care of him." ' (Lk. 10. 33,34).

The Jews called Jesus a Samaritan, having a demon (Jn. 8. 48). Why? Because our Lord told them the truth about Himself and themselves. To call Him a Samaritan was the greatest insult they could think of.

The Samaritan in the story that Jesus told is a beautiful portrait of the Saviour. He was an alien as far as the Jews were concerned, for 'the Jews had no dealings with the Samaritans' (Jn. 4. 9). This was our Lord's experience; He was as a stranger to His brethren (Ps. 69. 8). The Samaritan was on a journey, and so was the Saviour. He came from the Glory and was going to Golgotha. The Samaritan came to where the half-dead man was, and so did the Saviour, in His incarnation and humiliation.

The Samaritan had compassion on the wounded man; and who can assess the compassion of the Christ for a helpless lost humanity (Mk. 6. 34). The infinite measure of His compassion can only be computed at the Cross.

The Samaritan had resources to meet the man's every need: Oil, wine and bandages for his wounds; a donkey to carry him, and an inn where he was cared for, at the expense of the Samaritan. Our Lord, as the true Samaritan, has infinite resources to meet our every need. The comfort of the Holy Spirit, the care of the church; the promise of His return when every effort for him will be repaid.

Can you think of any other resources which the Lord Jesus, the true Samaritan, supplies?

August5

'For you were as sheep going astray; but now you have returned to the Shepherd and overseer of your souls.' (1 Pet. 2. 25).

In this part of his letter, the apostle Peter is emphasising the importance of submission on the part of the Christian; in society (2. 11-17), industry (18-25), the family (3.1-7) and in the assembly (8-12).

In the immediate context of the text quoted above, Peter is addressing household servants (2. 18) and how they should react to their masters. He reminds them that they were continually going astray, but now they were converted. They had turned from their sins to the Shepherd and Overseer of their souls. Thus, even if their earthly masters mistreated them physically, they had a Heavenly Master Who cared for them spiritually, like a Shepherd and a Guardian.

As the Shepherd of our souls, He guides us. Just as the eastern shepherd goes before the flock, so does our Shepherd lead our souls. But we, as His sheep, must follow in His steps. He has given us the example of a sinless walk, of untainted works and words (vs. 21, 22; Isa. 53. 9). He accepted verbal and physical abuse without retaliation (v.23). Indeed, when He was crucified, He prayed, "Father, forgive them." (Lk. 23. 34). In the midst of His final sufferings, He committed Himself to God, the Father (v.23; Lk. 23. 46).

As the Overseer of our souls, He guards us. Just as the eastern shepherd foresees the dangers and pitfalls which would overwhelm the flock and overcome them, so has our Overseer overcome every difficulty and danger which besets our souls. He carried, as a Sacrifice, our sins (v.24).

What is the greatest danger to confront the soul?

August6
The judge

'Let the heavens rejoice, and let the earth be glad; let the sea roar, and the fulness thereof; let the fields be joyful, and all that is therein. Then shall all the trees of the forest sing for joy, before Jehovah; for He comes; for He comes to judge the earth: He shall judge the world with righteousness and the peoples with His truth.'
(Ps. 96. 11-13).

King David assembled all Israel to Jerusalem, to bring up the ark of Jehovah to the place that he had prepared for it.   On that same day, notice was given to Israel through David that Jehovah   was coming to judge the earth (1 Chron. 16. 33).   The coming of the ark to Jerusalem was a symbol of this future event, when Jehovah in the Person of Jesus would return.   As Judge, He will do two things.   Firstly, He will punish sinners, and secondly, He will govern the world.

In at least three other places in the Old Testament Scriptures, this same intimation of the coming of the Judge is given to Israel.   'He will judge the habitable earth with righteousness;   He shall execute judgment upon the peoples with equity.' (Ps. 9. 8).   See also 96. 13   and 98. 9.   It is evident that all nations are included in these songs of victory, which foretell the formation of a renewed earth.   Observe, too, that the first letters of the first four Hebrew words at the beginning of   96. 11   are Y, H, W and H, spelling out the Name Jehovah.   Thus the sacred Name is stamped upon the heavens and the earth.

Gentiles are also given notice of the coming of the Judge by the apostle Paul in Athens on the hill of   Ares or Mars, the god of war (Acts 17: 31).   The Judge   is the Man, Christ Jesus, risen from the dead and appointed by God.   He will wage war on His enemies and bring peace to the earth.

How does the coming of the Judge   affect you, personally?

August 7
This rock

'And Jesus answered and said to him, "Blessed art thou, Simon , son of Jonah; for flesh and blood has not revealed it to thee, but My Father Who is in heaven; and I say also to thee, that thou art Peter, and upon this Rock I will build My church; and the gates of Hades shall not prevail against it." ' (Mat. 16. 17,18).

The God and Father of our Lord Jesus Christ had revealed the identity of His Son to Peter.   Acting as spokesman for the other disciples, Peter confessed that Jesus was the Christ, the Son of the living God.

After this revelation from God, the Father, Peter was given an additional revelation of the church, from God the Son.   Jesus said to him, "I say also to thee, that thou art Peter, and upon this Rock I will build My church."   Thus our Lord points out the equality between Father and Son.

The Saviour speaks of Himself when He refers to 'this Rock'.   He is the Foundation Stone of the church, the building of God, as well as its Final Stone.

The Lord Jesus is not only the church's Foundation, but He is also its Builder.   He said, "Upon this Rock I will build My church."   The same idea is found in the fact that He is both Offering and Offerer: He is also both Sheep (the Lamb of God) and Shepherd.

What kind of building is being erected upon 'this Rock'?   It is both a temple and a citadel, a basilica and a bastion.   It consists of 'living stones', of which Peter was one (1 Peter 2. 5).   All blood-bought believers of this present era are incorporated in this building.   The completion date of the building is fast approaching.   The Foundation Stone was laid at Golgotha, and the Final Stone will be added at our Lord's return to the air.

How can we help in the building of the church on 'this Rock'?

August 8
The scapegoat

'But the goat on which the lot fell to be the scapegoat shall be presented alive before Jehovah, to make an atonement with him, and to send him away as a scapegoat into the wilderness.' (Lev. 16. 10).

The scapegoat was one of two goats which were required on Israel's great Day of Atonement. This took place on the tenth day of the seventh month of each year, that is, towards the end of September.

One of the goats was appointed by lot to be slain in sacrifice, for a sin offering. Aaron, the high priest sprinkled its blood on and before the mercy seat. This was the cover on the ark of the covenant, in the Holy of Holies in the tabernacle. Only on this day was the high priest allowed to enter into the Holiest of all, firstly with incense, and then to sprinkle the blood. Here is a beautiful picture of our Lord Jesus, our great High Priest Who put away sin by the sacrifice of Himself. No repetition of this work is required. Once was enough since the Sacrifice was perfect
(Heb. 9. 26, 28). God's glory has been secured, and His righteous claims against sin have been met, fully, finally and perfectly, through the sacrifice of His Son.

On emerging from the tabernacle, Aaron laid both his hands on the head of the live goat. He confessed all Israel's sins and laid them on its head. It was then led away into the wilderness, to a solitary land. Again, in the scapegoat (literal meaning 'the goat of removal'), there is a wonderful picture of our Lord Jesus. All our sins were laid on Him at the Cross and He took them all away, never to be remembered any more.

How can we be sure that, when we believe on our Lord Jesus, all our sins are forgiven? See Colossians 2. 13; Titus 2. 14 and 1 John 1. 7, 9).

August 9

'But my God shall supply all your need according to His riches in glory in Christ Jesus.'
(Phil. 4. 19).

The apostle Paul is writing to the saints in Philippi. He is under house arrest in Rome (Acts 28. 30), awaiting his trial. A messenger has come from Philippi, bringing the saints' gifts to Paul: His name, Epaphroditus. He will return with Paul's letter.

The apostle sends them these words of encouragement in the above text. God, through these believers, has met his need, and just as surely He will meet their need. He is the Divine Provider: He brought all things into being; He made the stars and the sparrows, and us. But He is not only a powerful God, but also a personal God. We are of much greater value to Him than the sparrows, and even the very hairs of our head are all numbered. God loves us and gave His Son to die for us.

The text contains a sure promise - 'my God shall supply' (literally, shall 'fill full'). The word of the Lord through Elijah was fulfilled to the widow of Zarephath. The supply of flour and oil in jar and jug was maintained as long as it was needed. But the promise must be accepted by faith on our part.

The text also states that there is ample provision - 'all your need', whether it be spiritual or temporal. It comes from the heavenly store-room - 'God's riches in glory', but the source is Christ Jesus. All that God has for us is given to us in Christ Jesus. We are blessed with every spiritual blessing in the heavenly realms in Christ. (Eph. 1. 3). God's infinite resources are made available to us in Christ Jesus, the One Whom God appointed and anointed to be our Saviour, Jesus.

Notice that God promises to supply all our need - not our greed, nor our want - in Christ Jesus.

What is your greatest need to-day? It can be met in Christ Jesus, the Source of God's riches.

August 10
Prince of princes

' "And through his (anti-christ) policy also he shall cause craft to prosper in his hands; and he shall magnify himself in his heart, and by peace shall destroy many; he shall also stand up against the Prince of princes; but he shall be broken without hand." ' (Dan. 8. 25)

In the third year of the reign of Belshazzar, king of Babylon, Daniel had a vision. It concerned two animals, a ram and a goat.

The angel Gabriel was commanded by Someone, possibly the Son of God, to tell Daniel the meaning of the vision (v:16). The ram, with its two horns, represented the kings of Media and Persia. The goat, with a single horn originally, represented Alexander, the king of Greece. Just as the ram was destroyed by the goat, so Alexander destroyed the power of Medo-Persia. But at the peak of his career, Alexander died. He was only thirty-two years of age. His kingdom was divided into four parts which were ruled by four of his generals. This corresponds to the four horns which succeeded the single horn of the goat.

Then a little horn grew out of one of these four. It represents a king who will arise at the time of the end (v.17), in the time of wrath (v.19), in the distant future (v.26). This refers to the tribulation period of seven years which takes place after the Church is caught up.

This fierce-faced king who is a master of intrigue will become very strong. He will cause astounding devastation: He will succeed in all that he does: He will destroy mighty men and holy people: He will oppose the Prince of princes, our Lord Jesus Christ, and he will be broken without human agency. (2 Thes. 2. 8; Rev.19. 16-21).

Whom do you serve? Satan, the prince of the power of the air (doomed to destruction) or Jesus, Prince of princes (enthroned on high)?

223

August 11
The vinedresser

'He spoke also this parable: "A certain man had a fig tree planted in his vineyard; and he came looking for fruit on it, and found none. Then he said to the dresser of his vineyard, " Behold, these three years I come seeking fruit on this fig tree, and find none: Cut it down! Why does it even use up the ground?" And he answering said to Him, "Lord, let it alone this year also, until I dig around it and fertilise it; and if it bears fruit next year, fine! If not, cut it down." ' (Lk. 13. 6-9.).

A note of warning had been sounded by the Saviour, with solemn repetition. "Unless you repent, you will all likewise perish." (vs.3, 5). The warning was accentuated in this parable of the barren fig tree.

A fig tree in a vineyard was somewhat out of place. Evidently the owner had a taste for the sweet fruit. He arranged to have the fig tree planted, no doubt in some choice place. Usually, such a tree was most fruitful. Three crops were expected every year. The first figs ripened towards the end of June; the second crop came in August; the third crop in September consisted of smaller figs. It was in the third year that the owner came seeking fruit and found none. The barrenness of the tree had been confirmed. It must be removed, since it was even polluting the earth. But the vinedresser pleaded for a stay of execution. Meantime he used all his energy on it.

The story is a parable: The vineyard owner is God, the Father, and the vinedresser is God, the Son. The fig tree is the nation of Israel. For three and a half years, the heaven-sent Vinedresser had tended the Fig Tree, Israel, but no fruit was found. The nation was unrepentant. Therefore the axe was applied and the Tree was cut down.

What important lesson can we learn from this parable?

August 12
The chief shepherd

'The elders who are among you I exhort, - - - -: shepherd the flock of God which is among you, serving as overseers, not by constraint, but willingly; not for filthy lucre, but of a ready mind; neither as being lords over God's heritage, but being examples to the flock. And when the Chief Shepherd shall appear, you shall receive the unfading crown of glory.' (1 Pet. 5. 1-4).

The apostle Peter is addressing the elders, in this part of his circular letter. The term 'elder' implies maturity in the faith. He also exhorts them to be shepherds to the flock of God. The term 'shepherd' implies an ability to teach the word of God, in order to feed the flock of God. Moreover, he adds that elders should serve as overseers. The term 'overseer' implies a measure of administrative ability. Therefore elders (or 'presbyters') should also be shepherds (or 'pastors'), and overseers (or 'bishops').

As chief Shepherd, our Lord fills these three offices to perfection. He is the Author and Completer of faith. He is the good and great Shepherd, giving His life for the sheep, and guarding them with His resurrection power. He oversees our souls, and leads us in righteous paths for His Name's sake.

The elders ought to be examples for the flock, giving the sheep a pattern to follow. They should do their work willingly and readily, without any thought of personal gain. They, in turn, have a perfect example to follow, that of the chief Shepherd.

He is coming soon, to reward His under-shepherds, and reveal His glory to a wondering world. The reward will be the unfading wreath of glory.

Are you, whether you are an elder or not, following the example of the chief Shepherd, with a view to receiving a glorious crown from His pierced hand at His manifestation?

August 13

'Confounded be all those who serve graven images, those who boast in idols. Worship Him, all you gods.' (Ps. 97. 7).

Psalms 95 to 100 celebrate the return of Jehovah-Jesus to the earth to reign (Ps. 96. 10,13;   97. 5;   98. 9;   99. 1).   The central verse of this group of psalms summarises this theme: 'The heavens proclaim His righteousness, and all the peoples see His glory.' (Ps. 97. 6).   Our Lord referred to this event in His discourse on the mount of Olives: ' "But when the Son of Man comes in His glory, and all the holy angels with Him, then shall He sit upon the throne of His glory." '   (Mat. 25. 31).

The first part of Ps. 97.7 may be translated as follows: 'All who worship an image are put to shame, those who boast in nothings.' The Lord will root out all idolatry from His kingdom when He comes. We, as Christians, 'know that an idol is nothing in the world, and that there is no other God save One' (1 Cor. 8. 4).   But the non-entities are inspired by evil entities, the fallen angels.   They will be forced to worship the Son of Man at His return.   'Worship Him, all you 'gods' '   (or 'supernatural beings,' namely 'angels').'   The same word for angels is found in Ps. 8. 5, in connection with the creation of man by God: 'Thou hast made him a little lower than 'gods' (or 'angels').' This meaning is verified in Heb. 2. 7, in the New Testament.

The writer of Hebrews also verifies the context and the meaning of Ps. 97. 7. (Heb. 1. 6).   The preferred reading would be; 'When He again bringeth the First-born into the world - - - -.'   When our Lord returns to reign, all angels, both holy and fallen will worship Him as God.

If angels are called upon to worship the Son, how much more should we, who are redeemed by His blood?

August14
Transfigured

'And after six days Jesus takes Peter, James and John his brother, and brings them to a high mountain apart, and was transfigured before them; and His face shone as the sun, and His garments became white as the light.' (Mat. 17. 1,2).

Mount Hermon was the most likely location for the transfiguration scene. Its summit is about 9,000 feet (about 3,000 metres) above the Mediterranean Sea, and it is about 40 miles (about 65 kilometres) north-east of the Sea of Galilee. It is named the Holy Mount by Peter, because Jesus, the Holy One was there (2 Peter 1. 18).

The sequence of events is significant. First, there was the Father's revelation of His Son to Peter, followed by the Son's revelation of the church to His disciples. Then the Son revealed that He must suffer rejection, be put to death, and rise again after three days. Now, His glory is revealed as He is transfigured before His favoured followers. Peter, James and John were privileged to be given a glimpse of the coming kingdom glory of the Son of Man.

What did the three disciples see? They saw Jesus transfigured - the form of the Son shone through the form of the Servant. They were eye-witnesses of His majesty. Then they saw Moses and Elijah, who were speaking with Him of His 'exodus' which He would accomplish at Jerusalem. Then a shining cloud overshadowed them, and they heard the Father extolling His Son and commanding them to hear Him. Lastly, after Jesus came and touched them telling them to rise up and not be afraid, they saw no one but Jesus alone.

What encouragement can you derive from the words of the Transfigured One to His own towards the end of the episode?

August 15
The Nazirite

'This is the law of the Nazirite who has vowed his offering to Jehovah for his separation, in addition to what else he can afford, according to the vow which he vowed, according to the law of his separation.' (Num. 6. 21).

The name Nazirite means 'separated one'. Thus the individual who was a Nazirite vowed to be separated for God's service. This was perfectly true of our Lord Jesus. Every moment of His life was given over to do His Father's will, and to complete the work which He had been given to do.

There were four notable servants of God mentioned in Scripture who were Nazirites from their earliest days. They were Joseph, Samson, Samuel and John Baptist. There was an element of the supernatural in each of their conceptions. Their mothers were all barren. This is far more evident in the conception of our Lord Jesus, whose mother Mary was a virgin.

The Nazirite was bound by three important vows. He was forbidden to drink wine or alcohol of any kind. Although the Lord Jesus did drink wine (Mat. 11. 19), yet in a spiritual sense, He was a true Nazirite. Wine speaks of earthly joy (Ps. 104. 15). Jesus derived no joy from earth or Israel. His delight was to do the Father's will.

The Nazirite was forbidden to cut his hair. This was, naturally speaking, a reproach to a man. (1 Cor. 11. 14). Again, the spiritual fulfilment is found in Jesus, Who was always subject to the Father and willing to suffer reproach for His sake.

The Nazirite must avoid contact with the dead. Again our Lord fulfilled this spiritually; He was 'holy, harmless, undefiled, separate from sinners'. (Heb. 7. 26).

Are you marked out as a spiritual Nazirite ? (Romans 1. 1).

August 16

'Giving thanks to the Father, Who has qualified us to share in the inheritance of the saints in light. For He rescued us from the dominion of darkness and has translated us into the kingdom of the Son of His love: In Whom we have redemption through His blood, even the forgiveness of sins.' (Col. 1. 12-14).

Isaac was the son of his father's love. Yet God told Abraham to offer him as a burnt - offering on Mount Moriah. A substitute in the form of a ram was found for Isaac. There was no substitute for Jesus, the true Son of the Father's love, at Golgotha on that same Mount Moriah, many years later. Only the offering of the Father's Son in death could accomplish our redemption, and enable God to forgive sins.

Joseph was the son of his father's love. Jacob marked him out as distinct from his other sons by making for him a richly ornamented robe to wear (Gen. 37. 3). God, the Father marked out the Son of His Love by raising Him from the dead (Rom.1. 4).

Absalom was the son of his father's love. But he was a rebellious son. Yet when he was slain, hanging on a tree; king David his father mourned deeply for him. David would have died in his place, if it had been possible (2 Sam. 18. 33). The true Son of the Father's love was never rebellious. On the contrary, he was always obedient to the will of His Father, even to accepting death on a Tree.

Timothy was Paul's beloved son or child in the faith (2 Tim. 1. 2). Paul had led him to the Lord. Therefore there was a great bond of love between them. But the bond of love between Father and Son transcends this by far.

According to Colossians 1. 12-14, what benefits are the portion of those who are translated into the kingdom of the Son of the Father's love?

August 17

'Know therefore and understand that from the going forth of the commandment to restore and build Jerusalem unto the Messiah the Prince shall be seven 'sevens' and sixty-two 'sevens'; the street shall be built again, and the wall, even in troublous times. And after the sixty-two 'sevens' shall Messiah be cut off, and shall have nothing: - - - - .' (Dan. 9. 25, 26a).

The angel Gabriel had been sent to answer Daniel's prayer. Gabriel revealed to Daniel the great prophecy of the seventy 'sevens', or 490 years. This period was divided into three parts, namely, seven 'sevens' (49 years), sixty-two 'sevens' (434 years) and one 'seven' (7 years).

Two princes are mentioned in the prophecy, namely, the Messiah-Prince (the Christ) and the coming prince (the Anti-Christ). The final seven years (as yet unfulfilled) relate to the latter.

The first period of 49 years was fulfilled with the rebuilding of Jerusalem. The second period of 434 years was fulfilled with the coming of Messiah-Ruler to Jerusalem. This was the day when our Lord made His triumphal entry into Jerusalem, riding on a colt (Zech. 9. 9; Lk. 19. 36, 42). It is contended that the 483 prophetic years (namely, 173,880 days) were fulfilled exactly on that day.

A few days later, Messiah-Prince was 'cut off' by means of crucifixion. 'He was cut off out of the land of the living' (Isa. 53. 8). He was cut off, as if He was an evil-doer (Ps. 37. 9). But, on the Cross, He made atonement for iniquity. He received nothing - no earthly throne or kingdom. These await Him at His return.

Does Messiah-Prince have something from these lives of ours?

August18

'And when one of those who were reclining at table with Him heard these things, he said to Him, "Blessed is he who shall eat bread in the kingdom of God." Then said He to him, "A certain man was preparing a great banquet and invited many." ' (Lk. 14. 15, 16).

One of the Jewish rulers, a Pharisee, had invited our Lord Jesus to his house for a meal. During it, and because of our Lord's comments on the resurrection of the just, another guest spoke about the blessedness of eating bread in the kingdom of God. But the kingdom of God was there already, in the Person of the Son of God. So, in reply, the Saviour told the parable of the great banquet.

The banquet is great, because of the greatness of the Person providing it. The triune God is responsible for supplying the great need of all concerned. The cost of this great banquet was infinite, and was fully paid for in precious blood, that of God's own Son.

The banquet is great because of the greatness of the provision. The servant's message to the guests was that "all things are now ready". The menu includes the living Bread sent down from heaven and the Passover Lamb. Also there is living Water, rich Wine, and the Spirit's fruit. God's table groans with good things.

The banquet is great because of the greatness of the numbers invited. The Jewish leadership was invited but refused, with lame excuses. The lower strata of Jewish society responded more readily to the invitation. Then the outcasts of the Gentiles were constrained to come in, and yet there is room. In the end, every place in the Lord's house will be filled; and all is free to those who come.

With which characters in the parable can you identify?

231

August 19

'But there were false prophets also among the people, even as there shall be false teachers among you, who will secretly bring in destructive heresies, even denying the Master Who bought them, bringing swift destruction upon themselves.' (2 Pet. 2. 1).

The Greek word 'despotes' is translated 'master' in the above text.   This word describes someone who has absolute ownership and complete power.   It is therefore used of God on several occasions in the New Testament.   For instance, Simeon addressed God as 'Despotes', when he took the child Jesus into his arms (Lk. 2. 29).   Again, when Peter and John were released by the Jewish rulers and had returned to their own company, their prayer was addressed to God as 'Despotes' (Acts 4. 24).

Significantly, the word is also used to describe our Lord Jesus, as it is in the above text. Here is another proof of our Lord's deity.   This is the central doctrine which is denied by the false teachers, then, in the early days of the church's history, and now, in the last days.   These false teachers also deny that all Scripture is God-breathed.   They deny the truth of Creation and the entry of sin into the human race.   They deny the death of Christ, as a Substitute for sin, and His resurrection from the dead.

They deny the Master or Sovereign Lord Who bought them. Here is the scope of the death of Christ.   He died for the sins of the whole world (1 Jn. 2. 2).   But only those who believe on Him are saved from their sins.   He purchased even those who reject Him and deny Him.   But, this loving and merciful Despot is also a holy and righteous One.   He will judge and punish these false teachers.

As bond-slaves of the Master Who bought us at such awful price, what is our reaction? See 1 Corinthians 6. 20;   7. 23.

August 20

'I am like a pelican of the wilderness: I am like an owl of the desert places.   I watch, and am like a sparrow alone   upon the house top.'   (Ps. 102. 6, 7).

The writer to the Hebrews refers verses 25 and 26 of this psalm to God, the Son (Heb. 1. 10-12).   Therefore, there is good reason to assume that the rest of the psalm is Messianic in content.   This can be seen quite clearly in verses 1 to 11 of the psalm.

The superscription sets the scene: 'A prayer of the afflicted, when he is overwhelmed, and pours out his complaint before Jehovah.'   The afflicted One is the Messiah, as ultimately He is transfixed on the Tree at Golgotha.

Firstly, He describes the distress of His body (vs. 3-5).   He feels like a sick man whose strength is consumed by a burning fever.   His whole physical being is affected; His bones, heart, inwards and flesh.   He speaks of 'the voice of His groaning,' and we are reminded of Gethsemane.

Secondly, He describes the desolation of His soul (vs. 6, 7).   In His spiritual solitude, He depicts Himself as being like a pelican, an owl and a sparrow.   But the pelican is not in the water fishing, but alone in the wilderness, preparing to feed her young.   This reminds us of the soul-solitude   of our Lord, during the daylight hours, on the Cross. The owl, a nocturnal bird, is also alone,   preparing to find his prey in desolate places. This reminds us of our Lord's soul-solitude during the hours of darkness, on the Cross. His prey was Death, and He Death, by dying slew.   The sparrow, normally gregarious, seeks solitude upon the house top when bereft of its mate.   Our Lord felt completely alone when forsaken of God.

Thirdly, He describes the derision of men (v.8).   The leaders of the Jews hurled their insults at Him, there on the Cross.   But finally, He describes being discarded by God (vs. 9-11).   This was the severest solitude.

Why did God's Son become the Solitary One?

233

August 21

'And when they had come to Capernaum, those who collected the two-drachma tax came to Peter, and said, "Does your Teacher not pay the two-drachma tax?" '
(Mat. 17. 24)

This incident is recorded only in the gospel according to Matthew (vs. 24-27).   It would appeal to him, as an erstwhile tax-man.

The tax mentioned here was for the temple at Jerusalem.   It had its origin in connection with the construction of the tabernacle in the wilderness (Ex. 30. 11-16; 38. 25, 26).   The two-drachma coin was more than equal to a half shekel of silver then.

It was an annual tax and everyone was expected to pay it.   Even a beggar was expected to sell his coat, if he had one, to pay his dues.   So when Peter was questioned by the collectors, if their (i.e. the disciples') Teacher would pay, he said, "Certainly!"   Evidently he never considered the confession which he had made a short time ago of Jesus, as the Son of the Living God.   The temple at Jerusalem was His Father's house and He had no need to pay any tax. (Jn. 2. 16).

Our Lord anticipated Peter's query, when he entered the house, by asking him another question:-   "Who pays tribute to kings?   Their sons or strangers?"   Peter said, "Strangers."   "Then are the sons free," our Lord Jesus said: But, in order to avoid offence, He sent Peter to catch a fish!

Peter obeyed, of course: The first fish that took the hook already had a mouthful!   It was just as Jesus had said.   The fish had a coin in its mouth, called a 'stater'.   It was equal to four drachmas, the amount required to pay the tax for the Lord and Peter.

In this incident, what lessons can we learn from our Teacher?

August22
The red heifer

'And Jehovah spoke to Moses and to Aaron, saying, "This is the ordinance of the law which Jehovah has commanded, saying: Speak to the children of Israel that they bring to thee a red heifer without spot, wherein is no blemish, and upon which never came yoke." ' (Num.19. 1, 2).

Every offering in the Old Testament is a picture of the sacrifice of the Saviour. The offering of the red heifer cannot be an exception to this rule.

The colour red emphasises the uniqueness of the animal, and reminds us of the absolute uniqueness of Immanuel, God with us.

The fact that it had to be a heifer, a female animal, reminds us of the submissiveness of the Son of Man to God.

The flawlessness of the animal reminds us of the moral perfection of the Son of God.

The giving of it to Eleazar, the son of Aaron, the high priest of Israel, reminds us that Jesus, after His arrest in Gethsemane, was led away to Caiaphas, another son of Aaron.

The animal was taken outside the camp: Our Lord was taken outside the city wall. Another had to slaughter it, reminding us that the Roman power executed the Saviour.

Caiaphas said that it was better that one Man should perish for the people. (Jn. 18. 14). The priest sprinkled the blood of the sacrificed heifer seven times before the tent of meeting.

The sacrifice was wholly consumed by fire. Our Lord Jesus endured the flame of God's wrath against sin and exhausted it. Into the fire was cast cedar wood (the noblest of trees), hyssop (the humblest of shrubs), and scarlet wool. These all speak of Christ, the noblest and humblest of men, and the shedding of His blood. The ashes were put in a pot, and running water was added to produce water of purification.

What can you learn from the mention of the red heifer by the writer of Hebrews. (Hebrews 9. 13, 14)?

August 23

Firstborn over all creation

'In Whom (the Son of the Father's love) we have redemption through His blood, even the forgiveness of sins; Who is the Image of the invisible God, the Firstborn over all creation.' (Col. 1. 14, 15).

The passage in which these two verses are set is unique in Scripture, because of its description of the supremacy of Christ. In this passage, there are listed no less than nine characteristics of the deity of the Son of the Father's love.

He is the Image of the invisible God. The Lord Jesus said, "Anyone who has seen Me has seen the Father" (Jn. 14. 9). Just as a wax mould faithfully duplicates the article pressed into it, so the Son represents God in every detail.

He is the Firstborn over all creation. The Greek word translated here as 'firstborn' carries with it the ideas of supremacy and sovereignty. If the apostle had wanted to say 'first-created', he would have used another Greek word. Thus the description of Christ as the 'Firstborn' conveys the truth of His priority in time, and His sovereignty in rank, over creation.

He is the Creator of the universe. All things, whether visible or invisible, were created by Him, and for Him.

He was before all else began, in a past eternity with the Father and the Holy Spirit.

He is the Upholder of all things: It is by His power that everything holds together at this very moment.

He is the Head of the Body, the assembly of the redeemed, from Pentecost to the Rapture.

He is the Beginning, the Firstborn from among the dead (Rom. 1. 4). All God's fullness dwells in Him, and He is the Reconciler of all things. The Son is supreme.

Do we acknowledge His supremacy in our lives, as the Firstborn of all creation?

August 24

' "When Israel was a child, then I loved him , and called My Son out of Egypt." '
(Hos. 11. 1).

'And when they had departed, behold, the angel of the Lord appears to Joseph in a dream, saying, "Arise, and take the young Child and His mother, and flee into Egypt, and be there until I shall tell thee; for Herod will seek the young Child to destroy Him." When he arose, he took the young Child and His mother by night, and departed into Egypt; and he was there until the death of Herod; that it might be fulfilled which was spoken of the Lord by the prophet, saying, "Out of Egypt have I called My Son" ' (Mat. 2. 13-15).

The wise men, or magi, from the east, had brought their gifts to the Baby Jesus, and had departed homeward.

Then an angel of Jehovah warned Joseph, the legal human father of Jesus, to escape with the little Child and Mary, His mother, to Egypt. This was the second of Joseph's four dreams (1. 20; 2. 13, 19, 22).

Joseph was obedient to the heavenly messenger and left for Egypt with his little family, under cover of darkness. This was done in fulfilment of Hosea's prophecy, "I called My Son out of Egypt."

But the context in Hosea refers to the exodus of the nation of Israel from Egypt. At that time, Jehovah called Israel, His son, His firstborn (Exod. 4. 22).

There are other similarities between Israel and Messiah. Israel was sent down to Egypt by God, in order to escape the rigours of a famine (Gen. 46. 4). Messiah was taken there to escape destruction at the hands of Herod. Jehovah called His son Israel out of Egypt to fulfil the nation's short-term destiny. But He called His Son Jesus out of Egypt to fulfil the nation's long-term destiny.

In what ways is your long-term destiny linked with Jehovah's Son Jesus?

August25

'Then drew near to Him all the tax-gatherers and sinners to hear Him; and the Pharisees and scribes murmured, saying, "This (man) receives sinners and eats with them." ' (Lk. 15. 1, 2).

Our text for today brings before us two kinds of people. There were the tax-gatherers and sinners, and there were the Pharisees and scribes, or teachers of the law.

The first group was ostracised by the second group. The tax-gatherers were employed by the hated Romans, who governed the country as an occupying force. Moreover, these tax-collectors usually defrauded the people (19. 8). Therefore they were rejected by many. They shared this rejection with the 'sinners', who were immoral people.

The second group, the Pharisees and scribes, consisted of people who thought that they were righteous. Certainly, they were on a much higher moral plane than the first group, so they thought. Therefore, they condemned the Saviour because He received these sinners and ate with them. But the truth is that we are all sinners (Rom. 3. 23); even people like the proud Pharisees, because pride is a great sin!

Then our Lord told three parables to show that He is not alone in the business of receiving sinners. The first parable is about a shepherd who finds his lost sheep and brings it home. This is a picture of God, the Son, Who is the good Shepherd, giving His life for the sheep. The second parable is about a woman who searches carefully until she finds a lost silver coin. This is a picture of God, the Spirit, searching and finding lost souls. The third parable is about a father whose prodigal son returns home to be welcomed with open arms. This is a picture of God, the Father, welcoming lost sinners home. The Trinity is involved in this work of receiving sinners.

Has this Man, Christ Jesus, received you as a sinner? If so, when does He eat with you?

August 26
The promise keeper

'The Lord is not slack concerning His promise, as some men count slackness; but is longsuffering towards you, not willing that any should perish, but that all should come to repentance.' (2 Peter 3. 9).

Our Lord Jesus has made a solemn promise. He said, "I am coming again, and shall receive you to Myself, that where I am, there you may be also." (Jn. 14: 3). 'These words are trustworthy and true, " I am coming soon." ' (Rev. 22. 7). "See, I am coming soon, and My reward is with Me." (v.12). 'He Who has said all these things declares, "Yes, I am coming soon." ' (v.20). So we confidently expect our Lord to come for His own at any moment. He will come to the air, and summon all those who are His to Himself, to be forever with Him. (1 Thes. 4. 17).

But, in these last days, mockers come with their questions, "Where is this 'coming' He promised?" (2 Peter 3. 4). These false teachers argue that everything has remained exactly as it was since the first day of creation, as far back as anyone can remember. "Not true!" Peter says. They deliberately forget that God destroyed the world with a great flood: He will destroy it again with a great fire, when all ungodly men will perish.

Why does the Lord delay His coming? Firstly, because His reckoning of time is not like ours. The present Church age, which has lasted almost 2,000 years, is like two days in God's reckoning. Secondly, He delays His coming, because He is giving more time for sinners to repent and be saved. But the Lord will keep His promise to return.

He has made another promise which He will keep. It is the promise of new heavens and a new earth, wherein dwells righteousness (v.13). This will take place after the Millennium.

In view of the fulfilment of these promises, what kind of people ought we to be? (vs. 14, 15).

August27
The transgression remover

'As far as the east is from the west, so far has He removed our transgressions from us.'
(Ps. 103. 12).

Transgression against God is rebellion against Him.   It is committed when a known command of God is disobeyed.   It is a trespass against Him.

The first human transgression ever to be committed was in the garden of Eden.   On the sixth day of the creation week, God made Adam and put him in the garden. Jehovah Elohim commanded Adam not to eat of the tree of the knowledge of good and evil, for in the day that he ate of it, he would certainly die. (Gen. 2. 17).

Satan deceived Adam's wife, Eve, and she took of the fruit and ate, and gave also to her husband with her, and he ate (3. 6).   He was not deceived, but he transgressed. (1 Tim. 2. 14).   God's command was broken, and death, (both spiritual and physical), entered the human race.

Adam's sinful nature has been transmitted to every member of the human race with disastrous results. God says in His law, "Thou shalt not ----", man says, "I shall ----!" in blatant rebellion against Him.   But God, in His infinite mercy (Ps. 103. 11), sent His Son to be the Transgression-Remover to die on a Cross of shame.   There, He was wounded for our transgressions. (Isa. 53. 5).

What must we do?   We must confess our transgressions to the Lord. (Ps. 32. 5). Then He will blot them out (51. 1).   He will remove them, as far as east is from west. This illustration is very powerful.   We may travel east or west around planet Earth without ever coming to the end: East and west never meet.   Thus Jehovah has removed our transgressions from us eternally.

What is the condition, on our part, as stated in Psalm 103, for having our transgression removed?   See vs. 11, 13 and 17.   Have we fulfilled this condition?

August28
In the midst

' *"For where two or three are gathered together in My Name, there am I in the midst of them." '* (Mat. 18. 20).

Our text for today is set in the fourth discourse given by our Lord in the Gospel according to Matthew. The three preceding ones are found in chapters 5 to 7 (the Sermon on the Mount), chapter 10 (instruction given to the 12 apostles) and chapter 13 (the parables of the kingdom). In this fourth discourse, the Lord Jesus gives teaching on humility and forgiveness.

Earlier in the Gospel, our Saviour had introduced His church in its universal aspect, as the total number of the redeemed of this present era (16. 18). Now, He speaks of the church in its local aspect (18. 17), as the local community of believers.

It is evident from v.19 that our Lord Jesus is referring to the saints coming together for prayer. A particular matter must be resolved: There is harmonious agreement as to the resolution of the matter on the part of two believers. The Lord's faithful promise is then given; "It shall come to them from My Father Who is in the heavens."

Our Lord makes another faithful promise. It is given to those who gather together in His Name. That is, those who own His Lordship, His Saviourhood and His Messiahship, for He is the Lord Jesus Christ. And what is His promise? The promise of His Presence! "There am I in the midst of them." Even if there are only two, and if they meet in the humblest of places, the "I Am" has promised to be with them, when they meet in His Name. Where His saints are, His sanctuary is.

Let us never despise the meetings of the twos or the threes, by reminding ourselves of the Third or the Fourth, Jehovah Jesus, Himself.

What constraints are placed upon us when we realise that Jesus is in the midst?

August29
The bronze serpent

'And Moses made a bronze serpent and put it upon a pole, and it came to pass, that if a serpent had bitten any man, when he looked to the bronze serpent, he lived' (Num. 21. 9).

The people of Israel had sinned; it was by no means the first time, since they had escaped from Egypt. They grumbled against God and Moses. They despised God's provision for them. "There is no bread, and no water, and our soul loathes this miserable food!" They were referring to the manna.

So the Lord sent the serpents; their bite introduced a deadly fire into the victims' body. Many died. The sting of sin is even deadlier, since its wages is death, both physical and spiritual.

The people repented; they came to Moses and asked him to intercede for them, so that the Lord would remove the serpents. So Moses pleaded with God for the people.

The Lord prescribed the remedy; it was not what the people imagined. He told Moses to make a bronze serpent and set it upon a pole. Then everyone who was bitten could look at the bronze serpent and live.

Many centuries later, our Lord Jesus referred to this event, in conversation with Nicodemus (Jn. 3. 14,15). It provided a perfect picture of His work on the Cross. He is the Anti-type of the bronze serpent. The Son of Man became Sin Offering (2 Cor. 5. 21). The time-point was reached, when He cried on the Cross, "My God, My God, why hast Thou forsaken Me?"

Now, 'there is life for a look at the Crucified One.' There is no other way to obtain eternal life.

What other similarities can you find between the story of the bronze serpent and the Son of Man?

August30
The hope of glory

'Even the mystery which has been hidden from ages and from generations, but now is made manifest to His saints; to whom God would make known what are the riches of the glory of this mystery among the nations, which is Christ in you, the hope of glory.' (Col. 1. 26, 27).

The text explains the use of the word mystery in the New Testament. It refers to a truth, which was hidden in the past, but is now revealed in the present. This particular truth concerns Christ and the Church.

The Christ (or Messiah) had come to His people (the nation Israel) who had rejected Him and had put Him to death on a Cross. He rose from the dead and ascended again to heaven. Then He sent His Spirit on the day of Pentecost to begin a new work, namely the forming of the Church, the body of Christ. It is composed of both Jews and Gentiles. It is separate and distinct from the nation, Israel. Each member of it has the in-dwelling Christ by the presence of the Holy Spirit within. Thus, in the present 'Church age,' each person who receives Christ by faith has His Presence within. He is the Hope of Glory.

This hope is sure and certain, because it rests upon the Person and work of our Lord Jesus Christ. 'But, we also rejoice in the hope of the glory of God; and hope does not disappoint us, because God has poured His love into our hearts by the Holy Spirit, Whom He has given us' (Rom. 5. 2-5). 'Christ in you, the Hope of glory.' This hope will be fully realised when we are 'caught up - - - - to meet the Lord in the air - - - - to be with the Lord forever.' (1 Thes. 4. 17).

What practical effect should the Hope of glory have in our lives day by day? See :-
Titus 2. 13; Hebrews 3. 6; 6. 11, 18, 19; 1 Peter 3. 15; 1 John 3. 3.

August 31

'Now Jehovah prepared a great fish to swallow up Jonah. And Jonah was in the belly of the fish three days and three nights.' (Jonah 1. 17).

' "An evil and adulterous generation seeks after a sign; and there shall no sign be given to it, but the sign of the prophet Jonas. For as Jonas was three days and three nights in the belly of the great fish, so shall the Son of Man be three days and three nights in the heart of the earth. The men of Nineveh shall rise in the judgment with this generation and shall condemn it; because they repented at the preaching of Jonas; and, behold, a greater than Jonas is here." ' (Mat. 12. 39-41).

Firstly, there is a striking contrast between Jonah and Jesus. When the word of Jehovah came to Jonah, to preach against Nineveh, he ran away. It was never so with Jesus. He always did the things which pleased the Father. Also, when God had compassion on the penitent people of Nineveh and spared them, Jonah was angry. It was never so with Jesus. He always displayed the compassion of the Father's heart to poor and penitent sinners.

But, secondly, consider the comparisons between Jonah and Jesus. Jonah was a prophet and so was Jesus, but much greater. (Lk.24. 19). Jonah was from Gath-Hepher in Galilee, and Jesus was brought up in Nazareth, just 3 miles (5km.) away. Jonah went down 'to the bottom of the mountains' when thrown into the sea. Jesus descended into the lower parts of the earth. Jonah's experience inside the great fish was used by Jesus to symbolise His death, burial and resurrection. Jonah's prayer in the fish reminds us of Jesus' prayer on the Cross. (Ps. 22. 1; Mat. 27. 46). Jonah preached to the Gentile city of Nineveh: Jesus preaches to a Gentile world today (1 Tim. 3. 16).

What is the practical implication for us in the last statement?

244

September 1
The robe, ring, shoes, and calf

'But the father said to his servants, "Bring forth the best robe, and put it on him; and put a ring on his hand, and shoes on his feet; and bring the fatted calf and kill it; and let us eat and be merry: For this my son was dead, and is alive again; he was lost and is found." And they began to be merry.' (Lk. 15. 22-24).

The third part of this parable told by our Lord is concerned with a father and his two sons. The younger one had squandered his share of the inheritance, in a far country. Now he has returned home, repentant and wretched, to a father's welcome! Indeed, it would seem that the father was watching for him, since he 'saw him while he was yet a long way off.'

The son begins his rehearsed speech, but it is cut short by the father's rapid commands to the servants. The best robe was fetched and fitted; the ring was found and placed on his hand; sandals were brought and put on his feet.

All these items remind us of what awaits the poor, penitent sinner when he comes home to God, the Father. All of them speak of Christ and His work on our behalf.

The best robe reminds us of the righteousness of Christ imparted to us (Rom. 13. 14; Eph. 4. 24; Col. 3.10).

The ring reminds us of the dignity of Christ's Sonship conferred upon us (Eph. 1. 5).

The sandals remind us of the liberty which Christ has brought to us (Gal. 5. 1). Only free-men wore sandals.

The calf was kept ready for just such an occasion. It had to be slain before the feast could be made. It reminds us of the necessity of the sacrifice of Christ, before we could enjoy the Father's feast.

Are you entering into the joy of the Father's house, or are you, like the elder son, still outside?

September2

Our advocate, the righteous one

'My little children, these things I write to you, in order that you may not sin; and if any one sin, we have an Advocate with the Father, Jesus Christ the Righteous One.'
(1 Jn. 2. 1).

Our whole-hearted aim as believers is not to sin.   But if we sin, we have 'One Who speaks to the Father in our defence.' (N.I.V.)   This is the work of an advocate.

The basic meaning of the Greek word translated 'advocate' is 'one called alongside' to plead another's cause, to help and to succour.   It is translated 'Comforter', in the King James English translation, when referring to the Holy Spirit (Jn. 14. 16, 26; 15. 26; 16. 7).   Our Lord spoke of 'another Comforter' (14. 16),   that is Another of the same kind.   So the Lord Jesus was also a 'Comforter' or a 'Counsellor' to His disciples.

A good example of our Lord's advocacy is found in Luke 22. vs 31, 32,   when He is speaking to Simon Peter.   "Simon, Simon, Satan has asked to sift you (the Greek word is plural) as wheat, but I have prayed for thee (the Greek word is singular) that thy faith fail not."

This work of advocacy and intercession, is being maintained by our Lord on our behalf, in heaven now.   He is managing our affairs above, while the Holy Spirit is managing our affairs below.

Note that we have an Advocate with the Father.   When we are born again and enter the family of God, He becomes our Father.   When sin comes in, it will break our fellowship with the Father, but it will never break our relationship with Him.

Note too, that our Advocate is the Righteous One.   All that He says and does is right and just, and is based on His atoning sacrifice for our sins.

What can you find out about the comfort and advocacy of Jehovah-Messiah for Israel? See Isaiah 40. 1;   51. 3, 12;   61. 2;   66. 13.

September 3

'Jehovah said to my Lord, "Sit at My right hand, until I make Thine enemies Thy footstool." ' (Ps. 110. 1).

David the King is reporting a conversation which he heard between Jehovah-God, the Father, and Messiah-Jesus, the Son. He has been projected into the future to hear this conversation; it takes place when the Son returns to heaven, after His death, resurrection, and forty days of appearing to his disciples.

The New Testament witnesses to this important event in the following Scriptures: 'After the Lord Jesus had spoken to them, he was taken up to heaven and He sat at the right hand of God' (Mk. 16. 19).

'For David did not ascend to heaven, and yet he said, "The Lord said to my Lord, "sit at My right hand, until I make Thine enemies Thy footstool." " ' (Acts 2. 34, 35).

'God exalted Him (Jesus) to His own right hand as Prince and Saviour ---." ' (Acts 5. 31).

'---- (God's) mighty power which He wrought in Christ when He raised Him from the dead, and set Him at His own right hand in the heavenly realms.' (Eph.1. 19, 20).

'When He had by Himself purged our sins, He sat down on the right hand of the Majesty on high.' (Heb. 1. 3).

'But to which of the angels said He at any time, "Sit on My right hand, until I make Thine enemies Thy footstool." ' (Heb. 1. 13).

'But this Man after He had offered one sacrifice for sins for ever, sat down at the right hand of God, from henceforth expecting till His enemies be made His footstool.' (Heb. 10. 12, 13).

What does David's Lord promise us as overcomers? See Revelation 3. 21.

September 4

' "For the kingdom of heaven is like a landowner who went out early in the morning to hire men to work in his vineyard. He agreed to pay them a denarius for the day and sent them into his vineyard. " ' (Mat. 20. 1, 2).

Our Lord Jesus had been speaking already to His disciples about rewards. These would be apportioned at the 'regeneration' when He, the Son of Man, shall sit down upon His throne of glory. This will take place at the end of the tribulation period, when Israel will be re-born, in preparation for the thousand years of Christ's reign on earth.

At that time, our Lord's disciples will judge the twelve tribes of Israel. Also, whatever sacrifice has been made by individual believers will be recompensed one hundred times. They will also have eternal life, which is the gift of God to every believer. (Rom. 6. 23).

Then the Lord Jesus told the parable of a landowner: He needed workers for his vineyard. The first workers hired by him at sunrise agreed to be paid one denarius for a day's work. It was the standard wage for a labourer at that time.

The landowner then returned to the market place at nine o'clock, twelve noon, three, and five o'clock in the afternoon and hired others for 'whatever was just' (Mat. 20. 4).

At the end of the day, all were given the same pay of one denarius, even those who had worked for only one hour. When those who had worked all day grumbled, the landowner asserted his right to give to each servant what he thought to be appropriate.

The Lord Jesus will reward and judge His servants in whatever way He thinks best (Jn. 5. 22, 23).

Are you working in the landowner's vineyard? Many jobs must be done, such as digging, weeding, watering, protecting, feeding, pruning, and harvesting. Which of these jobs are you doing?

September5

'And he took up his parable, and said, "Balaam the son of Beor has said, and the man whose eyes are open has said; he has said, who heard the words of God, and knew the knowledge of the most High, who saw the vision of the Almighty, falling down but having his eyes open: I shall see Him, but not now: I shall behold Him, but not nigh: There shall come a Star out of Jacob ----." ' (Num. 24. 15-17a.).

The saga of the Star begins with Joseph's second dream, which he recounted to his brothers. He saw the sun, moon and eleven stars bowing down to him (Gen. 37. 9.). The sun represented his father, the moon his mother and the stars his brothers. This dream was fulfilled, when Joseph was exalted by Pharaoh in Egypt and his family came to him.

Then Balaam, the son of Beor, comes with the second episode of the Star. He was a diviner, (Josh. 13. 22.) and a prophet (2 Pet. 2. 16.). He was asked by Balak, king of Moab, to curse the people of Israel. If he did this, Balaam would be rewarded handsomely. But God prevented him from doing this: Indeed, Balaam could only bless Israel at that time.

Part of that blessing was associated with the Star. "There shall come a Star out of Jacob." Because of Balaam's next statement about the Sceptre, the Star must refer to Someone of the tribe of Judah (Gen. 49. 10.); king David is the likeliest candidate. Although David was a bright star, there was One far brighter than he - his Son, Jesus, Who is his Lord.

The third episode in the saga of the Star was after Jesus was born. Wise men came to Jerusalem seeking the King of the Jews, because they had seen His Star in the east, and had come to worship Him - which they did (Mat. 2. 2, 9-11.). Jesus is The Star out of Jacob.

In a practical way, how can we follow Jesus, the Star out of Jacob?

September 6

'For in Him dwells all the fulness of the Godhead bodily; and you are complete in Him, Who is the Head of all principality and authority'. (Col. 2. 9, 10.).

The apostle Paul is describing our Lord Jesus Christ here, in our text for today. Note that the present tense of the verb 'to dwell' is used. At this present moment, Christ Jesus possesses all the fulness of Deity, in a glorified human body, enthroned at the Father's right hand.

Then the apostle writes, 'and you are filled full in Him'. Just as a cup immersed in a basin of water is in the water, so are we in Christ. Also, as a consequence, just as the cup is full of water in the basin, so are we filled full in Christ. Thus, the cup is in the water, and the water is in the cup. Similarly, we are in Christ and Christ (in all His fulness) is in us. We cannot have any more of Christ than we have. We are complete in Him.

The greatness of our Lord Jesus cannot be over-emphasised. In the beginning, He was the creator of angelic principalities and authorities (Col. 1. 16). Through His death on the Cross, He disarmed and defeated all Satan's might, with his rulers and authorities (2. 15). But now, in His glorified Manhood, He is the Head of all principality and authority.

This headship of our Lord applies to the whole creation. It reminds us that He is a God of order. It is seen in the material universe; it is also seen in the structure of the human family, the assembly, human society, and in the angelic hierarchy.

How does the fact that Christ is the Head of all principality and authority affect you personally and practically?

September 7

' "I will surely assemble, O Jacob, all of thee; I will surely gather the remnant of Israel; I will put them together as the sheep of Bozrah, as the flock in the midst of their fold; they shall make great noise by reason of the multitude of men". The Breaker goes up before them; they have broken up, and have passed through the gate, and have gone out by it; and their king shall pass before them, and Jehovah at their head.' (Micah 2. 12, 13.).

Our Lord Jesus well deserves the name of 'Breaker.' During His three and a half years of public ministry, He broke the power of sin, disease, demons and death. Also, He broke through human pride, deceit, and hypocrisy, exposing men for what they were.

The Breaker is seen at work again on the Cross and subsequently. By His death, the Saviour has broken the power of Satan for ever, and has set free the captives (Heb. 2. 14, 15). By his resurrection, the Saviour has broken the bands of death and the bars of Hades. Moreover, 'as He was blessing them (i.e. His disciples), he was separated from them, and was carried up into heaven.' (Lk. 24. 51). 'Having ascended up on high He led captivity captives and has given gifts to men.' (Eph. 4. 8). The Breaker went up before them.

But the scene depicted in today's text is pre-eminently a millennial one. After the seven years of tribulation, the Breaker will return to earth and lead out His people, the remnant of Israel, through the breaches in the wall of Jerusalem. He is none other than Jehovah-Jesus, with king David in attendance.

What sinful practice have you to ask the Breaker to break, so that He can lead you to full liberty in His service?

September8

'And Jesus said to him, "This day has Salvation come to this house, forasmuch as he also is a son of Abraham; for the Son of Man has come to seek and save that which is lost." ' (Lk. 19. 9, 10).

Zacchaeus was chief tax-gatherer in the city of Jericho. He was despised by many of his fellow-Jews because of his work. He was collaborating with the Romans, who had occupied the territory. His name was derived from a Hebrew word, which means 'pure' or 'clean'! Thus, his name belied his character because he was 'a sinful man' (v.7).

In his desire to see Jesus, he climbed a tree, for he was small. When the Saviour came to that spot, He told Zacchaeus to hurry and come down, for He was going to visit him: Zacchaeus received Him joyfully.

Then came the announcement: 'Zacchaeus stood and said to the Lord, "Behold, Lord, the half of my goods I give to the poor, and if I have taken anything from any man by false accusation, I return to him fourfold." ' (v. 8; Ex. 22. 1). This hard-headed business man had been transformed. The evidence was there for all to hear and see. Salvation, in the Person of the Son of Man, had come to his house and his heart.

Our Lord describes him as a son of Abraham, which he was by birth, but now was by belief (Rom. 4. 16). Our Lord adds the word 'also,' since He Himself was that pre-eminently (Mat. 1. 1). In order to save the lost, Jesus, the true Son of Abraham had to be offered up as a Burnt Offering to God. (Gen. 22. 2).

Has Salvation come to your house? What practical changes have you made as a result?

September 9

'Whosoever commits sin transgresses also the law; for sin is the transgression of the law; and you know that He was manifested to take away our sins; and in Him is no sin'. (1 Jn. 3. 4, 5.).

When the Son of God entered into the world, through the virgin Mary, a completely new kind of humanity was introduced. The first man (Adam) was from out of the earth. The second Man is from out of heaven. (1 Cor. 15. 47). That heavenly origin was seen in His sinlessness. He said to the Jews on one occasion, "I always do what pleases Him (the Father)." (Jn. 8. 29); and again, "Can any of you prove Me guilty of sin?" (v.46). Of course, none of those present could. He was tempted in every way, just as we are - yet He was without sin. (Heb. 4. 15).

Our redemption depends upon this fact, namely, our Saviour's sinlessness. The apostle Peter writes, 'You were redeemed --- with the precious Blood of Christ, a Lamb without blemish or defect.' (1 Pet. 1. 19). The apostle Paul adds his testimony; 'God made Him Who had no sin to be sin (or, a sin offering) for us, so that in Him we might become the righteousness of God.' (2 Cor. 5. 21). In death, the sinless Lamb of God took away the sin of the world (Jn. 1. 29).

Now that he has risen from the dead, and ascended on high to take up His priestly ministry, there is 'One Who is holy, blameless, pure, set apart from sinners, exalted above the heavens.' (Heb. 7. 26). Also, He graciously imparts His sinless nature to all those who receive Him by faith: They become partakers of the Divine nature (2 Pet. 1. 4). They are indwelt by the Holy Spirit (Rom. 8. 9,10).

If His sinless nature dwells in us, what must we do to prevent ourselves from sinning? See 1 John 3. 6.

September 10

'Jehovah has sworn, and will not repent, "Thou art a Priest for ever after the order of Melchizedek." ' (Ps. 110. 4).

The psalm is concerned with a Prince Who is also a Priest. (None other than Messiah-Jesus). These two offices are the subjects of two Divine declarations in the psalm. The second of these declarations is contained in our text; it is extremely solemn and sure, because of its utmost importance.

Since our Lord Jesus was from the royal tribe of Judah (humanly speaking), He could not enter the Aaronic priesthood. This was the prerogative of the tribe of Levi. (Heb. 7. 14). So God introduced a different order of priesthood for His Son, after the pattern of Melchizedek. Just as Melchizedek combined the two offices of king and priest in himself, so did our Saviour. Thus the significant prophecy of Zechariah will be completely fulfilled, during Christ's millennial reign. "He shall be a Priest upon His throne." (Zech. 6. 13). Psalm 110 looks forward to that event.

The writer of the Epistle to the Hebrews refers to our Lord's Melchizedek Priesthood on a number of occasions, as follows:-

'Just as He said in another place, "Thou art a Priest for ever after the order of Melchizedek." ' (Heb. 5. 6).
'Called of God a High Priest after the order of Melchizedek.'(v.10)
'Jesus --- having become a High Priest for ever after the order of Melchizedek.' (6. 20).
'For it is declared, "Thou art a Priest for ever after the order of Melchizedek." ' (7. 17).
'The Lord has sworn and will not repent, "Thou art a Priest for ever after the order of Melchizedek." ' (v. 21).

**What does the Melchizedek Priesthood of our Lord Jesus mean to you today?
See Heb. 7. 25.**

September 11

The temple cleanser

'And Jesus went into the temple of God, and cast out all those who sold and bought in the temple, and overthrew the tables of the money changers, and the seats of those who sold doves, and said to them, "It is written, 'My house shall be called a house of prayer,' but you have made it a den of thieves." ' (Mat. 21. 12, 13).

This was not the first time that our Lord had cleansed the temple.   At the outset of His public ministry, He had come suddenly to His temple (Jn. 2. 13-16), in fulfilment of Malachi's prophecy (Mal. 3. 1).   But His work of cleansing proved only to be temporary. The abuses had resumed and had intensified.

What were these abuses?   Sacrificial animals were bought by the traders in the temple precincts at a low price;   then they were sold at a much higher price to the pilgrims. For example, a pair of doves sold in the temple courts cost fifteen times their 'street' value.   Why did people pay such elevated prices?   Because these animals had been vetted by the priests as being fit for sacrifice, although they were often flawed (Mal.1. 8, 14).   Also, foreign money had to be exchanged for the temple shekels, in order to pay the temple tax of one half-shekel per person per annum.   Of course, a charge was levied, part of which went into the pockets of the priests.   Indeed, these temple shops were known as 'the booths of Annas',   the high priest.

So now, at the end of our Saviour's public service, He repeated the cleansing of the temple, with an authority which was unquestionable.   He reminded them of what was written in the Scriptures (Isa. 56. 7;   Jer. 7. 11).   What ought to have been a house of prayer had become a den of thieves.   But judgment was tempered with mercy, as there, in the temple, the Son of David healed the blind and the lame. (Mat. 21. 14).

Why should it be the blind and the lame particularly who were healed by the Temple Cleanser?   See 2 Samuel 5. 6, 8.   What lesson can be deduced from this?

September 12
The sceptre out of Israel

' "---- and a Sceptre shall rise out of Israel, and shall smite the corners of Moab, and destroy all the children of Sheth." ' (Num. 24. 17b).

Balaam, the son of Beor, continues with his oracle concerning Israel. He has already revealed that a Star would come out of Jacob. Now he speaks of a Sceptre arising from Israel. Jacob needed the light of the Star to guide him through this world's darkness; and so do we. But Israel, 'the prince with God,' needed the power of the Sceptre in the hand of the Prince of Peace, to govern him; and so do we.

The sceptre or rod was a staff-like object carried by a ruler as an emblem of authority. In the case of Jesus, our Shepherd-Sovereign, His Sceptre or Rod has the following characteristics:-

In the context of our text for today, and elsewhere in Scripture, our Lord Jesus carries the Rod of judgment, with which He will smite all His enemies (Ps. 2. 9; Rev. 19.15). This will be fulfilled when our Lord returns in glory to the earth, at the end of the Great Tribulation.

It is the Sceptre of our Lord's strength, which Jehovah will stretch forth, so that Jesus will rule in the midst of His enemies. (Ps. 110. 2).

It is a Rod which comforts the Great Shepherd's sheep (Ps. 23. 4; Mic. 7. 14).

It is a Rod of correction which imparts wisdom to those subjected to it (Prov. 29. 15).

Yet how poignant it is to consider the treatment meted out by men upon 'the Sceptre of Israel' (Mic. 5. 1). Prior to His crucifixion, at His mock coronation, the Roman soldiers struck our Lord on the head again and again with a staff. What wonderful grace on the part of our Saviour to suffer such indignity.

To whose rule do you submit? Self, Satan or the Sceptre of Israel?

September 13
Christ our life

'When Christ, Who is our life, shall appear, then you also will appear with Him in glory.'
(Col. 3. 4).

Saul of Tarsus was on a deadly mission.   He was on his way to Damascus.   There he would pursue the Christians until he found them.   His avowed intention was to bind them and bring them to Jerusalem for trial and possible execution (Acts 9. 1, 2).   He had already witnessed and approved of the stoning of Stephen to death, in that city.

As he approached Damascus, he was stopped by a light from heaven.   He fell to the ground, and heard the voice of Jesus say to him, "Saul, Saul, why do you persecute Me?"   From that moment, the life of Saul was completely changed.   The proud Pharisaical law-keeper became a humble bond-slave of Jesus Christ.   Saul, the persecutor of Christ became Paul, the apostle of Christ.

Now, some twenty-five years later, he is writing from Rome to some fellow-Christians in Colosse, a city which he had never visited.   He reminds them of the fact that Christ is their life.   That He, Who is the Source of all life, became their life when they received Him by faith into their lives.

Paul reminds his readers of the security of their present spiritual position.   Their life is now hidden with Christ in God. (Col. 3. 3).

Then he reminds them of future glory.   They will be with Christ, their life, when He is manifested to a wondering world, at His return (Rev. 19. 8, 14;   2 Thess. 1. 10).

If Christ is your life, what difference does it make to you now?

September 14

' "But thou, Bethlehem Ephratah, though thou be little among the thousands of Judah, yet out of thee shall He come forth unto Me Who is to be Ruler in Israel; whose goings forth have been from of old, from everlasting." ' (Mic. 5. 2).

Already, in the Old Testament Scriptures, facts regarding the Messiah's origins had been predicted.

He would be the Seed of the woman (Gen. 3. 15) and not the man. This was fulfilled in the virgin Mary, who was the mother of our Lord.

He must be of the seed of Abraham (Gen. 22. 18; Gal. 3. 16), through Isaac and Jacob.

He would be of the tribe of Judah (Gen. 49. 10). The apostle John gave confirmation of this, as he looked at the Lion-Lamb in the midst of the throne in heaven (Rev. 5. 5).

He would be a Shoot, springing from the stem of Jesse (Isa. 11. 1), a fruit-bearing Branch.

He must be of the seed of David, the youngest son of Jesse (2 Sam. 7. 12).

But this Ruler in Israel must be born in Bethlehem Ephratah, David's city. Note the accuracy of prophecy; there was another Bethlehem of Zebulun, in the north of Israel. About seven hundred years later, Micah's prophecy was fulfilled in a most remarkable manner (Lk. 2. 4, 11).

Moreover, according to Micah, this Infant of days must also be the Ancient of Days, no less than God of very God!

What else is predicted of the Ruler in Israel, in Micah 5. 3, 4? What personal comfort can you find from these verses?

September 15

'And as they heard these things, He added and spoke a parable, because He was near Jerusalem, and because they thought that the kingdom of God should immediately appear. He said therefore, " A certain nobleman went into a far country to receive for himself a kingdom, and to return." ' (Lk. 19. 11, 12).

The hearers of this parable would be aware that it was based on historical fact. When Herod the Great died, one of his sons, Archelaus, travelled to Rome to ask Caesar for the inheritance. He was followed by fifty men who appealed to Caesar not to make him king. Caesar did not grant their request, but he reduced the authority of Archelaus.

Our Lord Jesus had much greater claim to a kingdom than a son of Herod. The Saviour was the Son of David, but He was also the Son of God. He is God's true Nobleman. In His life, He displayed a nobility of character not found in any other. His noble bearing was particularly evident in the events leading up to, and including His sufferings on the Cross.

When our Lord returned to heaven, His Father gave Him the Kingdom. He is seated at God's right hand; soon He shall come to reward His servants and crush His enemies.

In the parable, the nobleman entrusted each of his bondmen with one mina, which was equivalent to about 100 days' wages. We, as the bond-slaves of the Nobleman, have a much greater responsibility. Our Lord has entrusted us with the Word of the Gospel. He tells us to 'trade with it' until He returns. Then will be the time of review and reward for His servants, but of retribution for His enemies.

Can you think of ways which you can use to multiply the Word of God, thus obeying the command of the Nobleman?

September 16
The saviour of the world

'And we have seen, and testify, that the Father sent the Son to be the Saviour of the world.'   (1 Jn. 4. 14).

Today's text tells us, firstly, of the responsibility of our Lord's disciples.   What they saw of the Lord Jesus, as the Sent One and the Saviour, they were expected to report this to others.

John was a faithful witness.   In his account of our Lord's life, death and resurrection, he reveals to the reader what he saw.   For instance, he writes, 'And we have contemplated His glory (of the Word become flesh), a glory as of an only-begotten from alongside a father' (Jn. 1. 14).

John saw the crucifixion of his beloved Lord.   He stood by the Cross of Jesus, together with Mary, our Lord's mother, and other faithful women (19. 25).   He saw Jesus bow His head and deliver up His spirit.   Then he saw the blood and water flow from the pierced side of the Saviour.   'And he who saw it bears witness, and his witness is true, and he knows that he says true, that you also may believe.' (19. 35).

Secondly, the text tells of the Father's responsibility: 'The Father sent the Son.'   This plan of action had been discussed and agreed upon by the Godhead in a past eternity. The Son was the slain Lamb foreknown before the foundation of the world
(1 Pet. 1. 19, 20).   When the fulness of the time came, the plan was enacted.

Thirdly, the text speaks of the Son's responsibility.   He was sent to be the Saviour of the world.   He became the atoning sacrifice for the sins of the whole world
(1 Jn. 2. 2).   Because of the perfection of our Lord's work of salvation, the whole world can be saved.   Sad to say, there are those in the world who don't want to be saved.

Is the Saviour of the world your Saviour?   How do you bear witness to that fact?

September 17
The giver of gifts

'He has dispersed, he has given to the needy; his righteousness endures for ever; his horn shall be exalted with honour.' (Ps. 112. 9).

This text reminds us of the Man, Christ Jesus, and His liberality as a Man, as recorded in the Gospel of Luke, the Gospel of the Son of Man.

On the material level, He gave Simon and his partners enough fish to fill two ships (Lk. 5. 7). Also He gave a great crowd of people more than enough to eat from five loaves and two fishes (9. 17).

On the physical plane, His gifts were many and varied, and bestowed on a variety of people, all needy.

He gave health to a woman with fever (4. 39.), another with an issue of blood (8. 48.), and yet another with a deformed spine (13. 13.).

Men, too, received the gift of health from Him. Lepers were cleansed (5. 13; 17. 14); a man's withered hand was restored (6. 10); a centurion's servant was healed (7. 10.). Other individuals were cured of dropsy (14. 4.), blindness (18. 42) and a severed ear (22. 51.).

Even the dead were raised to life; the young son of a grieving widow (7. 15.), and the twelve year old daughter of a synagogue ruler (8. 55.).

On the spiritual plane, different persons were given deliverance from demons (4. 33; 8. 33; 9. 42.). Above and beyond that, a man who was paralysed, and a woman who was a sinner had their sins forgiven . (5. 20; 7. 48).

But the greatest gift of all was the life of the Lord Jesus given in death on the Cross. His precious blood paid fully for every other gift given.

How does the Giver of gifts dispense and disperse them today? How can you help in this task?

September 18
The curser of the fig tree

'And when He saw a fig tree in the way, he came to it, and found nothing on it but leaves only, and said to it, "Let no fruit grow on thee henceforward for ever."   And presently the fig tree withered away.' (Mat. 21. 19).

When our Lord cursed the fig tree, a miracle of judgment was performed.   It was the only one of its kind in our Saviour's ministry.   The next morning, the disciples saw that the fig tree which He had cursed, was dried up from the roots (Mk.11. 14,20,21.).   The Lord's curse had come into effect.

It was a symbolic act on the part of the Lord Jesus.   The vine, the olive tree and the fig tree are used in Scripture as symbols of the nation of Israel.   The vine is a picture of its past (Isa. 5. 1-7.).   Israel produced no fruit for God.   The olive tree is a picture of its future, when all Israel will be saved out of the Great Tribulation, to enter the millennial kingdom of Christ.   (Rom. 11. 24-26).

But during the present time, Israel is pictured as a fig tree (Matt. 24. 32.).   Our Lord exhorts us to learn the parable of the fig tree.   When the branch becomes tender and produces leaves, we know that summer is near.   We see these things presently;   Israel is a nation once more, surrounded by Arab nations - all the trees (Lk. 21. 29.).   Israel is still in unbelief - nothing but leaves.

When the disciples spoke about it to our Lord, He used it as an object-lesson in faith. If they had faith, they could say to this mountain (Zion - emblematic of the nation Israel) and it would be cast into the sea (of the nations).   It did happen!

Our Lord came looking for fruit in the fig tree and found none.   What fruit does He find in our lives?

September 19

' *"Jehovah thy God will raise up unto thee a Prophet from the midst of thee, of thy brethren, like unto me; unto Him you shall hearken." '* (Deut. 18. 15.)

Moses prophesied of the raising up of a Prophet like himself. He would arise out of the nation Israel, as Moses did. God would give Him the words to speak. In the end, the people will listen to the Prophet Jesus, when He returns to the earth as King.

Christ as Prophet was like Moses in a number of ways. Like Moses, He was born into a slave nation. In Moses' day, Israel was subject to Egypt; in Christ's day, Israel was subject to Rome.

In the providence of God, the life of Moses was preserved as a baby. When he was three months old, his mother made an ark, and put him in it; she placed it in the sedge on the bank of the river. Pharaoh's daughter discovered him and adopted him as her son thus saving him from death. The life of the little Child Jesus was also preserved in Egypt, from the wrath of Herod. (Mat. 2. 13).

Then there were the 'silent years', as both Moses and the Lord Jesus grew up into full manhood. But what a contrast in life-styles! Moses was brought up as the son of Pharaoh's daughter, while Jesus was the Son of a carpenter, as was supposed.

When the Lord Jesus embarked on His public ministry, He performed mighty miracles like Moses (Jn. 3. 2.), and even mightier.

Like Moses, the Lord Jesus was a Law-giver. In His 'Sermon on the Mount', our Lord enunciated the laws of His kingdom.

Moses was very meek (Num. 12. 3.): Jesus surpassed him in meekness
(1 Peter 2. 23.). Moses as a servant had deep fellowship with Jehovah his God. But Christ as the Son enjoyed constant communion with the Father (Jn. 10. 30).

When and why was communion broken between God and Christ?

September 20

Christ, all and in all

'Where there is neither Greek nor Jew, circumcision nor uncircumcision, barbarian, Scythian, bond nor free; but Christ is all, and in all.' (Col. 3. 11.). Christ is the Lord's Anointed, the Son sent by the Father. It was Christ Who died, was raised up, and is at the right hand of God; Who also intercedes for us. Who shall separate us from the love of Christ? Nothing and nobody. (Rom. 8. 34, 35.).

Also, the Christ did not please Himself, but in all that He did, He pleased the Father. Christ is all that the heart of God desired in a Man. The all-sufficiency of Christ transcends all human barriers. Differences in nationality disappear ('neither Greek nor Jew'): Religious differences are unimportant ('circumcision nor uncircumcision'): Cultural differences ('barbarian, Scythian') vanish, as well as social differences ('bond or free'). In Christ, the noblest Lord and his humblest servant are one.

Christ is all that the Christian needs. He has been forgiven all his sins; he is clothed with the righteousness of Christ, having put on the 'New Man'; he possesses eternal life, Christ in Him, the Hope of glory; he is indwelt by the Holy Spirit; he has a home in heaven; he has a peace which passes all understanding; He has the Word of God, a treasure beyond measure; and much much more.

Christ is in all God's plans for the present. A home is being prepared for the Church, the Bride of Christ, in the Father's house in heaven. The Bride is making herself ready for the return of Christ, to take her there.

Christ is in all God's plans for the future. He will return to earth with His Bride to set up His kingdom. He will reign on earth for one thousand years.

Is Christ all and in all in your life now?

September 21

'For the earth shall be filled with the knowledge of the Glory of Jehovah as the waters cover the sea.' (Hab. 2. 14.).

Habakkuk receives a vision from Jehovah.   It is for an appointed time, but at the end it shall speak.   It concerns the unrighteous man, whose soul is puffed up in him.   He is a proud, restless man, who enlarges his desire as Sheol.   He is like death - he cannot be satisfied.   He gathers to himself all the nations.   Surely, this is a portrait of the man of sin, the son of perdition, the Antichrist.

Then a remarkable thing happens: All these nations whom he has led astray pronounce five woes upon him (v. 6.).   These are because of his aggression, self-assertion, violence, inhumanity and idolatry.

But after the third woe, Jehovah of hosts intervenes, and brings all the efforts of the nations to nothing (v. 13.).   He has His own plan for mankind which centres in the Man, Christ Jesus.   This plan is revealed in today's text.

The Glory of Jehovah is a Person;   none other than the Lord's Christ.   Simeon, speaking to the Lord, described the Child in his arms as a Light to lighten the Gentiles and the Glory of God's people, Israel. (Lk. 2. 32.).   God's glory is the display of His attributes and perfections;   His goodness, holiness (His Name is holy), grace and mercy. (Exod. 33. 18, 19.).   All these, and infinitely more, are seen in Christ, the Outshining of God's Glory.   (Heb. 1. 3).

When all rebellion is put down, at the return of Christ, with His saints and holy angels, the knowledge of Jehovah's Glory will completely fill the earth (Isa. 11. 9.).   The millennium will have begun.

How can we fill our hearts now with the knowledge of the Glory of Jehovah?

September 22

'And when He drew near, even now at the descent of the Mount of Olives, all the multitude of the disciples began to rejoice and praise God with a loud voice for all the mighty works which they had seen, saying, "Blessed is the King Who comes in the Name of the Lord. Peace in heaven and glory in the highest." ' (Lk. 19. 37, 38.).

The King was coming to his city, Jerusalem. He needed suitable transport. He sent two of His disciples to find and fetch a donkey and her colt (Mat. 21. 2.). He was coming in peace, with meekness and humility. He was fulfilling the prophetic word, 'Behold, thy King cometh unto thee: He is just, and having salvation; lowly, and riding upon a donkey, and upon a colt, the foal of a donkey.' (Zech. 9. 9.). It was not the time for coming on a war-horse. (Rev. 19. 11.).

His steed required a saddle; so His disciples cast their own garments on the colt. The way into the city was prepared for Him, as His disciples strewed their garments before Him.

Then the multitude of the disciples burst into praise. They praised God for the mighty miracles they had seen. Sight had been give to the blind, and even the dead had been raised to life. They blessed the King coming in Jehovah's Name. (Ps.118. 26.). "Peace in heaven," they cried, "Glory in the highest." At the Saviour's birth, the angels said, "Peace on earth." That Peace on earth, in the Person of the King, was going to be transferred soon to heaven, by way of the Cross and the empty Tomb.

The crowd cried, "Hosanna!" Another crowd, in a few days, would cry, "Crucify!" Such is the fickleness of humanity. But such was the love of the Saviour, to accept it all. Jehovah's King was crucified: He will return.

The King's disciples gave Him their animals and their garments. What can we give Him?

September 23

'And we know that the Son of God has come, and has given us an understanding that we should know Him that is true, and we are in Him that is true, in His Son Jesus Christ. He is the true God and Eternal Life.' (1 Jn. 5. 20).

The Father's Son, Jesus Christ, is alive from the dead. He is seated at the Father's right hand in glory. He is God: Although He is a Man of flesh and bone, he possesses all the attributes of Deity: He is flawlessly righteous and holy: He is immeasurably loving and merciful: He is infinitely powerful and wise: He is present everywhere: He is Creator, Upholder and Redeemer: He is the Eternal One: He is equal with the Father and the Holy Spirit, yet distinct from them in His personality.

He is the true God; that is, He is real, genuine and ideal, as opposed to what is unreal, counterfeit and false. If there was no other statement in the Bible which declares the Deity of our Lord Jesus Christ, this one is enough.

The false theory of evolution, ancient or modern, has spawned a plethora of idols; such as humanism, materialism, pantheism and amoralism. These are all false gods, in contrast to the true God, Jesus Christ.

He is Life: In Him all other life had its source. This is true of spiritual life; each angel received life from His hand. It is also true of plant and animal life, as well as human life.

He is Eternal Life: Here is God's great gift to humanity. But each one must receive the Son individually and personally. 'He who has the Son has the Life; he who does not have the Son of God, does not have the Life.' (1 Jn. 5. 12.).

Can you find other Scriptures which teach that Jesus Christ is the true God and Eternal Life?

September 24

'The Stone which the builders rejected has become the Head Stone of the corner.' (Ps. 118. 22.).

Psalms 113 to 118 are called the 'Hallel,' or 'Praise' Psalms. At Passover, Psalms 113 and 114 are sung before the meal in a Jewish home: Psalms 115 to 118 are sung after it. Our Lord Jesus probably sang Ps.118 with His disciples after the 'Last Supper' (Mat. 26. 30; Mk. 14. 26.). Certainly, the Saviour quoted verses 22 and 23 of the psalm to His opponents, just a few days before His death. He was speaking of Himself as the rejected Stone which becomes the corner Stone.

Evidently, the Spirit of God has in mind the construction of some sort of building. Indeed, in today's text, He makes mention of the builders; and from our Lord's use of the text in the Gospels, the identity of these builders is revealed. They were the chief priests, the elders of the people, the teachers of the law, the Pharisees.(Mat. 21. 23, 45; Mk. 11. 27). They were building a house, the house of Israel (Acts 2. 36). They were the leaders of their nation.

They looked for suitable material to incorporate into the building of their house. So when this Carpenter from Nazareth came along, they examined Him - and rejected Him. Why? Because this Stone was composed of material which was perfect and pure. They were exposed as hypocrites in the dazzling splendour of His Presence. But for them, the deadly flaw was that of blasphemy; here was a Man, Who claimed to be God (Jn. 10. 33.). Apart from that , their own vested interests were threatened by Him. So they rejected Him and had Him crucified.

He will become the chief Corner Stone. When the broken house of Israel is raised again by Jehovah-Jesus, at His return as King, this will be fulfilled for the faithful remnant of the nation.

What practical encouragement can be derived from this history of the Corner Stone? See 1 Cor. 1. 27-29.

September 25

'But when the gardeners saw the son, they said among themselves, "This is the heir; come, let us kill him, and let us seize his inheritance." ' (Mat. 21. 38.)

Our Lord Jesus was preaching the gospel to the people: They were in the court of the temple in Jerusalem. He was confronted by the chief priests and elders, who asked Him about His authority. Our Lord chose not to answer them directly. He chose rather to answer them by telling them the parable which contains the verse quoted above.

The first person we meet in the parable is a landowner. He has planted a vineyard, put a wall round it, dug a winepress in it and built a tower. This part of the parable would be very familiar to our Lord's audience, since it is found in Isaiah 5. 1, 2. It also helps to identify the landowner as God (v.3.) and the vineyard as the house of Israel (v.7.). Just as the landowner had done everything for the benefit of the vineyard, so God had lavished His love on Israel.

Next, we are introduced to the gardeners, to whom the landowner has rented the vineyard. He then goes on a journey. These gardeners are a picture of Israel's leaders. How do they treat the bondmen of the landowner, sent at the time of harvest? They beat them, kill them and stone them, just as Israel's leaders dealt with the prophets.

Last of all, the landowner sent his son and heir. Here is a perfect description of the Son, Whom God has appointed Heir of all things (Heb.1. 2.). Just as the gardeners cast out the heir from the vineyard and killed him, so the leaders of the nation rejected God's rightful Heir, and crucified Him outside the city of Jerusalem. The 'Lord of the Vineyard' has an awful reckoning with these wretched 'gardeners,' on their own admission (Mat. 21. 41.).

What determines the measure of our inheritance with Christ, the Heir of all things? See Romans 8. 17.

September 26

'And the Commander of Jehovah's army said to Joshua, "Loose your sandal from off your foot; for the place where you stand is holy." And Joshua did so.' (Josh. 5. 15.)

The children of Israel had survived for forty years in the desert, because God provided them with food and water. They had crossed the river Jordan, because God caused the waters to stop flowing. Now they faced another formidable obstacle, the fortress of Jericho. It barred their entry into the land of Canaan.

God had appointed Joshua as the new leader in the place of Moses. God had promised to be with him, not to fail him nor forsake him. Joshua became aware of the Lord's presence with him near Jericho some time later. He saw a Man standing in front of him with a drawn sword in His hand. "Are you for us, or for our enemies?" Joshua asked. "Neither," the Man replied, "but as Commander of Jehovah's army I have now come." This Man was not merely an ally, but a Commander Whom Joshua must obey and worship.

This Warrior was none other than Jehovah Himself (6. 2). His command extends over all the myriads of holy angels, created by Him. Also, He commands and controls all the forces of nature, to accomplish His purpose (10. 11.). The army of Israel must be obedient to His command issued through Joshua. The people obeyed the Commander's instructions, although they must have seemed somewhat bizarre. The walls fell down, and Jericho was taken.

These interventions of Jehovah in human form were appropriate to the occasion. He appeared as a Traveller to Abraham at Mamre, as a Wrestler to Jacob at Peniel, as a Sufferer to Moses at Horeb, and as a Warrior to Joshua at Jericho.

Where do we find the orders of our Commander nowadays?

September27

'For they themselves report about us what kind of a reception you gave us, and how you turned to God from idols to serve the living and true God; and to wait for His Son from the heavens, Whom He raised from the dead, even Jesus, our Deliverer from the coming wrath.' (1 Thess. 1. 9, 10.).

The apostle Paul is writing to believers who are young in the faith. He reminds them of their response when he brought the good news to them.

It was a three-fold response: Firstly, they turned to God from idols. This was a work of faith (v.3.): Secondly, they began to serve the living and true God, instead of dead and false gods. This was a labour of love (v.3.): Thirdly, they were waiting for God's Son from the heavens. This proved that they possessed an enduring constancy of hope in our Lord Jesus Christ. (v.3.).

Their hope was centred in a Person - none other than God's Son, from eternity, possessing all the attributes of Deity. But the Son became their Saviour, Jesus, to die for their sins on a Cross of shame. But God raised Him up, having loosed the pains of death, since it was not possible that He should be held by its power. (Acts 2. 24.). He is now in the heaven of heavens, at the Father's right hand.

We, too, await His return at any moment, to rescue us from coming wrath. 'God has not destined us for wrath, but for obtaining salvation through our Lord Jesus Christ.' (1 Thess. 5. 9.). This coming wrath is referred to in many scriptures, such as Zeph. 1. 15-18; 3. 8; Rev. 6. 16, 17; 14. 19; 15. 1; 16. 1, 19; 19. 15. Thus Jesus will rescue His saints of this present era by catching them up to Himself, before the Day of the Lord's Wrath begins. (1 Thess. 4. 17.).

What is your response to the One Who rescues from the coming wrath?

September 28
The chief musician

'Jehovah Adonai is my strength, and He will make my feet like hinds' feet, and He will make me to walk upon my high places.   To the Chief Musician   on my stringed instruments.'   (Hab. 3. 19).

Habakkuk wrote his prophecy just before the capture of Jerusalem by Nebuchadnezzar, king of Babylon.   Thus he was a contemporary of Jeremiah.   His name means 'embracing' or 'wrestling.'   He certainly wrestled with Jehovah-God
(1. 2.), as he sought for answers to the problems of human injustice (v.4.) and justice (2. 4.).   Although his prophecy begins with a sigh, it ends with a song.

His song or psalm is contained in chapter 3.   It begins 'A prayer of Habakkuk the prophet upon Shigioneth.'   The word 'Shigioneth' or 'Shiggaion' is also found at the beginning of Psalm 7, and means 'to cry aloud in trouble.'   We are reminded immediately of our Lord's cry on the Cross,   "My God, My God, why hast Thou forsaken Me?"

The prophet's psalm is addressed 'to the Chief Musician.'   He would be the Levite in charge of the temple choir and orchestra.   Yet some ancient translations of the Old Testament give other renderings for this phrase;   such as, 'to the praise,' or, 'to the Giver of victory.'   We are reminded immediately of the apostle Paul's statement, 'But thanks be to God, Who gives us the victory through our Lord Jesus Christ.'
(1 Cor. 15. 57.).

Our Lord is pre-eminently the Chief Musician.   He puts music in our hearts and a new song in our mouths (Ps. 40. 3.).   He teaches us to sing praises to Him Who is our Redeemer.

Can you praise the Chief Musician for giving you a song in a time of sorrow?

September 29

'And He said to them, "The kings of the Gentiles exercise lordship over them, and those who have authority over them are called benefactors. But not so with you; but let the greater among you be as the younger, and the leader as the servant. For who is greater, the one who reclines at table, or the one who serves? Is it not the one who reclines at table? But I am among you as the One Who serves." ' (Lk. 22. 25-27.).

Our Lord Jesus was with His apostles, sharing the last Passover meal together. Judas Iscariot was there, who would betray Him; Simon Peter was there, who would deny Him. Also, they were arguing among themselves about who would be the greatest in the coming kingdom! So the Lord Jesus taught them what was necessary for leadership in His kingdom.

First, He told them not to be like earthly rulers, who ordered their subjects about, and praised themselves for their good deeds.

He then exhorted them to follow His example. He Who was their Leader became their servant. They saw the principle enacted, as our Lord rose from the table, took a towel and a basin of water, and washed their feet (Jn. 13. 4, 5.). He performed the most menial task of the humblest household servant. But this was only a faint picture of the amazing reality of His service. The 'I Am,' Who appeared to Moses in the burning bush, was among His people - not to be served, but to serve, by giving His life a ransom for many. It is truly astounding that Jehovah-God should become a Servant-Saviour; that He should be counted as a criminal and die on a Cross.

How can we follow the example of the One Who serves?

273

September 30

'Grace be with you, mercy and peace, from God the Father, and from the Lord Jesus Christ, the Son of the Father, in truth and love.' (2 Jn. 3.).

This short letter is understood to be written by the apostle John. He describes himself as the elder, as in his third letter (3 Jn. 1.). He addresses the letter to the chosen lady and her children, thus introducing the concept of a family.

The church (as the aggregate of the redeemed of the present era) is described as the bride of Christ (Eph. 5. 25-27.). Also, the local company of believers is described by the apostle Paul as a chaste virgin whom he had espoused to one Man, to present her to Christ (2 Cor. 11. 2.). So the idea of the chosen lady could fit into that concept. Also, the saints are chosen in Christ before the foundation of the world (Eph. 1. 4.). God has from the beginning chosen them to salvation through sanctification of the Spirit and belief of the truth (2 Thess. 2. 13.).

God, the Father, is the Head of this family. He is bringing many sons to glory through the suffering of the Son, the Pioneer of their salvation. He is not ashamed to call them brothers (Heb. 2. 10, 11.). He is the true Son of the Father. What the Father is, He is; what the Father does, He does (Jn. 5. 19.). Our Lord Jesus said to the Jews on one occasion, "I and the Father are One." (Jn. 10. 30.).

'Thou art the everlasting Word, the Father's only Son.
 God manifestly seen and heard; and heaven's beloved One.
 Worthy, O Lamb of God art Thou,
 That every knee to Thee should bow.'

According to the text, what blessings can be ours from God, the Father and the Father's Son?

October 1

'My soul faints for Thy salvation; I hope in Thy word. My eyes fail for Thy word, saying, "When wilt Thou comfort me?" For I have become like a bottle in the smoke; yet I do not forget Thy statutes.' (Ps. 119. 81-83.)

The author of Psalm 119 uses the Hebrew alphabet as its literary basis. Thus the psalm has 22 sections corresponding to the 22 letters of the Hebrew alphabet in their regular sequence. Each section has eight verses; each verse begins with a word which starts with the letter of that particular section. Every verse, with very few exceptions (such as vs.122 and 132), contains a reference to the word of God, in one form or another.

Today's text consists of the first three verses of the section associated with the letter 'K'. The first verse begins with the Hebrew word whose meaning is 'faints' or 'perishes': This sets the scene of the section. It could be entitled: "The suffering servant is sustained by God's word."

No-one suffered like our Saviour. Truly He could say that He was like a skin bottle in the smoke. But there was a reason for putting the wineskin in the smoke. It had to be dried, before it could fulfil its purpose. Therefore the Christ must suffer and then enter into His glory.

He suffered in life to succour us (Heb. 2. 18; 5. 8.). He suffered in death to save us (1 Peter 3. 18.). He never forgot God's decrees concerning Him. They were engraved on His heart, and He fulfilled them all.

When we are called to suffer affliction, what should be our reaction to it?
See James 1. 2; Romans 5. 3;   2 Corinthians 4. 17.

October 2

'And Jesus answered, and spoke to them again in parables, and said, "The kingdom of the heavens is like a certain king who made a wedding feast for his son." '
(Mat. 22. 1, 2.)

This is now the third parable told by our Lord to the religious leaders of the Jews in Jerusalem, during 'Holy Week'.

The Lord Jesus described, by means of this parable, what the kingdom of the heavens would become, after Israel had rejected it and its King. The kingdom of the heavens is God's rule upon earth. It is a sphere of profession, includi.ıg all those who profess allegiance to the King, now absent in heaven. So now the kingdom is seen in its mystery form. At the return of Christ to the earth, it will be manifested in its material form, with His millennial reign.

In the parable, the 'certain king' is God. His son is the Christ. The marriage banquet is the gospel feast. But note that the king prepared the wedding feast for his son. Similarly, the feast of good things prepared by God in the gospel is for the glory and delight of His Son.

Note, too, that the son's bride is not mentioned, although she must be present. She would be at the top table, by the son's side. Similarly, and secretly, the true Church, the Bride of Christ, is being formed presently from His wounded side, to be at His side continually and eternally. This is the work of the Spirit of God sent down on the Day of Pentecost. He works through His servants, bringing the gospel invitation to all, both evil and good. Israel was judged for their rejection of the Son. The people were destroyed and Jerusalem was burned in 70A.D. Now the gospel feast is for all.

What is the meaning of the man without a wedding garment (vs.11-13.)?

October 3
The angel of Jehovah to Gideon

'And there came an angel of Jehovah, and sat under an oak which was in Ophrah, that belonged to Joash the Abi-ezrite; and his son Gideon threshed wheat in the winepress, to hide it from the Midianites. And the Angel of Jehovah appeared to him, and said to him, Jehovah is with thee, thou mighty man of valour." ' (Judges 6. 11, 12.)

The Midianites were everywhere; they were like locusts in number. They devoured all the produce of the land. Many of the Israelites had been forced to live in caves. But Gideon was determined to save some of the harvest. He was threshing wheat in the seclusion of the winepress, to keep it from the marauding hordes.

But the God of heaven was interested in what Gideon was doing. The Christ appeared to him in human form (vs. 14, 16, 22.), as the Angel of Jehovah, and spoke encouraging words to him. Jehovah had chosen him to rescue Israel from the bondage of Midian.

Gideon's confessed weakness was evident in the number of questions which he asked. If? Why? Where? (v.13.) How? (v.15.) If? (v.17.). But the Lord reassured him with the promise of His Presence. "I will certainly be with thee." (v.16.).

Gideon brought an offering to the Messenger of God and presented it (v.19.) - a most generous three-course meal in such austere times! A basket of goat meat, a pot of broth, and unleavened cakes made from about 20 litres of flour. The Divine Visitor touched the food with His staff, and fire consumed it all. Gideon's fears were dispelled by Jehovah's word of peace. Gideon built an altar, and named it 'Jehovah- Shalom' ('the Lord is Peace'.).

What kind of offerings can we bring to the Lord which will be acceptable to Him? See Psalm 51. 17; Romans 12. 1; Philippians 2. 17; 4. 18 ; Hebrews 13. 15, 16; 1 Peter 2. 5.

October4

'For the Lord Himself shall descend from heaven, with a loud command, with the voice of the archangel, and with the trumpet call of God; and the dead in Christ will rise first. Then we who are alive and remain shall be caught up together with them in the clouds, to meet the Lord in the air; and so shall we ever be with the Lord.'
(1 Thes. 4. 16, 17.)

Our Lord Jesus will not entrust such an event to any other, not even the highest archangel. The Lord Himself shall descend from heaven. He will give the first part of the loud command, "Come out!" The graves in the earth and in the sea will release the remains of the departed saints of this present era. They will be fashioned into bodies of glory and re-united with their owners, who will descend with the Lord from heaven. These are the dead in Christ who will rise first. Every blood-bought born-again believer, since that day of Pentecost when the Church was inaugurated, will be included. 'This corruptible will put on incorruptibility.' (1 Cor. 15. 53).

Our Lord will then give the second part of the loud command, "Come up!" The bodies of those saints who are alive then on earth will be transformed. 'This mortal will put on immortality,' (1 Cor. 15. 53.). It will happen in an instant, in the twinkling of an eye. They will then be translated into the immediate presence of the Lord, to meet Him in the air. They will, in no way, precede the dead saints whose bodies are raised. All will meet the Lord simultaneously. So 'the dead shall be raised incorruptible, and we shall be changed,' (1 Cor. 15. 52.).

This stupendous event may take place at any moment. It is the hope of the Christian (1 Thes. 2. 19.).

What is the practical outcome of having such a hope?

October 5

'Sing, O daughter of Zion; shout, O Israel; be glad and rejoice with all thy heart, O daughter of Jerusalem. Jehovah has taken away thy judgments, He has cast out thine enemy. The King of Israel, Jehovah, is in the midst of thee; thou shalt not see evil any more.' (Zeph. 3. 14, 15.)

Zephaniah (meaning, 'Protected by Jah') prophesied in Judah about 70 years after Isaiah and Micah. He was contemporary with good king Josiah, who tried to bring the people of Judah back to God. His predecessors, Manasseh and Amon, had turned the people away from God.

Zephaniah's message is one of judgment and recovery. He prophesied that the Day of Jehovah was coming, when God will pour out His judgment upon the nations (3. 8.). However, a remnant of Israel will be protected and recovered, (v.13.).

The apostle Paul taught the Thessalonian believers about the Day of the Lord. It would not come until the Man of Sin, the Son of Perdition would be revealed (2 Thes. 2. 3.). This will take place at the beginning of the tribulation period, which lasts for seven years. At the end of this time, our Lord Jesus will return to earth and cast out this Antichrist, the enemy of God's people (v.8.). He will be cast into the lake of fire which burns with brimstone (Rev. 19. 20.).

So, Jehovah, King of Israel is Jesus, the Messiah. He must reign (for one thousand years) until He has put all enemies under His feet (1 Cor. 15. 25.). At His return, with His saints, to reign, the nation Israel will be re-instated and recovered. He will be in the midst of them, like a Shepherd tending His sheep (Zeph. 3. 13.). Their sorrow and trouble will be over, and their heart will be filled with joy and gladness.

What spiritual blessings akin to those relating to Israel in vs.14-20, have you received from Jehovah the King?

October 6
Chosen instead of Barabbas

'And they cried out all at once, saying, "Away with this (man), and release unto us Barabbas" (who for a certain sedition made in the city, and for murder, was cast into prison).' (Lk. 23. 18, 19.)

Pontius Pilate, the Roman governor, was confronted with Jesus, the Carpenter, from Nazareth. The encounter took place in Pilate's judgment hall in Jerusalem. It had been engineered by the Jewish leaders, who were now demanding the death of Jesus. But Pilate could find no basis of a charge against Him.

So Pilate sought another way of ridding himself of his responsibility. At the time of the Passover, it was the custom to release one prisoner - the people's choice. So Pilate said to them, "Whom shall I release? Barabbas, or Jesus, Who is called Christ?"

Consider the contrast between those two men, Barabbas and Jesus. Barabbas (meaning, 'Son of the Father') had all the characteristics of his father, the devil. He was a rebel leader, just like Satan who leads his followers to confusion and destruction. He was a murderer, just like the devil (Jn. 8. 44.). He was a robber (18. 40.), just like Satan, who would rob God of His glory.

Jesus, the true Son of the Father is a Shepherd-Leader with a heart of love like His Father's. He is a Life-giver, both of physical and spiritual life. He is the Divine Benefactor, giving bread to the hungry, water to the thirsty, sight to the blind, strength to the powerless and peace to the tormented.

They selected Barabbas, and sent Jesus to His death. Some weeks later, the apostle Peter said to them, "You disowned the Holy and Righteous One, and asked that a murderer be released to you." (Acts 3. 14.)

What are the advantages of choosing God's Man, rather than Satan's man?

October 7

'John to the seven churches in Asia: Grace to you and peace from Him Who is, and Who was, and Who is to come, and from the seven Spirits which are before His throne; and from Jesus Christ, the faithful Witness, the Firstborn from the dead, and the Prince of the kings of the earth - - - - .'   (Rev. 1. 4, 5.)

The apostle John is a prisoner of Rome, banished to the island of Patmos, because of the word of God and his witness to Jesus.

Here, he greets his readers with a benediction of grace (a Greek blessing) and peace (a Hebrew blessing) from the triune God.   The One Who is and Who was and Who is to come is a description of the Eternal Father.   The seven Spirits refer to the Holy Spirit, in the fulness of His ministry.   He is the Spirit of Jehovah, of wisdom and understanding, counsel and strength, knowledge and the fear of Jehovah. (Isa. 11. 2.).

Jesus Christ, the Son of God, is given a three-fold description: It has to do with the past, present and future activities of our Lord Jesus, as He fulfils the offices of Prophet, Priest and King.

In the past, He witnessed faithfully to men concerning God (Isa. 55. 4;   Jn. 18. 37.).   But His witness as God's Prophet was not believed by men, so they put Him on a Cross to die.

In the present, He is the Firstborn from the dead.   This title declares our Lord's pre-eminence in resurrection.   He rose, never to die again.   He is the Firstfruits of a great harvest to follow (1 Cor. 15. 23.).   Presently, He is our Great High Priest in heaven.

In the future, He will be the Ruler of the kings of the earth.   He will enter into His office of King   at His return to earth to reign. (Rev. 19. 16;   Ps. 2. 6.).

What should be our reaction to this three-fold revelation of Jesus Christ, as Witness, Firstborn and Prince?   See Revelation 1. 5, 6.

October8

Scourged

'The ploughers ploughed upon my back; they made long their furrows.' (Ps. 129. 3.)

Undoubtedly, Israel as a nation has suffered in the past. Right at the beginning, in Egypt, the people endured the lash of the taskmasters. Even when they settled in the land of Canaan, they were oppressed by the surrounding nations. Then they were carried away into exile by the Assyrians and the Babylonians. They suffered terribly under Antiochus Epiphanes, the Syrian (170B.C.), and Titus, the Roman (70A.D.).

But the deepest furrows ploughed in Israel's back were made in more recent years. During the second world war (1939 to '45), six million Jews from all over Europe perished in Hitler's death camps. This awful ploughing produced a joyful reaping - the state of Israel, which was inaugurated in Tel Aviv on May 14,1948.

Israel's ploughing has not yet ended. After the church is caught up to be with her Lord, there will be a time of unprecedented sorrow for Israel. It is called the time of Jacob's trouble (Jer. 30. 7.). Our Lord spoke of it as 'great tribulation' (Mat. 24. 21.). It will last for three and a half years.

Our Lord Jesus also endured the ploughing of His back. Although Pilate found no fault in Him, he gave the order for Jesus to be scourged. It was a common precursor to crucifixion. The victim was so weakened by his ordeal that he would be half-dead already. The flesh of our Lord's body and face would have been so torn as to make Him almost unrecognisable; also, the Scripture was fulfilled, "I can count all My bones." (Ps. 22. 17; Isa. 50. 6.).

All this God incarnate endured, and much, much more, because of His love for us.

As we contemplate the scourging of the Saviour, what response does it elicit in our hearts?

October 9

'While the Pharisees were gathered together, Jesus asked them, saying, "What do you think concerning the Christ, whose son is he?" They say to Him, "David's." He says to them, "How then does David in the Spirit call him Lord, saying, The Lord said to my Lord, Sit at My right hand, until I make thine enemies thy footstool." If David then calls him Lord, how is he his son?" ' (Mat. 22. 41-45.)

During this day in the last week, before our Lord went to the Cross, He was confronted by the Jewish leaders in Jerusalem. Every shade of opinion was represented.

First, the chief priests and elders of the people challenged His authority for His deeds. (21. 23; 22. 14.). They represented the religious class.

Second, disciples of the Pharisees, together with the Herodians, tried to trap Him in His words (22. 15-22.). They failed miserably. They represented the political class.

Third, the Sadducees came to Him with a question about the resurrection. (22. 23-33.). They represented the wealthy upper class.

Fourth, the Pharisees sent their representative to test Jesus with a question. (22. 34-40). They represented the intellectual middle class.

Finally, the Lord Jesus had a question for the Pharisees (22. 41-45.). In essence, it was this: The Scriptures declare that the Messiah must be a descendant of David, that is, David's son. (2 Sam.7. 12-16.). How can he also be David's Lord? (Ps. 110. 1.) The Answer was the One standing before them. In order that David's Lord should also be his son, God must become Man. After that, they had no more questions to ask Jesus.

Is David's Son your Lord? If this is so, what does that imply? See Psalm 45. 11.

October 10
The Angel with the wonderful name

'And Manoah said to the Angel of Jehovah; "What is your name, so that we may honour you when your word comes true?" And the Angel of Jehovah said to him, "why do you ask My Name, seeing it is Wonderful." ' *(Judges 13, 17, 18.)*

The Philistines had oppressed Israel for forty years. Now God was going to send a deliverer. He appeared to a woman who was barren; He promised her a son. She told her husband, Manoah, and he believed her.

Manoah prayed to God for further instructions. His prayer was answered by a second appearance of the Angel of God to the woman. She ran and fetched her husband, who offered food to the 'Man'. He refused it, but suggested that Manoah should offer a burnt-offering to Jehovah. When Manoah asked Him what His Name was, He replied that it is Wonderful, or 'Incomprehensible'.

God's Wonderful Name is described in the Psalms. It is Majestic (Ps. 8. 1, 9.), Good (52. 9.), Glorious (72. 19.), Great (76. 1.), Jehovah (83. 18.), Great and Terrible (99. 3.), Holy (103. 1.), Exalted (148. 13.). But God's most Wonderful Name is Jesus, which means, the 'I Am' (is our) Saviour. His Name is like perfume poured out (S.of S. 1. 3.).

But the One with the Wonderful Name did a wonderful thing. When Manoah offered the young goat and the grain offering to Jehovah, He did wondrously. As the flame blazed up from the altar to heaven, the Angel of Jehovah ascended in the flame. Here is another beautiful picture of the Cross, where the Christ offered Himself without spot to God. (Heb. 9. 14.). That was indeed the most wonderful work.

The woman did have a son, in accordance with the word of the One with the Wonderful Name. She called the child Samson.

What help do you find in the facets of the Wonderful Name in the Psalms, and elsewhere in Scripture? For instance, see Proverbs 18. 10; Isaiah 9. 6; Acts 4.12.

284

October 11

Our hope

'Paul, an apostle of Christ Jesus, according to the command of God our Saviour, and of Christ Jesus our Hope, to Timothy, my true child in the faith: Grace, mercy and peace from God the Father and Christ Jesus our Lord.' *(1 Tim. 1. 1, 2.)*

Young Timothy had been converted to Christ, through the preaching of Paul. Now, he receives this letter of instruction and encouragement from his spiritual father.

Paul begins his letter by describing how he became an apostle, or 'sent one'. He had received his commission from God, and from Christ Jesus. Also, he reminds Timothy, and us, that God is our Saviour, and Christ Jesus is our Hope. The order is significant; there is no hope without salvation. The worldling is without God as Saviour, and therefore has no hope in Christ.

Hope may be defined as the happy anticipation of good. This state can only be achieved when a person receives God's Salvation, the Lord Jesus Christ. He then becomes that person's Hope. Christ in us is the Hope of Glory (Col. 1. 27.).

This Hope is good (2 Thes. 2. 16.), better (Heb. 7. 19.), living (1 Peter 1. 3.), and is presented in the Gospel (Col. 1. 23.). This Hope, which is Christ Jesus, is as an anchor to the soul, both sure and steadfast (Heb. 7. 19.). This Hope will be fully realised at the return of our Lord for His saints. (Titus 2. 13.).

This Hope makes us pure (1 Jn. 3. 3.), and joyful (Rom. 5. 2; 12. 12.): It does not disappoint (5. 5.), and it makes us bold (2 Cor. 3. 12.).

With such a Hope within us, what should we be ready to do? See 1 Peter 3.15 and Hebrews 6. 11.

October 12

'For thus says Jehovah of hosts, "Yet once, it is a little while, and I will shake the heavens, and the earth, and the sea, and the dry land; and I will shake all nations, and the Desire of all nations shall come; and I will fill this house with glory," says Jehovah of hosts.' (Hag. 2. 6, 7.)

It was a time of great excitement for the returning Jews. About 50,000 of them had gone back to Jerusalem after 70 years of captivity in Babylonia. This was in fulfilment of the prophecy of Jeremiah. (Jer. 29. 10.). Two years later, the foundation of the temple was finished with great joy, as well as tears, on the part of the people. (Ezra 3. 8-13.).

Then the work stopped and languished for fourteen years. So God raised up the prophet Haggai to encourage the people to recommence building. (Hag. 2. 4.). In this, his second of four messages, Haggai encourages them by declaring to them three important things.

Firstly, Jehovah of hosts had promised to be with them. (Exod. 29. 45, 46.). His Presence was enough to vanquish all the might of men.

Secondly, Jehovah would shake the physical universe and the nations. These cataclysmic events will take place during the Tribulation period, prior to the Millennium. (Rev. 6. 12-17; 16. 18-21; Heb. 12. 26, 27.).

Thirdly, the Desire of all nations, Jesus-Messiah, will come and fill the Millennial temple with His glory. (Ezek. 43. 5; 44. 4.). All the nations desire permanent peace and prosperity. Only the Prince of Peace can secure these conditions at His return to reign.

What conditions are needed for us, as individuals, to enjoy spiritual peace and prosperity from the Desire of all nations?

October 13

'And the people stood beholding: And the rulers also with them derided Him, saying,
"He saved others;   let Him save Himself, if this is the Christ, the Chosen of God." '
(Luke 23. 35.)

The rulers of the Jews had attained their goal: The carpenter of Nazareth was on the Cross.   They heard Him saying, possibly as the iron spikes were hammered into His hands and feet, "Father, forgive them, for they know not what they do."   This was the first of seven sayings uttered by Jesus on the Cross.   He, Himself, had already forgiven the sins of a paralysed man (Lk. 5. 20.), and a sinful woman (7. 48.), thus signing His own death warrant.   Now, He limits Himself to His humanity, and pleads with His Father to forgive His enemies.   It was in ignorance they did this terrible deed. (Acts 3. 17.).

Yet these notable members of the Jewish council, chief priests, scribes and elders, were at the Cross to sneer at Him.   They had been unsuccessful in persuading Pilate to change the inscription above Jesus' head to read, "He said, I am king of the Jews." Pilate replied, with strange resolve, "What I have written, I have written."
(Jn. 19. 21, 22.)

These Sanhedrists continued to pour scorn on the silent Sufferer.   "If He is the Christ, God's Chosen One, let Him save Himself!"   They knew not the Scriptures, that Jesus was the Messiah, the holy and mighty One chosen from the people.   (Ps. 89. 19; Isa..42. 1.).   Also, they knew not the power of God - Christ crucified (Mat. 22. 29; 1 Cor. 1. 23, 24.).

Because Jesus was God's Chosen One, He would not save Himself.   God had chosen Him for this very task of suffering and dying on that Cross, to save others from their sins.

What kind of people does God choose for His service, and why?
See 1 Corinthians 1. 27-29.

October 14

The first and the last

'And when I saw Him, I fell at His feet as dead. And He laid His right hand upon me, saying, "Fear not; I am the First and the Last; I am He who lives, and I became dead, and behold, I am alive for evermore, and have the keys of death and of hades." '
(Rev. 1. 17, 18.)

The apostle John was given a vision of the Saviour. He described in graphic detail what and Whom he saw. He saw One Who was not only truly human ('like a son of man') but also One Who possesses all the attributes of Deity.

A human figure was clothed with a robe of divine origin. Human emotions were constrained by divine righteousness. A human head and hair bore the mark of divine wisdom. Human eyes were endowed with divine discernment. Human feet moved in divine judgment. The radiance of His face was like the sun in its strength. It is not surprising that John fell at His feet as dead.

Then John felt the touch of the Lord's hand upon him, and heard Him say, "Be not afraid." He continued, "I am the First and the Last". John would be reminded of similar words in the prophecy of Isaiah; 'Thus says Jehovah, - - - -, " I am the First and I am the Last, and there is no God besides Me - - - - -. Do not tremble and do not be afraid." ' (Isa. 44. 6, 8.)

Undoubtedly, John was confronted with Deity in human form; He existed eternally before all else, and He shall exist after all else. He is Creator of all things and Concluder of all things.

John had no cause for fear, when he had his Creator as his Companion.

In what aspects can you say that the Son of God is the First and the Last in your Life?

October15

'Behold how good and how pleasant it is for brethren to dwell together in unity! It is like the precious oil upon the head, coming down upon the beard, even Aaron's beard; coming down to the hem of his garments; as the dew of Hermon, coming down upon the mountains of Zion; for there Jehovah commanded the blessing, life for evermore.' (Ps. 133. 1-3.)

King David is the author of this psalm of brotherly unity. Probably he wrote it after his son, Absalom, was slain and his rebellion put down. David bowed the heart of all the men of Judah, even as the heart of one man. (2 Sam. 19. 14.)

The final fulfilment of the psalm will take place during the Millennium. Then the Spirit will be poured upon the people of God from on high, and the wilderness will be a fruitful field (Isa. 32. 15.). God has promised to make the children of Israel one nation in the land, upon the mountains of Israel (Ezek. 37. 22.).

This state of unity is like the precious anointing oil. Aaron, the high priest of Israel, was anointed with this oil, to consecrate him for God's service in the tabernacle. (Exod. 29. 7; Lev. 8. 12.). The oil came down from the head even to the hem of his garments. This is a beautiful picture of our Lord Jesus, entering into His priestly ministry in the heavenly tabernacle. The comfort, power and fragrance of the Holy Spirit, as symbolised in the oil, come down from the Head and pervade the whole body.

This state of unity is also like the dew of Hermon. Again, it came down upon the mountains of Zion. It happened in Jerusalem on the day of Pentecost when the Holy Spirit descended. The Lord commanded the blessing of eternal life.

How can we enjoy fully the fragrance, fulness, and fruitfulness of the Holy Spirit?

October 16

' "For then shall be great tribulation such as was not since the beginning of the world to this time, no, nor ever shall be." ' (Mat. 24. 21.)

The temple in Jerusalem was the centre of Jewish worship, when our Lord was here on earth.   He predicted the destruction of this temple.   He said, "Not one stone will be left on another; every one will be thrown down." (Mat. 24. 2.)   His prediction was fulfilled in July, 70A.D. when the invading Roman army, under Titus, broke into Jerusalem, and the temple was burned.   The gold on the walls melted and ran into the cracks between the stones.   The soldiers tore them apart to recover the gold.   Thus the words of our Saviour were fulfilled exactly.

He also said,   "Behold, your house is left to you desolate." (23. 38.)   This word was fulfilled when the Romans put down another Jewish rebellion led by Bar Kochba in 135 A.D.   All Jews were banished from the land.   Its name was changed to Palestine in honour of the Philistine.   The name 'Jerusalem' was changed to 'Aelia Capitolina'.

Again, Jesus foretold that the Jews would return to the land in unbelief.   He said that the fig tree (an emblem of Israel) would produce leaves, but no fruit (24. 32.).   The state of Israel was set up on May 14, 1948.

Also, He revealed to His disciples that there will be a time of great tribulation (v.21.). Comparing Scripture with Scripture, this will take place after the Church is caught up to be with the Lord. (1 Thes. 4. 17.).   It will last three and a half years prior to our Lord's return to earth.   It is called 'the time of Jacob's trouble' (Jer. 30. 7.).

But the Lord also taught that, at His return as King to the earth, Israel will be reborn (Mat. 19. 28.).   It is also described as the times of restoration of all things. (Acts 3. 21.).

What kind of future does the Revealer of Israel's future have in store for you?

October 17

'Then Samson went down, and his father and his mother, to Timnath, and came to the vineyards of Timnath; and behold, a young lion roared against him. And the Spirit of Jehovah came upon him mightily, so that he tore him as one tears a kid, and he had nothing in his hand; but he did not tell his father or his mother what he had done.' (Judges 14. 5, 6.).

Although Samson often followed his own desires, there are, in his history, things that remind us of God, the Son. The meaning of the name 'Samson' is possibly 'Like the Sun'. In some ways, the life of Samson reflected the glory of the Sun of righteousness, our Lord Jesus. Samson is mentioned in the Hebrew epistle as one of the heroes of faith. (Heb. 11. 32.).

Samson's mother was told by the Angel of Jehovah that her child was to be separated to God from the womb.

This was perfectly and spiritually fulfilled in our Lord Jesus, Who was holy, harmless, undefiled, separated from sinners. (Heb. 7. 26.).

Samson's desire for a Gentile bride turned out to be of Jehovah (Judges 14. 4.). The Son of God came down to earth to win a bride, the Church, composed mainly of Gentiles.

Samson, by the Spirit, tore a lion apart with his bare hands. The Son of God, through His death on the Cross has rendered powerless him who had the power of death, that roaring lion, the devil. (Heb. 2. 14.).

On his return for his bride, Samson found honey made by a swarm of bees in the carcase of the lion. He ate some of it. At His return, the Servant of Jehovah shall see of the fruit of the travail of His soul and shall be satisfied. (Isa. 53. 11.).

What spiritual honey is available to us, to refresh and equip us for God's service? See Psalm 19. 10; 119. 103.

October 18

'For there is one God, and one Mediator between God and men, the Man Christ Jesus.'
(1 Tim. 2. 5.)

The apostle Paul exhorts Timothy to encourage the believers to pray for everyone, especially for those in authority.   Our prayers for the salvation of others is in keeping with the desire of God.   He wants all to be saved.   Sadly, all do not want to be saved.

But God has done all that He can to bring His salvation to all.   There is one God, Who created the universe and Who controls it.   However, this Unity of God is contained in a Trinity of Persons, the Father, the Son and the Holy Spirit:

> 'Holy, holy, holy, merciful and mighty.
> God in three Persons, blessed Trinity.'

So God, in His mercy, provided a Mediator, Someone to bridge the gulf between God and Man.

The original Greek word for 'mediator' has the literal meaning of 'a go-between'.   In order to be an effective 'go-between' or 'mediator', the person who is mediating must understand and act for both parties.   This is pre-eminently true of Christ Jesus.   As the Son of God, He fully represents God;   as the Son of Man, He fully represents man.

It is important to note that Christ's mediation is unique.   There is only One Mediator between God and men, the Man   Christ Jesus.   No other mediators are required, whether they are angels or humans.   Only Christ Jesus could pay the perfect ransom price on behalf of all men.   Thus, at the Cross, the claims of a holy God against sin were completely satisfied, and a way was opened up for penitent sinners to be accepted by a Holy God.

In the context of the above verse, what is our responsibility regarding the truth that Christ Jesus is the One Mediator between God and men?   Read 1 Timothy 2. 5-7.

October 19

' "In that day," Jehovah of hosts declares, " will I take you, Zerubbabel son of Shealtiel, My servant," declares Jehovah, "and will make you like My signet ring; for I have chosen you," declares Jehovah of hosts.' (Hag. 2. 23.)

Haggai, the prophet, is given a fourth and final message from Jehovah. It is addressed to Zerubbabel, the governor of Judah.

Zerubbabel was a descendant of king David. His name is found in the genealogies of our Lord Jesus, given by Matthew and Luke. (Mat. 1. 12; Lk. 3. 27.). It would appear that his Chaldean name was Sheshbazzar. (Ezra 5. 16; Zech. 4. 9.). He was sent by Cyrus, king of Persia, to lead a contingent of Jewish exiles back to Jerusalem. He was commissioned to rebuild the temple there. He was entrusted with 5,400 vessels of gold and silver, which were taken from Solomon's temple, destroyed by Nebuchadnezzar. Despite opposition, the new temple was completed.

This is a faint picture of Jesus, David's greater Son, the anti-type of Zerubbabel. He was sent by the King of heaven to build a spiritual temple. He endured great opposition and even death itself, in order to lay its foundation. But the work of building goes on, as living stones are added. At His return, the building will be completed, and His authority, as Jehovah's Signet Ring, will be acknowledged by all, in that day.

But Jehovah's promise to Zerubbabel will also be kept. After the Great Tribulation, when the Old Testament saints are raised from the dead, Zerubbabel will be given special authority during the Millennium.

God chose Zerubbabel to accomplish His plan at that time. Why has God chosen us? See 1 Corinthians 1. 27-29; Ephesians 1. 4.

October20
The living one

'And as (the women) were terrified, and bowed their faces to the ground, (the men) said to them, "Why do you seek the Living One among the dead?   He is not here, but He is risen; remember how He spoke to you, while He was yet in Galilee - - - ." '
(Lk. 24. 5, 6.)

Who were these faithful women, who had already observed the events of our Lord's crucifixion and death?   When Joseph of Arimathea and others carried the body of Jesus to the garden tomb, they followed.   They saw the tomb, and saw how the Lord's body was placed in it.

Here are the names of these devoted women:-

Mary of Magdala, who had been indwelt by seven demons until she met the Saviour.

Mary, wife of Clopas, mother of James the less, and of Joseph.   Early church history asserted that Clopas was the brother of Joseph, the supposed father of our Lord.

Salome, mother of the sons of Zebedee, the sister of Mary, the mother of our Lord.

Joanna, the wife of Chuza, who was the steward of Herod Antipas.

There was, at least, one other, whose name is not given. (Lk.24.10.).

At dawn, on the first day of the week, they arrived at the tomb.   To their surprise, the great stone at its entrance had been rolled away.   They could not find the body of the Lord Jesus.   Two angels appeared and rebuked them gently.   The Living One was not to be found here, among the dead.   He had risen from the dead as He had said.
(Mat. 17. 23.).   It was impossible for death to keep its hold on Him. (Acts 2.24.).   The women remembered what the Lord had said, and returned from the tomb to tell the others.

What certainty of hope does the Living One give to His own?   See John 14. 19.

October 21

' "And to the angel of the church in Philadelphia write: These things says the
Holy, the True, He who has the key of David, He who opens and no one shuts, who
shuts and no one opens." ' (Rev. 3. 7.)

The church in Philadelphia is the sixth of seven churches to which John is told to write
letters.   The Lord Jesus gives a four-fold description of Himself to this church.

He reminds this assembly that He is holy.   He expects His followers to be holy also
(1 Peter 1. 16.);   that is, set apart for His use.

He reminds this church that He is true.   Indeed, He describes Himself as the Truth. (Jn.
14. 6.).   Our Lord expects His followers to obey the truth.   He commended the church
in Philadelphia for having kept His word.

He reminds the company that He has the key of David.   In the days of king Hezekiah,
Eliakim was given authority over the king's household and treasury. (Isa. 22. 22.).   This
type is fulfilled in our Lord.   He, as Son, is over His house, whose house are we. (Heb.
3. 6.).   In Him are hidden all the treasures of wisdom and knowledge.
(Col. 2. 3.).

Also, the Lord Jesus is able to open and shut doors;   He has the key of the King.   He
had opened a door of opportunity for the church in Philadelphia. (Rev. 3. 8.).   On the
other hand, He will not allow the church to enter into the hour of trial, which is about to
come upon the habitable world (v.10.).   The church will not go through the tribulation
period, but will enter the open door into heaven, at the Lord's return for her. (4. 1.).
He is coming soon (3. 11.).

**What doors has God's Key Man opened or closed for you?   With what results?
See 1 Corinthians 16. 9;   2 Corinthians 2. 12;   Colossians 4. 3;   Acts 16. 6-10.**

October 22

'I, Wisdom, dwell with prudence; I possess knowledge and discretion.' (Prov. 8. 12.)
'Jehovah possessed Me in the beginning of His way, before His works of old. I was
appointed from eternity, from the beginning, before the world began.' (vs. 22, 23.)

Wisdom is the mastery of the art of living in accordance with God's expectations. It is
the ability to make the right choices at the right time. The reverential fear of Jehovah
is the beginning of Wisdom. All this can be said of God the Son in His relationship
with God, the Father. The Son is Wisdom personified.

In the context of Proverbs 8, Wisdom was the eternal Companion of Jehovah. The
Father possessed the Son in eternity past. (v.22.). God, the Son was the only-
begotten of God, the Father, in eternity, before the beginning of creation. (Jn. 1. 1, 2.).

Then Wisdom became a master Craftsman. During the creation of the heavens and the
earth, Wisdom in the Person of the Son was there, as the divine Artisan (v.30.). God
made all things in the universe by Him. (Col. 1. 16; Heb. 1, 2.).

Wisdom, in the Person of the Son, was daily the delight of the Father. (Prov. 8. 30.).
The Father's delight in the Son continued during His incarnation. (Isa. 42. 1.). He
always does the things that please the Father. (Jn. 8. 29.).

Also, Wisdom delighted in mankind. (Prov. 8. 31.). This love of the Son for humanity
compelled Him to become a Man, and to die a felon's death. He did this in order to
redeem human beings who repent of their sin and believe on Him.

Moreover, Wisdom is the divine Life-giver (v.35.). He who has the Son has life; he who
has not the Son of God has not life. (1 Jn. 5. 12.).

What is the alternative to finding Wisdom and life? See Proverbs 8. 36.

October 23

' "For as the lightning comes out of the east, and shines even to the west, so shall be the coming of the Son of Man." ' (Mat. 24. 27.)

The Lord Jesus has been outlining to His disciples the sequence of events during the Tribulation period.   Now, in His prophecy, He has arrived at the end of this period of seven years.   It is then, that He, as Son of Man, will return to the earth.   At least seven years prior to this event, the Lord will descend from heaven and summon from the world His own, to meet Him in the air, to be forever with the Lord.
(1 Thes. 4. 16, 17.).

Daniel, in his vision of the four beast-like kingdoms, saw One like a son of man.   He came with the clouds of heaven, and was given everlasting dominion. (Dan. 7. 13, 14.)
Our Lord uses this scene, here in His discourse, on the Mount of Olives.

He shows that His coming as Son of Man, will be observed by all.   It will be like lightning shining east to west.   (Mat. 24. 27.).

There shall also appear the sign of the Son of Man in the sky, which is the Son of Man Himself. (v.30.)   They shall see the Son of Man coming on the clouds of the sky with power and great glory.

The coming of the Son of Man will be just like the days of Noah.   Normal activities will be pursued without a thought of imminent danger and disaster. (vs. 37-39.).

Even the elect must be ready, because the Son of Man will come at an unexpected hour. (v. 44.).

The Son of Man will come in His glory, and all the angels with Him; He shall sit on His glorious throne. (25. 31.).

Why should the return of the Son of Man motivate us to live holy lives?
See Titus 2. 11-14.

October 24

' *"Who are you?" he asked. And she answered, "I am Ruth, your handmaid; spread therefore your covering over your handmaid, for you are a kinsman-redeemer." '*
(Ruth 3. 9.)

Boaz had gone to sleep on the threshing floor, at the far side of the heap of grain. In the middle of the night he awoke with a start, to discover a woman lying at his feet. She was a young widow named Ruth, the Moabitess. She was following the advice of her mother-in-law, Naomi, who was also a widow.

After Ruth revealed her identity, she said a very significant thing. "Spread therefore your covering (literally, 'wing') over your handmaid, for you are a kinsman- redeemer." Now Boaz had already used the same concept, on their previous encounter. He had said that she had come to take refuge under the wings of Jehovah, the God of Israel. (2. 12.). So, in effect, Ruth was saying to him, "You are the representative of Jehovah for me. Please, take care of me, as my 'kinsman-redeemer' (Hebrew, 'goel'.). It must be understood that Ruth's intentions were absolutely pure, and based upon the law of God. (Deut. 25. 5, 6.).

As 'goel', Boaz must prove that he has the right to redeem, the power to redeem, and the will to redeem. There was a nearer kinsman who, when challenged by Boaz, was unable to meet all of these requirements. So Boaz was willing to redeem the land belonging to Elimelech, Naomi's deceased husband. He was also willing to marry Ruth. He had won the right to do that, and he did. Their great grandson was David, king of Israel.

Christ is our heavenly Boaz (meaning, 'in him is strength'.) As Son of Man, He has the right to redeem; as Son of God, He has the power to redeem; as God become Man, He has the will to redeem.

What price was paid by our great 'Goel' for our redemption? See Ephesians 1. 7.

October25
God manifest in flash

'And without controversy, great is the mystery of godliness: God was manifested in the flesh, justified in the Spirit, seen of angels, preached among the nations, believed on in the world, received up into glory.' (1 Tim. 3. 16.)

Undoubtedly the incarnation of the Son of God is a great mystery. God has revealed it to us through His word by His Spirit. It is the mystery of a pure, perfect piety which was unique to the Man, Christ Jesus.

This poem in praise of piety has three couplets. Each couplet contains opposing ideas. In the first couplet, two opposing powers, the flesh and the Spirit, are brought together. In the second, there are two opposing groups of personalities, angels and Gentiles. In the third, there are two contrasting provinces, the world and glory.

The poem begins with the incarnation:

> 'Veiled in flesh the Godhead see!
> Hail, the Incarnate Deity!
> Pleased as Man with man to dwell,
> Jesus, our Emmanuel.'

Also, He was put to death in the flesh, but made alive in the Spirit. (1 Peter 3. 18; Rom. 1. 4.).

Emmanuel was seen by angels, when they ministered to Him in the desert and in the garden. (Mk. 1. 13; Lk. 22. 43.). The witness of the Incarnation and the Cross was taken to the Gentiles. (1 Tim. 2. 7; 1 Cor. 1. 23.).

There was a ready response to this witness, on the part of those in the world who believed it and received it. (Rom. 1. 8; Col. 1. 6.). The Subject of that witness, the Man Christ Jesus, had been received up in glory. The climax to this great mystery of godliness is the presence of a perfect Man in the glory. Jesus takes the highest place, and has the greatest Name, in the heaven of heavens. (Phil. 2. 9; Eph. 1. 20, 21.).

Where can we fit into this poem in praise of piety, and with what results?

October 26

'I saw by night, and behold a Man riding upon a red horse, and He stood among the myrtles, in a ravine; and behind Him were red, reddish-brown, and white horses.' (Zech. 1. 8.)

Zechariah (meaning, 'Jah has remembered') was contemporary with the prophet Haggai (Ezra 5. 1; 6. 14.).   Both ministered to the Jewish exiles who had returned to Jerusalem after the Babylonian captivity.   Zechariah was given a series of night visions in the second year of Darius Hystaspes, king of Persia: This was around 520 B.C.

The first of these visions shows that Jehovah had not forgotten Jerusalem or the Jewish remnant there.   The prophet sees a Man among the myrtles in a ravine.   He is riding upon a red horse.   This Man is none other than the Angel of Jehovah.
(Zech. 1. 11.).   It is a pre-incarnate appearance of God, the Son, in human likeness.

The red horse upon which the heavenly Rider sat is a picture of battle and bloodshed. Jehovah is jealous for Jerusalem, and angry with the complacency of the nations.   The myrtle in the ravine is a picture of Israel in humiliation, yet precious to God.   The myrtle is an evergreen bush whose blossom is white and fragrant.   Queen Esther's Hebrew name was Hadassah (meaning 'Myrtle'.)   So the Angel of Jehovah was there to protect and avenge His people.

Then Zechariah is privileged to hear God, the Son questioning God, the Father, concerning the plight of Jerusalem (v.12.)   The prophet is given the answer: The temple and the city of Jerusalem will be rebuilt.   Jehovah will comfort Zion and shall yet choose Jerusalem to be His earthly capital. (vs.16, 17.).

What do you find helpful for yourself, in this vision of the Man among the myrtles?

October27

Jesus, in the midst

'And as they were saying these things, Jesus Himself stood in the midst of them, and said to them, "Peace be unto you." ' (Lk. 24. 36.)

The first human being to see the Risen Christ was Mary Magdalene. (Mk.16.9.). It was early on Easter Sunday morning. Then other women saw Him, as they ran to Bethany to tell His disciples. (Mat. 28. 8-10.). These women probably were Mary, wife of Cleopas, and Salome, wife of Zebedee.

Later, that same day, the Risen Lord met with Cleopas and his companion, on their way to Emmaus. There was also a private meeting which Jesus had with Simon Peter. (Lk. 24. 34.).

The fifth and final appearance of our Lord, on that momentous day, was to the apostles (except for Thomas) and their companions. Cleopas and his friend were just finishing the account of their experience with the Risen Saviour, when He appeared, standing in the midst of them. Barred and bolted doors were no deterrent to Him.

Our Lord's word of greeting, "Peace be unto you," did not dispel their terror and fear. So He invited them to behold His hands, feet and side. No one but Jesus, crucified and risen from the dead, could bear these awful marks of identity. He asked for some food: They gave Him part of a cooked fish, which He ate before them.

So they saw Him with their eyes, with their ears they heard Him speak to them, they handled Him with their hands. (Mat. 28. 9; 1 Jn. 1. 1.). Slowly, the amazing fact was beginning to dawn in their minds, that Jesus was alive, there in their midst. Things would never be the same again.

Can you think of other instances in Scripture, when Jesus is in the midst?
See Luke 2. 46; Matthew 18. 20; Revelation 5. 6.

October 28

' "And to the angel of the church in Laodicea write: These things says the Amen, the faithful and true Witness, the Beginning of the creation of God." ' (Rev. 3. 14.)

The Lord Jesus described the church in Laodicea as being neither cold nor hot. Literally, it made him vomit. What was it about this church which nauseated Him? These professing Christians had compromised with the world. The city in which they lived was rich, and they too had become rich. They had no need of the Lord, so He was outside.

Laodicea means 'requirements or rights of the people'. This was the character of the assembly. What the people said and did was of paramount importance to them. So the Lord and His Word were demoted to second place.

This is why, in His letter to this church, our Lord Jesus introduces Himself as 'the Amen'. In the Old Testament, God described Himself as the God of Truth, or literally, the God of 'the Amen'. (Isa. 65. 16.). God's 'Amen' means 'It is', or 'It shall be': Man's 'Amen' means 'So be it'. But all God's promises find their 'Yes' answer in Christ, since He is the 'Amen' of God. (2 Cor. 1. 20.).

If the church in Laodicea recognised, not their own so-called rights, but those of the Amen, the faithful and true Witness, the Executor of God's creation, they would obey Him. Then He would sell them spiritual wealth (gold), clothing (white garments), and sight (eye-salve to heal their blindness).

What price must be paid to secure such spiritual assets from the Amen?
See Isaiah 55. 1, 2.

October 29

'Wisdom has built her house, she has hewn out her seven pillars: She has slaughtered her cattle; she has mingled her wine; she has also furnished her table. She has sent out her maidens; she calls on the tops of the heights of the city.'
(Prov. 9. 1-3.)

The building of Wisdom's house was a work of God (Lk. 1. 35.). 'The Word became flesh', referring to our Lord's conception in Mary's womb, 'and tabernacled among us' (Jn. 1. 14.), referring to His birth. On one occasion, the Lord Jesus said, "Destroy this temple, and in three days I will raise it up" (Jn. 2. 19.). He spoke of the shrine of His body.

The hewing out of seven pillars by Wisdom gave perfect strength to the House. This strength was seen in our Lord's life. There was the strength of His purity, and the power of His peace; the strength of His gentleness and submissiveness; His mercy and fruitfulness, impartiality and sincerity. (Js. 3. 17.).

Wisdom then proceeds to the slaughter of her 'slaughtering' (literally). Both redemption and provision come from this part of Wisdom's work at Golgotha.

The mingling of the wine brings us to Wisdom's work on the day of Pentecost, when the Holy Spirit was poured out upon the disciples. Others who were there said, mockingly, "They are full of new wine." (Acts 2. 13.).

The Gospel table was then prepared, and Wisdom's servants were sent out with the invitation. Their message is comprehensive. The hearer is exhorted to turn, eat, drink, forsake, live and go in the way of understanding. (Prov. 9. 4-6).

What is the criterion imposed by Wisdom for entering into the enjoyment of her work? Do you fulfil this criterion? See verse 4.

October 31
The coming bridegroom

' "And at midnight there was a cry made.   Behold, the bridegroom comes;   go out to meet Him." '   (Mat. 25. 6.)

The text quoted comes from the second of three consecutive parables told by our Lord during His Olivet discourse.   He begins the parable with the word 'then', which can be paraphrased or meaning 'at that time'.   He is referring to the time when He comes to earth as Bridegroom with His bride, the Church.

Jesus is describing a scenario which was common enough at the time.   A considerable period of time had elapsed since the betrothal had taken place; and the bride-price paid; perhaps even as long as one year.   Then the bridegroom summoned his bride to his father's house, where he had prepared a place for her. (Jn. 14. 2, 3.).   After several days together in private, the bridegroom together with his bride attended a public wedding banquet.   Members of both families, friends and other guests were present at this marriage supper.   Our Lord's parable refers to this point in the marriage procedure.

When the bridegroom arrived (with his bride, of course) at the banqueting house, he was met by five virgins or bridesmaids.   They were ready for his coming.   Their torches were burning brightly, as was required, since it was midnight.   Our Lord called them prudent, because they had carefully prepared for the coming of the bridegroom.   They had vessels of oil with them to keep their torches burning.   There were five foolish virgins who had no supply of oil.   They were not allowed into the banquet;   the bridegroom did not know them.

What will happen to those who are unprepared for the coming of the Bridegroom?   How do you react to this?

October 31

' "The adversaries of Jehovah shall be broken in pieces; out of the heavens shall He thunder upon them.   Jehovah will judge the ends of the earth.   He will give strength to His King, and exalt the horn of His Anointed." ' (1 Sam. 2. 10.)

Hannah's prayer to God for a son had been answered.   She named him 'Samuel' (meaning 'Heard of God'.) because God had heard and granted her request.   Now, she was in Shiloh, at the house of God, the tabernacle, before Eli the priest.   She was fulfilling her vow to give her son to Jehovah all the days of his life. (1. 11.).   In other words, he was to be a Nazirite. (Num. 6.).

As she leaves Samuel in the care of Eli, Hannah prays to God.   She begins her prayer by rejoicing in the salvation of Jehovah. (1 Sam. 2. 1.).   She then praises Him for His holiness, strength, wisdom and sovereignty (vs. 2 to 5.).   He is the God of resurrection, Who raised up His son from the dead.   Hannah has this hope of the resurrection of the dead, which is also shared by Abraham, (Gen. 22. 5; Heb. 11. 17-19.) and Job (Job 19. 25-27.), in those ancient times.

Hannah foretells the coming of Jehovah's 'Anointed One' or 'Messiah'.   This is the first reference to the title 'Messiah' in Scripture.   Hannah prophesies His exaltation, after the destruction and judgment of Jehovah's enemies.   Her son, Samuel, was destined to anoint David as king of Israel, by pouring the contents of a horn of oil over his head. But great David's greater son and Lord, Jesus, is truly the Lord's Anointed. (Ps. 2. 2; 45. 7;   Lk. 2. 26.).

What else in Hannah's prayer is an encouragement to you personally?
See 1 Samuel 2. 8, 9.

November 1

'......*our Saviour Jesus Christ, Who has abolished death, and has brought life and incorruptibility to light through the gospel.'* (2 Tim. 1. 10)

The appearing of our Saviour, Jesus Christ has changed everything. Nothing will be the same again.

During His lifetime here below, He demonstrated His power over death. A widow's son, a ruler's daughter, and a beloved brother were brought back to life. Sad to say, all three had to die again.

But the abolition of death had to wait until later in our Lord's own experience. To be our Saviour, He must die. The Lamb of God was slain to take away the sin of the world. Christ also loved the church, and has delivered Himself up (in death) for it. The apostle Paul wrote of the Son of God 'Who loved me and gave Himself (in death) for me'. (Gal. 2. 20).

Spiritual and eternal death is separation of the person from the presence of God. This was the experience of the Christ on the Cross. In the darkness, he was heard to say with a loud voice, "My God, my God, why hast Thou forsaken me?" The separation of an Infinite Being from His God for a finite period of time cancelled the separation of finite beings from God for an infinite period of time. Thus believers in Jesus are saved from eternal death, and possess eternal life.

Also, physical death is separation of the person from his body. Again, this was Christ's experience on the Cross. At the end of His sufferings, He dismissed His spirit and died. But he re-inhabited His incorruptible body on the third day, and abolished physical death. He is the First-fruits of those who have fallen asleep.

What other things are abolished? **See Romans 6. 6;** **1 Corinthians 13. 8, 10;** **15. 24, 26;** **Galatians 5. 4, 11;** **Hebrews 2. 14.**

November 2

'For thus says Jehovah of hosts, "After the glory has He sent Me to the nations who spoiled you; for he who touches you touches the apple of His eye. For, behold, I will shake My hand upon them, and they shall be a spoil to their servants; and you shall know that Jehovah of hosts has sent Me." ' (Zech. 2. 8, 9).

Note, firstly, the Person who speaks: He is none other than Jehovah of hosts, the One who commands the armies of heaven. This title of God occurs more than fifty times in the prophecy of Zechariah.

Note, secondly, the people who are being addressed. The nations are said to have spoiled them. Therefore, they must be the people of Israel. Again, they are described as Zion, who dwells with the daughter of Babylon (v.7). They are truly the apple of God's eye (v.8).

Note, thirdly, the period of history referred to: 'After the glory'. This awaits fulfilment, at the return of our Lord Jesus in glory to the earth, as Son of Man.
(Mat. 25. 31).

Note, fourthly, the purpose which will be accomplished. The One who is sent, namely, the One who is speaking, Who identifies Himself as Jehovah of hosts, will shake His hand upon the offending nations. They will become plunder for their slaves.

Then will the people of Israel know that Jehovah of hosts has sent the Saviour, who is also Jehovah of Hosts. 'The Father sent the Son to be the Saviour of the world.'
(1 Jn. 4. 14).

In that day, the daughter of Zion will rejoice. Jehovah-Jesus will dwell in her midst. She shall know that Jehovah of hosts has sent Him to her. (Zech. 2. 10, 11).

What comfort can you derive from the fact that the Father sent the Son to be your Saviour ?

November3

'In the beginning was the Word, and the Word was with God, and the Word was God. He was in the beginning with God. All things came into being through Him, and apart from Him not one thing came into being which has come into being.' (Jn. 1. 1-3).

God gave the apostle John the task of writing the fourth Gospel. It was written some decades after the others, and after the destruction of Jerusalem and the temple by the Romans in 70 A.D.

Each Gospel paints part of a portrait of Christ. Matthew portrays Him as King: Mark depicts Him as Servant: Luke describes Him as the perfect Man. But John presents a picture of the Son of God. However, all fit harmoniously into a complete presentation of our Lord Jesus Christ.

There is no need for John to begin his Gospel with a genealogy, as is given in the Gospels of Matthew and Luke; the Son of God dwells in eternity, and is without beginning of days. John begins, appropriately, with a description of our Lord as 'the Word'.

As the spoken word reveals the invisible thought, so 'the Living Word' reveals the invisible God. The Spirit of God answers, through John, some important questions regarding 'the Word'.

Where was 'the Word'?   He was there, in eternity before the ages began.
With Whom was 'the Word'?   He was with God, the Father and Holy Spirit.
Who was 'the Word'?   This same person was God.
What was the work of 'the Word'?   He did the work of creation.
What was in Him?   He was the Source of life.
What did He become?   He became flesh at conception (v.14).
Where did he live?   In a tent-like body, at birth and forever - but glorified in resurrection.

What has 'the Word' said to you today?

308

November 4

'And I wept much, because no one was found worthy to open the scroll, or to look into it. And one of the elders says to me, "Do not weep; behold the Lion of the tribe of Judah, the Root of David, has overcome so as to open the scroll, and its seven seals." ' (Rev. 5. 4,5).

The apostle John was taken up to heaven, by the Spirit, and was given a vision of the throne of God. The One who sat upon the throne had a scroll in His right hand. It was sealed with seven seals, and represents the title deed to the earth.

A search was made throughout the universe for a worthy inheritor, without success, so John wept. Then one of the twenty-four elders told him not to weep. An Heir to all the kingdoms of earth had been found. He was the Lion of the tribe of Judah, the appointed Heir of all things (Heb. 1. 2).

The picture of our Lord as the Lion is used by Jacob, in his final prophetic words to Judah. The Lion, with its nobility, strength and courage, is a fitting emblem for our Lord Jesus. (Prov. 30. 30). In the prime of His youth, like a young lion, the Lord defeated all His foes at the Cross. Death became His prey. (Gen. 49. 9). He has gone up to heaven.

He rests like a lion at the right hand of God. Who will rouse Him up? When the time comes, after the Rapture and the Tribulation, the Father will send him to put down all rebellion. The Lion will roar from on high, and the nations will be vanquished. (Jer. 25. 30-33).

How comforting to know that we can have the Lion of Judah with us, to guard us from all danger. Have you the protective presence of the Lion of Judah? If your answer is "Yes", what do you think is your part in this relationship with the Lion?

November 5

'He who is surety for a stranger will surely suffer, but whoever refuses to strike hands in pledge is safe.' (Prov. 11. 15).

A person who is surety is someone who is both willing and able to pay another's debt, whatever it may be. When Judah spoke with his father, Israel, about taking young Benjamin to Egypt, he said, "I myself will be surety for him - I will guarantee his safety. You can hold me personally responsible for him." (Gen. 43. 9).

The time came, when Joseph was going to keep Benjamin with him in Egypt, that Judah had to make good his pledge. He said to Joseph (not knowing that he was Joseph), "Your servant became surety for the lad to my father......please let your servant remain here as my lord's slave in place of the lad, and let the lad return with his brothers." (44. 32,33).

Because of the kindness of Joseph, the suretyship of Judah was not required. But Judah's descendant, the Lord Jesus did become Surety of a better covenant.
(Heb. 7. 22). In contrast to Judah's situation, we were strangers to the covenant of promise, having no hope and without God in the world (Eph. 2. 12). Our Lord became Surety for strangers, like us.

He surely suffered as our Surety, there at Golgotha. He was 'sore broken', as another rendering puts it. Reproach broke His heart, and he was overwhelmed. (Ps. 69. 20):
He was utterly broken. (Ps. 38. 8). Yet it was the will of Jehovah to crush Him.
(Isa. 53. 10). The price of the pledge had to be fully paid - and it was. No further payment from us is required.

In light of today's study, how would you interpret the second part of the verse quoted at the beginning?

November6

' *"After a long time, the Lord of those bondmen comes and reckons with them." ' (Mat. 25. 19)*.

Today's verse comes from the last of a series of parables told by our Lord Jesus in His Olivet discourse.

The key figure in the parable is a man who is very wealthy. It is a fitting picture of the Lord Jesus Himself. Although, in manhood, He chose humble circumstances, yet he was still the mighty God, Possessor of heaven and earth.

The man was leaving the country on a long journey. Again, we are reminded of how our Lord left the land of the living, by way of the Cross. His journey was back to heaven, to the Father's house.

Before leaving, the man entrusted his possessions to his own bondmen. As their Lord, he knew their abilities. Therefore, to one, he entrusted five talents, to another, two, and to another, one talent, and left immediately. In those days, a silver talent could pay the wages of a working man for ten years! Similarly, our Lord gives to each of His bondmen His possessions of time, truth and talents. These privileges are of great value. Israel was especially blessed in this aspect.

When the Lord of these bondmen returned, there was a time of reckoning. The two bondmen who had doubled what had been entrusted to them were called good and faithful. They were rewarded with greater responsibility. The one who had buried his talent was called wicked and slothful. The talent was taken from him, and he was cast out into the outer darkness.

So it will be when the Son of Man comes to earth in His glory, at the end of the Tribulation. Privileged Israel will be judged. The faithful enter, and the wicked are expelled from the kingdom.

What are you doing with the privileges which your Lord has given to you?

311

November 7
David and Goliath

' *"Your servant slew both the lion and the bear; and this uncircumcised Philistine shall be as one of them, seeing he has defied the armies of the living God."* So David prevailed over the Philistine with a sling and a stone, and smote the Philistine, and slew him, but there was no sword in the hand of David.' *(1 Sam. 17. 36, 50).*

There are many aspects in the early life of David which reminds us of David's Son, our Lord Jesus. The name David means 'Beloved'. Our Lord was declared to be God's beloved Son, at His baptism in Jordan, and at His transfiguration.

When Samuel anointed David with oil, the Spirit of Jehovah came upon him.
(1 Sam. 16. 13). When our Saviour was baptised, the Spirit of God came upon Him, as a dove. (Mat. 3. 16).

The father of David, Jesse of Bethlehem, sent him to the battle with help for his brothers. They were soldiers in the army of king Saul. On a much higher level, 'the Father sent the Son to be the Saviour of the world.' (1 Jn. 4. 14).

David was scorned by his eldest brother, Eliab. The Son of God came to His own things, and those who were His own rejected Him. (Jn. 1. 11).

David slew a lion and a bear to save his sheep. Our Lord overcame the evil strength of the devil (Lk. 4. 13), and the crushing embrace of the world. (Jn. 6. 15).

The epic encounter between David and Goliath has an important spiritual fulfilment at the Cross. Goliath (meaning 'to strip and enslave') is a type of the flesh; David called him 'this uncircumcised Philistine'. David vanquished Goliath with a sling and a stone. God chooses the weak things to put to shame the strong things. God uses the seeming weakness of a Man dying on a Cross to show that the flesh has no place in His reckoning. (1 Cor. 1. 27-29).

What application has this account of David and Goliath in your own life?

November8

'Henceforth there is laid up for me a crown of righteousness, which the Lord, the righteous Judge, will award to me on that day; and not to me only, but also to all who love His appearing.' (2 Tim. 4. 8).

The apostle Paul is writing his final letter to Timothy his beloved child in the faith. The Roman emperor Nero has condemned Paul to die. Soon, he expects to be taken from prison to the place of execution. Indeed, he views himself as being poured out already, as a drink offering, upon the final sacrifice of his ministry (v.6). For him, it will be a joyful release, like a ship set free from her moorings.

He reviews his own Christian career as a soldier of the Cross, a runner in the race, and a keeper of the faith (v.7). Soon his final battle will be fought, his course will be completed, his guardianship of the gospel will be at an end. He will be at home with his Lord, which is much better than being in the body.

Then he must await the coming of the Lord to the air, at the end of the church era, when he will be re-united with his body, which will be fashioned like our Lord's body of glory. (Phil. 3. 21;   1 Thes. 4. 16,17).

Then will come the Day of Review, when he and all the saints of this present era will stand before the Judgment Seat, or 'Bema', of Christ, the righteous Judge. What a contrast between Jesus and Nero!

The apostle is confident that he will be awarded the victor's crown of righteousness, by the righteous Judge, in that day. This reward is not exclusive to Paul. It will be given to all who long for and love their Lord's appearing.

What qualifications are required to receive other crowns from the righteous Judge at the Bema? See 1 Corinthians 9. 25;   James 1. 12;   1 Peter 5. 4;   Revelation 2. 10.

November 9

'Here now, O Joshua the high priest, and your fellows who sit in front of you, who are men of portent; for, behold, I will bring forth My Servant the Branch.' (Zech. 3. 8).

In this vision, Zechariah saw Joshua (or Jeshua) the high priest, standing before the Angel of Jehovah.

The command was given for Joshua's filthy garments to be removed. They were replaced with rich festal robes, or robes of state. Also, his iniquity was taken away from him. Moreover, a royal diadem was placed on his head. Thus he was equipped to represent Jehovah and serve the people.

Joshua and his fellow priests were to be a portent, or a symbol of things to come.

After Israel entered the land of Canaan under the leadership of another Joshua, of the tribe of Ephraim, God raised up judges to lead his people. The epoch continued for about 400 years, and ended with Samuel, around 1050 B.C.

But Israel resolved to be like the surrounding nations, and demanded a king. So, from the selection of Saul to the deportation of Zedekiah to Babylon in 586 B.C., kings ruled the people.

But now, with the rebuilding of the temple in Jerusalem in 516 B.C., there was going to be a new order. The people would be governed by the priesthood, led initially by Jeshua, of the tribe of Levi. That was the portent of the vision seen by Zechariah; and into this state of affairs, Jehovah brought forth His Servant, the Branch or Shoot. He was Jeshua, of the tribe of Judah. He was condemned to death by the Sanhedrin, led by Caiaphas, the high priest. The charge was blasphemy. A Man claimed to be God - but it was true.

In your own service for God, how can you emulate Jehovah's Servant the Branch ?

November 10

'No one has seen God at any time; the only begotten Son, Who is in the bosom of the father, He has declared Him.' (Jn. 1. 18).

This verse in the Amplified New Testament reads as follows:-
'No man has ever seen God at any time; the only unique Son, the only-begotten God, Who is in the bosom (that is, in the intimate presence) of the Father, He has declared Him - He has revealed Him, brought Him out where He can be seen; He has interpreted Him; He has made Him known.'

'The Only Begotten', when used of God the Son, refers to His unique relationship with God, the Father from eternity.   The expression is used in connection with Isaac and Abraham. (Heb. 11. 17).   Again, it is the uniqueness of Isaac as a son which is of paramount importance, contrasting with Ishmael, who was the elder son of Abraham.

The expression, 'the Only Begotten', is used of Christ five times in the New Testament, and only by the apostle John. (Jn. 1.14,18;   3. 16,18;   1 Jn. 4.9).

In the first occurrence, stress is put on the eternal glory possessed by the Son, as 'the Only Begotten' of the Father. (Jn. 1. 14).   John and others were privileged to contemplate that glory, on the Mount of Transfiguration, and on other occasions.

The eternal love between the Son and the Father is the truth declared in verse 18.   The Only Begotten is eternally in the bosom of the Father.

John 3.16 declares the infinite gift of God's love, His Only Begotten Son.   Unbelief in the Name of the Only Begotten Son of God secures judgment   (v.18).

God's Only Begotten Son is the Source of our spiritual life.   (1 John 4. 9).

How has the Only Begotten revealed the Father to you?

November 11

'And I saw, and behold, in the midst of the throne and of the four living creatures and in the midst of the elders, a lamb standing as slain, having seven horns and seven eyes, which are the seven Spirits of God sent into all the earth.' (Rev. 5. 6)

An elder had told John that the Lion of Judah was the rightful Heir to the earth. But when John looked, he saw a Lamb as slain, standing in the centre of the throne. The Lion overcame all His foes by becoming a slain Lamb, a willing Sacrifice, and then rising from the dead. The slain Lamb was alive!

John saw his beloved Lord in heaven as a Lamb freshly slain. The redeemed will be reminded of the sufferings and death of their Redeemer throughout eternity.

> "And when, O Lord, Thou comest again,
> And I Thy glory see,
> Forever as the Lamb once slain,
> I will remember Thee."

The final part of John's vision of the slain Lamb describes His Deity. The Lamb has seven horns. In Scripture, the horn is a symbol of political power. (Dan. 7. 24; Zech. 1. 18, 19). More significantly, it is a symbol of Divine power. (Ps. 18. 2; Hab. 3. 4). The number seven denotes spiritual perfection. Thus the seven horns symbolise perfect power; so the slain lamb is all-powerful or omnipotent. This is a mark of Deity. The risen Christ said to His own, "All authority is given to me in heaven and in earth." (Mat. 28. 18).

Also, the Lamb has seven eyes. The eye is a symbol of discernment. Thus the slain Lamb is all-seeing or omniscient. (Zech. 3.9; 4.10; Jn. 21.17). This is a mark of Deity. Moreover, the seven Spirits of God sent into all the earth speaks of the Lamb's omnipresence; another mark of Deity.

How should these marks of the slain Lamb's Deity affect your daily living?

November 12

'A man of many companions may come to ruin, but there is a Friend Who sticks closer than a brother.' (Prov. 18. 24).

When Rehoboam, the son of Solomon, became king of Israel, he sought advice on how to rule the people. He rejected the good counsel of the older men, and followed the bad advice of his contemporaries. This resulted in the break-up of the kingdom. The first part of today's verse found a fulfilment in this history. Rehoboam ought to have sought, from the beginning, the help of Jehovah, his only true Friend.

The second part of this proverb by king Solomon is in complete contrast with the first part. The following poetic translation of the text shows the contrast clearly:

> 'There are friends who rend us,
> But there is a Lover Who sticks closer than a brother.'

Solomon certainly knew of such an example of love. It was the love of Jonathan, son of Saul, for David, son of Jesse, and father of Solomon. (1 Sam. 18. 1). The death of Jonathan on Mount Gilboa robbed David of that love. (2 Sam. 1. 26).

But consider the contrast between Divine love and human love. Because of His great love for us, Christ entered into death itself, and overcame it by His resurrection. Now He offers His abiding Presence to all who trust Him as Saviour and Friend. Consequently, nothing is able to separate them from the love of God in Christ Jesus our Lord. (Rom. 8. 38,39).

He is a Friend and Lover Who sticks closer than a brother.

If Jesus is our close Friend, how should we respond to His love? See John 15. 14; 1 John 3. 16.

November 13

' "When the Son of Man shall come in His glory, and all the angels with Him, then shall He sit upon the throne of His glory; and all the nations shall be gathered before Him, and He shall separate them one from another, as the shepherd separates the sheep from the goats." ' (Mat. 25. 31,32).

It will be helpful to give answers to some questions relating to the text, as follows:

When will this separation take place? When the Son of Man comes in His glory, with His angels and His saints. (2 Thes. 1. 7-10; Jude 14). When he sits on His glorious throne. (Ps. 2. 6).

Where will this separation take place? It will take place on earth, in the valley of Jehoshaphat. (Joel 3. 2, 11-16). It is not to be confused with the Judgment Seat of Christ, which precedes this event; neither should it be confused with the Great White Throne Judgment, which will take place 1000 years later.

Who will be involved in the separation process? The One Who will judge is the Son of Man, returning to earth to reign. Those who will be judged are the living nations.

What criterion will be used in the separation process? The 'brothers' of the King will preach the gospel of the kingdom to the nations, during the Tribulation. Those who accept the gospel will accept and succour its messengers, and vice versa. So the works of these Gentiles will declare their belief or unbelief of the good news. Thus Christ's criterion for recognising 'sheep' is their treatment of His 'brothers'.

What will be the result of the separation process? The righteous 'sheep' will enter into the millennial kingdom and eternal life. The accursed 'goats' will depart into eternal punishment.

What marks you out as one of the Shepherd's sheep?

318

November14

'And David said to him, "To whom do you belong, and where are you from?" And he said, "I am a young man of Egypt, the slave of an Amalekite". ......And David said to him, "Can you bring me down to this company?" And he said, "Swear to me by God, that you will neither kill me, nor deliver me into the hands of my master, and I will bring you down to their company." ' (1 Sam. 30. 13,15).

David, and his men, had returned to Ziklag, only to find it destroyed by fire, and their families gone. It was a bitter blow for David, but worse was to follow.

He had been hunted out of his country by Saul, then driven from the camp of the Philistines, his erstwhile allies. Now Amalek had plundered his city, but worst of all, his own people spoke of stoning him. So David suffered rejection in a little measure, like that experienced by his Son, our Lord Jesus. But David never experienced that utter rejection which our Lord endured, when on the Cross He was forsaken by God. (Mat. 27. 46).

David set out with his warriors in pursuit of the Amalekite raiding party. His men found an Egyptian youth who had been forsaken by his Amalekite master. They gave him food and water, and brought him to David. The servants of 'the Beloved' ought to be engaged in a similar work of finding abandoned slaves of Satan, caring for them and bringing them to Jesus.

The youth confessed his part in the evil activities of the raiding band. Then he led David to the Amalekites, 'and David recovered all'. (1 Sam. 30. 18). In a much deeper spiritual sense, our Saviour 'restored that which He took not away'. (Ps. 69. 4).

In what ways can you fulfil our Lord's request to bring Him down to the company all around you?

November 15

'To Titus, my true child in a common faith. Grace and peace from God the Father and Christ Jesus our Saviour.' (Tit. 1. 4).

The birth of Jesus was announced to some shepherds by an angel, who said, "For unto you is born this day in the city of David a Saviour, Who is Christ the Lord." (Lk. 2. 11).

The presence of Jesus was announced to some Samaritan men by a woman, who said, "Is not this the Christ?" (Jn. 4. 29). After two days, they said to her, "We know that this One is indeed The Saviour of the world." (v.42).

The Person of Jesus was announced to Titus by Paul as 'Christ Jesus our Saviour' (Tit.1. 4). A Saviour announced to the Judean shepherds became the Saviour to the Samaritan men. But for saints like Paul and Titus (a Jew and a Greek, Galatians 2.3.), he becomes our Saviour. 'Christ is Head of the church, He Himself being the Saviour of the body.' (Eph. 5. 23).

The Cretans needed a Saviour; they were liars like the devil; they were evil beasts, typical of the world; they were idle gluttons, feeding the flesh. (Tit. 1. 12). Christ alone could save them, and us, from the world and its ways, the flesh and its pride, the devil and his deceit.

Our Saviour, through His death, has rendered the devil powerless. (Heb. 2. 14). The Cross of our Saviour has destroyed the wisdom of the wise. Our Saviour pours out the Holy Spirit on each believer, enabling him to overcome the lusts of the flesh. Moreover, our great God and Saviour, Jesus Christ, is coming soon to remove us from the world. (Tit. 2. 13).

If the Saviour is your Saviour, from what has He saved you, does he save you and will save you?

November 16

'Then he answered and said to me, "This is the word of Jehovah to Zerubbabel, saying, "Not by might, nor by power, but by My Spirit", says Jehovah of hosts. "Who are you, O great mountain? Before Zerubbabel, you will become a plain; and he shall bring forth the Headstone with shoutings, crying, Grace, grace to it." ' (Zech. 4. 6,7).

Zerubbabel, the governor of Jerusalem, needed encouragement. Jehovah of hosts gave him this in the vision of the lampstand, and the attendant dialogue.

Zechariah saw a golden lampstand with seven lamps. They were supplied with oil which flowed through seven channels. The channels were connected to a bowl which acted as a reservoir for the oil. The oil in the bowl was replenished from the branches of two olive trees on either side of it.

The first lesson was clear. The lamp of testimony will continue to burn brightly. Although Jehovah is pleased to use men like Zerubbabel the prince and Joshua the priest, the witness will be maintained by His Spirit, as portrayed in the 'golden oil'. Ultimately, God will use a Man Who is both Prince and Priest to accomplish His purpose.

The second lesson was this: The mountain of deception, discouragement and fear will be removed. (Ezra 4. 1-4).

The third lesson was this: The temple will be completed. The one who began the building would finish it; and so it was. It is known as the temple of Zerubbabel.

Soon, the spiritual temple of the church will be completed. (Mat. 16. 18). Our Lord Jesus, the Headstone, will have His place of pre-eminence: Grace and glory to Him!

How can you ensure that our Lord has the supreme place in your life?

November 17

'The next day, John sees Jesus coming to him, and says, "Behold the Lamb of God, Who takes away the sin of the world." '
'Again, the next day John stood and two of his disciples; and looking upon Jesus as He walked, he says, "Behold the Lamb of God." ' (Jn. 1. 29, 35, 36)

A most significant announcement was made by the banks of the river Jordan, almost two thousand years ago. "Behold the Lamb of God!"

Who made this announcement? A man sent from God, whose name was John (meaning, 'Jehovah is gracious'). He described himself as the voice of one crying in the wilderness, "Make straight the path of the Lord". He was the half-cousin of our Lord Jesus.

When did John make this announcement? It was made on two occasions, on the second and third days of a week at the outset of our Lord's public ministry. If the wedding in Cana was on a Wednesday, according to Jewish custom, the two announcements would have been made on a Friday and a Sabbath respectively. There is a progression, too, in our Lord's activity. On the first day, He is standing; on the second day, he is coming to John; on the third day, He is passing by.

What was the meaning of this announcement? Here was the Lamb of God's providing, flawless and perfect. (Gen. 22. 8; 1 Pe.1. 19). God's Lamb also fulfilled the part of the scapegoat, with this great difference. The scapegoat carried away the sins of one nation for one year. The Lamb of God took away forever the sin of the whole world. The scope of Christ's sacrifice is unlimited, but the individual must appropriate it by faith.

Is your reaction to this announcement similar to that of Andrew and John? What has your reaction prompted you to do?

November 18

'And they sing a new song, saying, "Thou art worthy to take the scroll, and to open its seals; for Thou wast slain and hast redeemed us to God by Thy blood out of every tribe, and tongue, and people, and nation; and hast made us to our God kings and priests; and we shall reign over the earth." ' *(Rev. 5. 9,10).*

John sees twenty four elders seated on thrones around the throne of God in heaven. But when the slain Lamb claims the scroll, they fall before Him and sing a new song.

The oldest song recorded in Scripture was sung at the foundation of the earth, by the 'morning stars'. (Job 38. 7). The elders' song is new, because redemption is its theme, redemption purchased by the blood of the Lamb.

Their song extols the worthiness of the slain Lamb to reveal God's prophetic plan for the world. The Lamb has the sovereign right to inherit the earth: He was slain. But, by His blood, He has brought from all nations a people for Himself; and by His grace, the Worthy One involves His saints with Himself in reigning over the earth, during the millennium.

The myriads of angels around the throne also extol the worthiness of the slain Lamb. (vs.11, 12). He is worthy (they say) to receive power and riches to accomplish His purpose; wisdom and strength to plan and execute it perfectly; honour and glory from God, angels and mankind; blessing from all His subjects. Jesus is the Lamb upon the throne of the universe, and He is worthy!

What power, riches, wisdom, strength, honour, glory and blessing do you possess? How can you put them at the disposal of the Worthy One?

November 19

'Who has ascended up into the heavens, and descended? Who has gathered the wind in his fists? Who has bound the waters in a mantle? Who has established all the ends of the earth? What is His Name, and what is His Son's Name, if thou knowest?' (Prov. 30. 4).

These are the words of Agur (meaning 'Gathered'), the son of Jakeh (meaning 'Pious'). They were spoken to Ithiel (possibly meaning 'God with me') and Ucal (meaning 'I am strong'). Thus the thoughts expressed have been gathered by the son of a pious man, and given to those who are strengthened by the presence of God.

The writer confesses his stupidity and lack of intelligence, his lack of wise instruction and knowledge of the Holies. The only other occurrence of this Name for God is earlier in the book of Proverbs, where it is written, 'The fear of Jehovah is the beginning of wisdom, and the knowledge of the Holies is intelligence.' (Prov. 9. 10).

The sage asks five questions which demand the same answer. Only God has freedom of access between the physical and spiritual realms. Angelic agents do so at His bidding. It is a reminder of the Son of God Who descended and ascended again as Son of Man. (Jn. 3. 13). Only God can control the wind and contain the waters. Only He can fix the boundaries of the continents.

His Name is thrice Holy; Father, Son and Spirit. His Son's Name is Jesus-Jehovah, the Messiah; it is also Emmanuel (meaning 'God with us'). His Name is called the Word of God (Rev. 19. 13); upon His thigh as He rides to war, a Name written, 'King of kings and Lord of Lords'. (v.16).

How can we know the Name of God's Son in a practical way?

November 20
The prostrate one

'And he went a little further, and fell on His face, and prayed, saying, "O my Father, if it be possible, let this cup pass from Me; nevertheless not as I will, but as Thou wilt".' (Mat. 26. 39).

Our Lord had led His disciples to the garden of Gethsemane (meaning 'Oil Press'), at the foot of the Mount of Olives.

After leaving the 'eight', He took the 'three' (Peter, James and John) with Him to pray. Then he was alone, prostrate before the Father.

The sorrow of the Saviour's soul is described by His own words and those of the Gospel writers. It was the spiritual counterpart of the crushing of the olives in the oil press. He had already used the word 'straitened' or 'pressed down'. (Lk. 12. 50). Now He is 'sore amazed' and 'oppressed in spirit' (Mk. 14. 33), as He anticipates the horror of Golgotha. His soul is overwhelmed with sorrow unto death (v.34). But the crushing of the soul of Christ on the Cross has resulted in the out-pouring of the oil of the Holy Spirit on men.

Falling on His face, he pleads thrice with His Father to remove the cup from Him; but he adds, "Not as I will, but as thou wilt." Thus He received strength to drink to its bitter dregs the cup of God's wrath against sin, on the Cross. There, God made Him to be sin for us, that we might become God's righteousness in Him. (2 Cor. 5. 21). From the place of the winepress comes to us the cup of blessing, filled to overflowing with the vintage of heaven.

What were the closest disciples doing, while their Master was prostrate before his Father? What lessons can we learn from this? Read Matthew 26. 37-46.

November 21

David and Mephibosheth

'And David said to him, "Fear not; for I will surely show thee kindness for Jonathan thy father's sake, and will restore thee all the land of Saul thy father; and thou shalt eat bread at my table continually." ' *(2 Sam. 9. 7).*

Here is a lovely illustration of the relationship between Christ and the sinner.

Mephibosheth is an apt picture of the sinner. There was such promise in his name, which means 'Dispeller of Shame'. His other name was Merib-Baal, which means 'Contender with Baal'. (1 Chron. 8. 34). So his two names were complementary.

However, his ability to contend with Baal was curtailed from a very early age. When he was five years old, news came that his father and grand-father, Jonathan and Saul, had been slain in battle. As his nurse fled with him, he fell and became lame.

He was summoned from Lodebar (meaning 'Place of no Pasture') across the Jordan to meet King David. The king showed him the kindness of God. He restored all his inheritance, and welcomed him to eat bread at the king's table continually.

The fallen sinner is at a distance from the Lord. He is not only ruined by the "Fall", but perishing: He is part of a condemned race. Notwithstanding, the King shows him kindness by inviting him near, to eat bread at His table continually. He is given an inheritance which is reserved in the heavens for him. (1 Pe. 1. 4).

David showed Mephibosheth kindness for Jonathan's sake. God shows the sinner kindness for Jesus' sake.

How can we show our gratitude to the King for giving us a place at His table?

November 22

'Who being the brightness of His glory, and the expression of His substance, and upholding all things by the word of His power, having made purification for sins, He sat down at the right hand of the Majesty on high.' (Heb. 1. 3).

Our Lord Jesus Christ is God's full and final revelation to mankind. The writer of this treatise to Hebrew believers gives an eight-fold description of our Lord, which declares His surpassing greatness.

First, He is the Son of God; this is His relationship with the Father in a past eternity. He is equal with the Father in every attribute of deity. This relationship never ceased when our Lord became a Man. The announcement at His baptism proves this. The Voice from heaven was heard to say, "Thou art my beloved Son; in Thee have I found my delight". (Lk. 3. 22). The announcement was also repeated at our Lord's resurrection. (Ps. 2. 7; Acts 13. 33; Heb. 1. 5). "Thou art my Son; this day have I begotten Thee."

Second, our Lord Jesus is heir of all things. The inheritance of the universe is His by right, because (third) He made it; but it is also His by blood because He redeemed it.

Fourth, our Lord, the Man of Nazareth, is the radiance of God's glory; and in that outshining, He expresses (fifth) the being of God exactly. Sixth, He is not only Creator, but Sustainer of the universe. Seventh, He alone made purification for sins, by His death on the Cross. Eight, He has taken His rightful Place at God's right hand, the place of honour.

The brightness of God's glory shone out on the transfiguration mount, and at Gethsemane when His captors fell to the ground.

How does the Son reveal the brightness of God's glory to us now?

November 23

The man whose name is the Branch

' "And speak to him (i.e. the high priest), saying; Thus speaks Jehovah of hosts, saying, "Behold the Man whose Name is the Branch, and He shall grow up out of His place, and He shall build the temple of Jehovah." ' (Zech. 6. 12).

Zechariah the prophet was instructed by Jehovah to make a royal diadem. The silver and gold used in its manufacture were gifts from three men who had returned from the Babylonian captivity.

Then the prophet was told to put the tiara, composed of many crowns, on the head of Jeshua ben Jehozadak, the high priest. It was a sign of things to come, when the two offices of priest and prince would reside in one Person, Jeshua ben David. He would be a priest for ever, after the order of Melchisedek. King Uzziah of Judah had attempted to usurp the priestly office, but Jehovah smote him with leprosy. This dignity is reserved for His Son.

The dual office of king-priest is for the Man whose Name is the Branch (or Shoot). He is the King-Branch (Jer. 23. 5,6), as depicted in the Gospel of Matthew; He is the Servant-Branch (Zech. 3. 8), as depicted in the Gospel of Mark; He is the Man-Branch, as portrayed in the Gospel of Luke, and the Branch of Jehovah (Isa. 4. 2), as portrayed in the Gospel of John.

He shall be as a root out of the dry ground of Israel. He shall grow out of His own stock; of the seed of Abraham, the tribe of Judah, the family of David. He shall be of humble origin, from Bethlehem and Nazareth, but of noble destiny. He shall build the millennial temple of Jehovah; the house of prayer for all nations. (Isa. 2. 2-4; 56. 6,7; Mic. 4. 1-7; Ezek. 40. 48). He shall be a priest upon His throne.

The Man-Branch is building a temple, in this present dispensation. What is your part in its construction?

November 24

'Then answered the Jews and said to Him, "What signs showest Thou to us, that Thou doest these things?" Jesus answered and said to them, "Destroy this Temple, and in three days, I will raise it up." ' (Jn. 2. 18,19).

During the first Passover of our Lord's public ministry, He went to Jerusalem. This was evidently His custom. (6. 4;   11. 55;   12. 1;   13. 1). It was predicted in the Old Testament, that the Lord would come suddenly to His temple.   (Mal. 3. 1-3).   Now, it happened.

It was the first of two occasions when the Lord Jesus cleansed the temple, which He called His Father's house.   (The second cleansing took place at the end of His public ministry.)   His disciples remembered the Scripture, "The zeal of Thy house consumes Me".   (Ps. 69. 9).   Who could stand against such holy anger?   None!   All fled before Him.

The Jews demanded proof of our Lord's authority to do these things.   They had to do something, in order to obtain such proof, according to our Lord's enigmatic reply. "Demolish this Sanctuary, and in three days I will rebuild it."

Their demolition work was thorough.   His back was gouged with a Roman scourge;   His head was pierced with a crown of thorns;   His face was marred and scarred; His hands and feet were torn with iron spikes;   His side was pierced with a soldier's spear. It was very thorough.

The rebuilding work was even more thorough.   On the third day after His death, the Sanctuary of our Lord's body was raised, a body of glory.   It was the work of God; Father, Son and Holy Spirit. (Rom. 8. 11;   Eph. 1. 19,20).

What practical results follow, as a result of the rebuilding of the Temple of our Lord's body?   See 1 Corinthians 15. 12-20.

November 25

'And when He had opened the fifth seal, I saw under the altar the souls of those who had been slain for the word of God, and for the testimony which they held; and they cried with a loud voice, saying, "How long, O Sovereign Ruler, Holy and True, dost Thou not judge and avenge our blood on those who dwell on the earth?" '
(Rev. 6. 9,10)

The Lamb in the midst of the throne in heaven has opened the fifth seal of the scroll. The Lamb is our Lord Jesus Christ.

Then the apostle John sees the souls of Israeli saints, who will be martyred during the tribulation period. The catching up to heaven of saints of the present era takes place before this period begins.

This event connected with the opening of the fifth seal is described by our Lord in His discourse on the mount of Olives. He said, "Then shall they deliver you up to be afflicted and shall kill you." (Mat. 24. 10). Now they are depicted as the ashes of a burnt sacrifice, offered on the anti-type of the bronze altar in heaven.

They cry to the Lamb, identifying Him as Sovereign Ruler, the One who possesses supreme authority. It is a title used of our Lord on several occasions (2 Tim. 2. 21; 2 Pet. 2. 1; Jude 4.), and of God. (Lk. 2. 29; Acts 4. 24).

Then they describe Him as Holy and True, as our Lord Jesus also describes Himself (Rev. 3. 7). Because He is Holy, He must judge sin; because He is True, His judgment will be impartial and righteous.

Should we pray, like these martyrs, for vengeance upon our enemies?
See Luke 23. 34; Acts 7. 60.

November26

'There are three things which are too wonderful for me, and four which I know not: the way of an eagle in the heavens; the way of a serpent upon a rock; the way of a ship in the midst of the sea; and the way of a man with a maid.' (Prov. 30. 18,19).

The prophecy, or oracle, of Agur continues, as he cites four things that are a mystery to him. His examples are all drawn from common experience. But in these four pictures may be discerned a prophecy concerning our Lord Jesus.

The way of an eagle in flight is a fitting picture of God, the Son descending from His home in the heavens, in matchless love and grace.

> 'O, the wonder of His love,
> See Him coming from above,
> To atone and die for thee,
> Praise Him, praise Him cheerfully.'

The way of a serpent upon a rock depicts the unique humanity of Immanuel, God with us. Christ, the Rock was perfect and flawless. That old serpent, Satan, came and found no imperfection in Him.

The way of a ship in the midst of the sea is a graphic description of the sufferings, death and resurrection of Christ. All the waves and billows of God's wrath overwhelmed Christ on the Cross. But he emerged triumphantly in His resurrection.

The way of a man with a maid describes the present ministry of the Man, Christ Jesus. Just as Abraham's servant was sent to seek a bride for Isaac, so the Holy Spirit is presently finding a bride for Christ, the Son of the Father's love.

As you consider the wonders of our Lord's deity, and humanity, His passion in the past, and His plan in the present, which, in your view, is the greatest wonder?

November 27

'Then Judas, who delivered Him up, when he saw that He was condemned, filled with remorse, he returned the thirty pieces of silver to the chief priests and the elders, saying, "I have sinned in having delivered up Guiltless Blood." But they said, "What is that to us? See thou to that." ' (Mat. 27. 3,4).

Here is a most fitting description of the Son of Man - 'Guiltless Blood'. It was given to Him by Judas Iscariot, or Ish Kerioth (meaning 'Man of the Cities'). Judas was a man of the world, who followed Jesus for gain. Judas was a thief, and carried the common purse, helping himself from it. (Jn. 12. 6). The Saviour named him the son of perdition (or, destruction) (17. 12). Our Lord also described him as a devil, that is, a false accuser (6. 70).

His love of possessions was so powerful that he sold Jesus to the chief priests and elders for thirty silver coins. It was the price of a slave who had been fatally gored by a neighbour's ox. (Exod. 21. 32).

To do this terrible deed of betrayal, Satan entered into Judas. (Jn. 13. 2,27). Perhaps he was encouraged to see the display of Jesus' power at Gethsemane, when the armed men fell to the ground. But now his plan was shattered - Jesus was condemned. Overwhelmed with remorse, he cried, "I have betrayed Innocent Blood!"

What Judas said was true, more true than he could ever have imagined. What God demanded was a perfect sacrifice, whose poured-out precious Blood could cleanse away every single sin from the heart of every believing sinner. God's demands were met in the 'Guiltless Blood'.

What lessons can we learn from the life of Judas Iscariot, the betrayer of 'Innocent Blood'?

November28

' "But will God indeed dwell on the earth? Behold the heavens, and the heaven of heavens cannot contain Thee; how much less this house which I have built!" '
(1 Kings 8. 27).

King Solomon was correct in what he said about God: His presence is everywhere. Yet God was pleased to show that He was with His people, Israel. There was the fiery cloud which settled upon the tabernacle in the wilderness, when the glory of Jehovah filled it. (Exod. 40. 34).

A similar event took place at the completion of Solomon's temple in Jerusalem. The house of Jehovah was filled with a cloud; for the glory of Jehovah had filled the house of God. (2 Chron. 5. 13,14). Also, when Solomon had finished his prayer of dedication, fire came down from the heavens, and the glory of Jehovah filled the house (7. 1). He had found a dwelling place on earth. But, about 360 years later, this temple was destroyed by the Babylonian army, led by king Nebuchadnezzar. The glory of Jehovah had departed. (Ezek. 10. 18).

But God did come to dwell on the earth. He was born of a virgin in Bethlehem. The Ancient of Days became the Infant of days. "And the Word became flesh and 'tabernacled' among us, and we have contemplated His glory, as of an only-begotten from alongside a father, full of grace and truth." (Jn. 1. 14). He was given no welcome by the leaders of the people; instead, they gave Him a Cross, upon which to die, and then to be received up in glory, by the Father.

But God will again dwell on the earth at Christ's return. The glory of Jehovah will fill a new temple. (Ezek. 43. 1-9). He will dwell among the Israelites for ever.

In this present era, in what sense does God dwell on the earth? Give Scriptural backing for your answer.

November29

'And of the angels He says, "Who makes His angels spirits, and his ministers a flame of fire." But to the Son he says, "Thy throne, O God, is for ever and ever; a sceptre of righteousness is the sceptre of thy kingdom." ' (Heb. 1. 7, 8).

Here the writer shows the tremendous contrast between the angels and the Son.

Angels are created beings: God made them. He made them to be His messengers, moving swiftly like the wind to do His will. He made them to be His ministers, serving Him in the pure holiness of His presence, for our God is a consuming fire.

The Son is an uncreated being: The Son of God is God, the Son. In a past eternity, the Son was co-equal with the Father and the Holy Spirit, three Persons, one God. When the Son became a Man, He was still God. He was Immanuel, God with us. During the years of our Lord's public ministry among men, His words and His works witnessed to His deity. When the Son expired on the Cross, He was still God. When He rose from the dead, the event declared His deity. Now enthroned in majesty, he is worshipped as God. When he returns to earth, to set up His kingdom, He is God. The Father issues the Divine decree, "Thy throne, O God, is the age of the age."

He is the mighty God (Isa. 9. 6); Jesus Christ is our great God (Tit. 2. 13). When confronted with the risen Christ, Thomas exclaimed, "My Lord and my God". (Jn. 20. 28).

In what ways does the deity of our Lord Jesus affect your life-style?

November 30

' "Rejoice greatly, O daughter of Zion; shout, O daughter of Jerusalem! Behold thy King comes to thee; He is just and having salvation, lowly and riding upon a donkey, even upon a colt, the foal of a donkey." ' (Zech. 9. 9).

It is evident, from what follows in this prophecy, that the coming King is none other than Jehovah, who will appear over His people (v.14). Confirmation of this is found in the book of the prophet Jeremiah: Jehovah declares that He will raise up of David a righteous Branch, Who will reign as King. His name will be Jehovah our Righteousness. (Jer. 23. 5, 6).

But here, in Zechariah's prophecy, a seeming contradiction would present itself to the readers contemporary with the prophet. On the one hand, Zion's King is pictured as coming, not riding on a war-horse, but upon a donkey. He is coming, yes, endowed with salvation, but also with all humility. On the other hand, he appears as Jehovah, and His arrow shall go forth like the lightning; He shall save His people from their enemies, in that day. (Zech. 9. 14-16).

How could these two views be reconciled? The answer is obvious now. There would be two advents of Messiah, with an indeterminate period of time between them. First, He must come and be rejected and suffer death; then he must return and be accepted by His people, as their King.

The New Testament confirms this view. Both Matthew and John show that the prophecy of Zechariah 9. 9 was fulfilled, when our Lord made His solemn entry into Jerusalem. (Mat. 21. 5; Jn. 12. 15).

How can we acquire this salvation which the coming King was endowed with?

December 1

'There was a man of the Pharisees, named Nicodemus, a ruler of the Jews: The same came to Jesus by night, and said to Him, "Rabbi, we know that Thou art a Teacher come from God, for none can do these things that Thou doest, unless God be with him." ' (Jn. 3. 1,2).

Nicodemus had the highest credentials. As a Pharisee, he kept the law. As a ruler of the Jews, he was a member of the Sanhedrin. Our Lord addressed him as the teacher of Israel, that is, the nation's foremost teacher. But he was still in nature's night. He had not yet been born from above. But what he could do, he did: In his darkness, he came to Jesus. He set a good example for all to follow.

Nicodemus, (meaning 'Innocent Blood') hailed Jesus as a Teacher come from God. Evidently, Nicodemus and others of his peers (since he said, "We know....") had arrived at this conclusion, as a result of the miraculous signs performed by the Saviour (2. 23). They had not yet concluded that Jesus was the Lord, the Angel of the covenant, coming suddenly to his temple. (Mal. 3. 1; Jn. 2. 13-16).

Nicodemus had confessed Jesus to be a Teacher come from God. So the Saviour proceeded to teach him some basic truths: How he or his fellows or his nation could see and enter the kingdom of God, through the new birth. (Mat. 19. 28).

Then our Lord told him of heavenly things: The lifting up of the Son of Man by sinful men, and the giving of the Son of God by His Father God, in order that eternal life could be offered to everyone who believes in Jesus.

What heavenly things has the Teacher from God been revealing to you recently?

December 2
The man-child

'And a great sign appeared in heaven; a woman clothed with the sun, and the moon under her feet, and upon her head a crown of twelve stars; and she, being with child, cried, in travail and in pain to give birth.' (Rev. 12. 1,2).
'And she brought forth a Man Child, who was to rule all nations with a rod of iron; and her Child was caught up to God and to His throne.' (v.5).

Three personages are prominent in this part of the book of Revelation. (Rev. 12. 1-6). They are a woman, a Man Child and a dragon. Each has a part to play during the end times.

The woman is Israel, as viewed from heaven, from God's stand-point. She is clothed with Christ's authority, as depicted by the sun. She has put down subordinate authority, as depicted by the moon, under her feet. She is invested with royal dignity and governmental authority, as depicted by the crown of twelve stars.

The Man Child is Christ: He is the Son of Abraham, the Son of David, the Son of Mary, the seed of the woman. After the tribulation and during the millennium, He will rule all nations with a rod of iron. (Mic. 5. 2;   Rev. 19. 15).   After His birth, the Son (the Male Child) was caught up to God and to His throne. His life, death and resurrection are not mentioned.

The dragon is clearly identified in the immediate context as the devil and Satan. (Rev. 12. 9). Reference is made to his initial rebellion, when he succeeded in bringing with him one-third of the angels. He has always sought to destroy the Man Child, without success.

In what ways does the rule of the Man Child affect you now?

December 3

A poor wise man

'There was a little city, and few men within it; and there came a great king against it, and besieged it, and built great bulwarks against it. Now there was found in it a poor wise man, and he by his wisdom delivered the city; yet nobody remembered that poor man.' (Ecc. 9. 14,15).

The poor wise man did the city a great service. How did he deliver it? It would appear that he himself had no resources, except his wisdom; and, in his wisdom he cried out in prayer to heaven, and heaven answered. This was the experience of Hezekiah, king of Judah, when the Assyrians besieged Jerusalem. In answer to the king's plea, Jehovah sent an angel, who annihilated the Assyrian army.
(2 Chron. 32. 20,21).

But the city under siege contains a deeper meaning. The little city is a picture of the world. How tiny it is, when compared with the sun and the stars. The city's few inhabitants is a picture of humanity.

The great king, building his great bulwark against the city, is a potent picture of Satan, the Prince of darkness. He lays siege to the city of Man's soul.

The Poor Wise Man is a most fitting description of our Saviour. For He who was infinitely rich became indescribably poor, in order to bring his wealth within our grasp. (2 Cor. 8. 9). Also, He is both the power and the wisdom of God.
(1 Cor. 1. 24). That wisdom was displayed in all its glory at the Cross. It was there that the 'great king' was defeated, and his engines of war destroyed.

Yet, it is true to say that, in general, His own nation Israel does not remember the Poor Wise Man. (Isa. 53. 3).

How often do you, as an individual, remember the Poor Wise Man, according to His own request? (1 Corinthians 11. 24,25).

December 4

'And Jesus stood before the governor; and the governor asked Him, saying, "Art Thou the King of the Jews?" And Jesus said to him, "Thou sayest." ' (Mat. 27. 11).

The day of our Lord's death had dawned. His Jewish captors led Him to Pontius Pilate, the Roman governor. He had the authority to impose the death penalty. Pilate asked the Jewish leaders what the charges were, which they brought against Jesus.

They accused Jesus of three things; firstly, He was subverting the nation; secondly, he opposed payment of taxes to Caesar; thirdly, He claimed to be Christ, a King. (Lk. 23. 1,2). Pilate ignored the first two accusations, but took up the third, by asking our Lord the question, "You are the King of the Jews?" The Saviour replied, "Yes, it is as you say." Pilate had Jesus flogged, and handed Him over to be crucified.

The soldiers took Jesus into their barracks and gave Him a mock coronation. After all, he claimed to be the King of the Jews! A king has a robe, so they put a scarlet cloak on Him. A king has a crown, so they wove a crown out of thorns, and set it on His head. A king has a sceptre, so they put a reed in His right hand. A king has subjects, so they knelt before Him, and said, in mockery, "Hail, King of the Jews." A king is anointed, so they spat upon Him. A king's crown must be secure, so they beat Him on the head, again and again.

After His crucifixion, they set over His head His accusation, written, "This is Jesus, the King of the Jews." And so they mocked their rightful King.

What can we learn from the wise men who sought and found the King of the Jews? See Matthew 2. 2, 11.

December 5

'And she said to the king, "It was a true report that I heard in my own land of thine acts and of thy wisdom. Howbeit, I believed not the words, until I came and mine eyes had seen it; and behold the half was not told me; thy wisdom and prosperity exceeds the fame which I heard." ' (1 Kings 10. 6,7).

The queen of Sheba (or the Sabeans) is addressing King Solomon. She has journeyed from the ends of the earth for this interview with the king. (Mat. 12. 42).   She had heard of Solomon's fame; she came to prove him with hard questions. He answered them all, to her entire satisfaction. Also, when she saw his court and courtiers, and his ascent to the house of Jehovah, she was overwhelmed. She exclaimed, "The half was not told me!"

Solomon resembles the Christ in several ways. He was king of Israel; our Lord is King of kings. Solomon's reign was characterised by peace. (1 Chron. 22. 9). His name means 'Peaceful'; our Lord is the Prince of peace. He made peace through the blood of His Cross. Solomon was noted for his building of the temple; our Lord is building a spiritual temple, the church. Solomon was noted for his wisdom; Christ is God's power and wisdom. Solomon was noted for his wealth; in Christ are hidden all the treasures of wisdom and knowledge. The whole universe belongs to Him. Solomon's kingdom stretched from the river Euphrates to the border of Egypt, and endured (through his descendants) for several centuries; our Lord's kingdom is universal and eternal. Jehovah his God made Solomon exceedingly great; our Lord said, "A greater than Solomon is here." (Mat. 12. 42).

In what ways does the queen of Sheba remind you of a repentant sinner coming to Christ?

December6

' "And Thou, Lord, in the beginning hast laid the foundation of the earth; and the heavens are the works of thine hands: They shall perish, but Thou remainest; and they shall grow old as a garment; and as a covering shalt Thou fold them up, and they shall be changed; but Thou art the Same, and Thy years shall not fail." ' (Heb. 1. 10-12).

In his quote from Psalm 102, the writer reveals that God, the Father, is speaking to God, the Son. The Father attributes the beginning and ending of the present material order to the Son. But the Father is careful to point out the difference between the creation and the Creator. He says, "They shall perish, but Thou remainest; ....they shall change, but Thou art the Same".

The Hebrew word, translated 'the Same' (meaning 'the self-existent One') is used on several occasions in the Old Testament as a name of God. The following examples are given:

In the song of Moses, he reasons that because God is the Same, He is sovereign. Therefore the Son of God is sovereign. (Deu. 32. 39).

Because God is the Same, He will keep His promises to king David. (2 Sam. 7. 28).

In a time of great stress, King Hezekiah prayed to Jehovah, God of Israel, who sits between the cherubim, the Same, the God of all the kingdoms of the earth. (2 Kings 19. 15).

When king Jehoshaphat was afraid, he said to God, "Art not Thou the Same, - God in the heavens." (2 Chron. 19. 6).

The God who is the Same is our Lord, Jesus Christ.

What other advantages accrue to those who are associated with One whose name is the Same? See Nehemiah 9. 6,7; Psalm 44. 4; Isaiah 41. 4; 43. 10,13; 46. 4; 51. 9,10; 52. 6.

December 7

'And I said to them, "If you think good, give me my wages; and if not, forbear." So they weighed for my wages thirty pieces of silver. And Jehovah said to me, "Cast it to the potter", the magnificent price at which they priced me! So I took the thirty pieces of silver, and cast them to the potter in the house of Jehovah.' (Zech. 11. 12,13).

The prophet Zechariah is instructed by God to play the part of Messiah, the good Shepherd (4-14). Then Jehovah tells him to play the part of Anti-Messiah, the idol shepherd (15-17).

As the representative of the good Shepherd, the prophet pastured the flock marked for slaughter. He paid particular attention to the afflicted of the flock, as did our Lord Jesus, the good Shepherd. Israel's leaders were false shepherds who oppressed the flock.

But the flock of Israel detested him and rejected him, as they did their Messiah. So he broke his two staves, called 'Favour' and 'Union'. This was done to show that God's gracious covenant with the nations was revoked. Also, the breaking of the staff named 'Union' showed that God had broken the bond between Judah and Israel.

As the good Shepherd, Zechariah asked for, and received his wages; thirty silver pieces, the price of a slave! (Ex. 21. 32). Jehovah told Zechariah to cast the money to the potter in the house of Jehovah. Judas Iscariot did exactly that with the thirty silver pieces which he received from the chief priests for the betrayal of Jesus.

What is your assessment of the worth of Jesus, the good Shepherd, who gave his life for the sheep?

December 8

' "He who has the bride is the Bridegroom; but the friend of the Bridegroom, who stands and hears Him, rejoices greatly, because of the Bridegroom's voice. This my joy therefore is fulfilled." '   (Jn. 3. 29).

John the Baptiser adds to his previous witness regarding the identity of the Messiah. Already, he has declared that Jesus is the Lamb of God (Jn.1. 29,36), and the Son of God (v.34). Now John reveals that Jesus is the Bridegroom.

This was the Baptiser's mission; he was 'the Friend of the Bridegroom', 'the Groom's Man'. His task was to prepare the Bridegroom's path, and introduce Him to the Bride. Then his joy will be complete.

The pattern of events follows Jewish custom, prevalent at that time. The Son of God had come from the Father's house in heaven. He is introduced to the family of His prospective bride. The dowry or Bride-price must then be paid, namely the precious blood of the Bridegroom. Thus a solemn and binding covenant was made between Bride and Groom (1 Cor. 11. 25), sealed by drinking a cup of wine.

Then Christ returned to His Father's house. He is preparing a place there for His Bride. (Jn. 14. 2). Soon, He shall come again to take His Bride (the Church) home to that prepared place (v.3). He shall be accompanied by an angelic escort.
(1 Thes. 4. 16,17). During this waiting period, the Bride is preparing her wedding garments. (Rev. 19. 8).

After at least seven years (corresponding to the tribulation period) the Bridegroom will reveal His Bride to a wondering world. (Col. 3. 4).

What can you do, to prepare for the Bridegroom's return?

December 9
Faithful and true

'And I saw heaven opened, and behold a white horse, and He who sat upon it is called Faithful and True, and in righteousness He judges and makes war.' (Rev. 19. 11).

Here is a portrait of Christ as the Warrior-King. He comes out of heaven, riding upon a white horse, as befits His regal dignity. He comes to judge the world. The seven years of tribulation have run their course; the thousand years of peace are about to begin. But, first, all opposition to Messiah's rule must be dealt with.

The identity of the Rider on the white horse is easy to discern. He is that same Jesus, who once rode into Jerusalem on a donkey. Then, He came in peace, to make peace through the blood of His Cross. Now, He comes in wrath, to wage war and consume His enemies with the breath of His mouth. (2 Thes. 2. 8).

His Names also declare His identity. He is called 'Faithful and True', and so He is, in His dealings with God and men. This is in sharp contrast to another man, the Antichrist, who is an unfaithful liar, like his father the Devil.

The Saviour has 'a secret Name'. It is written, but only He can decipher it. His Name is also 'the Word of God': He is the visible expression of the mind of God. He has another written Name; 'King of kings and Lord of lords'. These three names encompass, in measure, the history of the Son of God. His 'unknown Name' describes Him in eternity past. 'The Word of God' relates particularly to His first advent. At His return to reign, His Name is 'King of kings and Lord of lords'.

In what ways have you proved, in your own experience, that the Lord is 'Faithful and True' ?

December 10
The servant-prince, walking

'There is an evil which I have seen under the sun, as an error which proceeds from the ruler: Folly is set in great dignity, and the rich sit in a low place. I have seen servants upon horses, and princes walking as servants upon the earth.' (Ecc. 10. 5-7).

'The Preacher' (Hebrew, 'Koheleth'), or 'Convener of Assemblies' is king Solomon. (1 Kings 8. 1,2,5). In his sermon, he refers to his wisdom (Ecc. 1. 16.), his pleasures (2.3), his great projects (vs.4-6), his slaves (v.7), and his wealth (v.8).

In his wisdom, he has this insight. He observes that sometimes fools are exalted to honour and dignity in the state, but the worthy are abased. One example of this is found in the history of Saul and David. Saul was rejected by God, yet he still acted as king of Israel. David was anointed by Samuel, but he had to live in a cave.

The most notable example of this double anomaly is seen in the history of our Lord Jesus, just prior to His death. There were several 'servants upon horses'. Caiaphas, the high priest of Israel was a slave to an ecclesiastical system. He murdered the Messiah to maintain it. Herod Antipas was tetrarch of Galilee, but he was a slave to his own selfish whims; he murdered John Baptist to secure them. Pilate, the governor of Judea, was a slave to his own worldly ambition; he sacrificed the Christ on that altar.

In stark contrast, we see the Servant-Prince walking towards Calvary, carrying His Cross. He must complete His journey, which led inexorably to the Place of a Skull. (Lk. 13. 32,33).

What does it mean to you, to walk with Jesus, the Servant-Prince every day?

December 11

The crucified one

'*And they crucified Him, and parted His garments, casting lots; that it might be fulfilled which was spoken by the prophet, "They parted My garments among them, and upon My vesture did they cast lots." '   (Mat. 27. 35).*

The crucifixion of Christ is the greatest event in the history of the universe.   It is the paramount theme of   Holy Scripture.   In the Old Testament, the Cross is depicted in prophecy, in types and shadows.   In the New Testament, in the four Gospels, the crucifixion is described historically.   In the epistles of the New Testament, the doctrinal significance of the Cross is revealed.   In the last book of the Bible, the slain, yet living Lamb is seen by the apostle John, standing in the centre of the throne in heaven.   The Crucified One is supreme in eternity.

On a number of occasions, our Lord Jesus forewarned His disciples of His death, even by crucifixion. (Mat. 20. 19;   26. 2).   They were unable to accept such an eventuality, until after His resurrection.   (Lk. 24. 21).   To the Jews, a crucified Christ was an offence.

The Crucified One heard no encouraging word from heaven, as at His baptism and transfiguration.   The only encouragement He received from men was from one of the criminals crucified alongside Him.   "Remember me," he said, "when Thou comest in Thy kingdom."

All nature was convulsed at the Cross: Darkness descended over all the land for three hours: The temple veil was torn from top to bottom: The earth shook, the rocks were split, and the tombs were opened.   The unthinkable transpired when God incarnate expired, on the Cross.

What was the most important part of the work done by the Crucified One on the Cross?

December 12

'And all the congregation made a covenant with the king in the house of God. And he said to them, "Behold the king's son shall reign, as Jehovah has said of the sons of David." ' (2 Chron. 23. 3.).

Jehoram, king of Judah married Athaliah, the daughter of Jezebel, wife of Ahab, king of Israel. Jezebel (a Phoenician princess) introduced the worship of Baal to Israel. Her daughter, Athaliah did the same evil thing in Judah, as the wife of king Jehoram.

When Jehoram became king, he murdered his six brothers. This resulted in the judgment of God. The Philistines and Arabs invaded Judah and killed all his sons, except his youngest, Jehoahaz or Ahaziah. When he became king, Ahaziah followed the counsel of Athaliah, his mother. His destruction was of God; he was slain by Jehu.

When Athaliah learned of the death of Ahaziah, her son, she destroyed all the royal family of the house of Judah. But one of her grandsons escaped, because of the intervention of Ahaziah's sister and her godly husband, Jehoidah, the priest. They hid the one-year-old child in the house of God. His name was Joash.

When Joash was seven years old, Jehoidah and other loyal subjects made him king, and slew Athaliah, that wicked woman (24.7.). So the regal, legal line of Messiah from David was preserved.

Our 'Joash' (meaning 'The One whom Jehovah has given'), the Lord Jesus, was rescued from death, and is presently hidden in heaven. When He is revealed, He, as the king's Son shall reign.

What can we learn from Colossians 3. 1-3, regarding our present and future association with the king's Son who shall reign?

December 13

'For it became Him, for whom are all things, and by whom are all things, in bringing many sons to glory, to make the Captain of their salvation perfect through sufferings.' (Heb. 2. 10).

God, the Father, has a plan for the material universe. He created it for His pleasure and purpose, He sustains it by His power, despite the devastating effect produced by Adam's sin.

He also has a plan for the spiritual universe. He is bringing many sons to glory. These are not the holy angels, because they are already in glory. These are human beings who have been born again, and are part of the family of God. They have been born of the Spirit and washed in the blood of the Lamb. They are sons of Adam who have become brothers of God's Son. He is not ashamed to call them such.

He is the Captain of their salvation; its Author, Originator and Leader. But, in order to fulfil the Father's plan of salvation, He had to be made perfect through sufferings, that is, in His human experience. His moral perfection, as God the Son, is inviolate.

Our Lord suffered the confines of His mother's womb. He suffered being born and brought up in a family in Nazareth. He suffered rejection by His own people and nation. He suffered the agonies of Gethsemane, Gabbatha, and ultimately Golgotha. His 'salvation sufferings' ended, when he cried on the Cross, "Finished!", and delivered up His spirit.

In what respect does the Captain of our salvation suffer presently? Give Scriptural backing for your answer.

December 14

'And one shall say unto Him, "What are these wounds in Thine hands?" Then shall He answer, "Those with which I was wounded in the house of My friends." "Awake, O sword, against My Shepherd, and against the Man that is My Fellow," saith Jehovah of Hosts. "Smite the Shepherd, and the sheep shall be scattered; and I will turn My hand upon the little ones." ' (Zech. 13. 6;7.).

God, the Father and the Son were constant companions in eternity past, before the universe was created. They delighted in each other's presence. Then they, together with the Holy Spirit, participated in the creation of the universe.

Even when the Son took His place in the likeness of men, the fellowship between Father and Son was unbroken. The Son was Jehovah's Shepherd, finding, feeding and leading the lost sheep of the house of Israel. At our Lord's baptism, and again on the Mount of Transfiguration, Jehovah expressed His delight in His Son, the One who is His Fellow.

Then there was the wounding of the Shepherd-Companion in the house of His friends: They hammered the iron spikes into His hands to fasten Him to the Cross. But this was only the beginning of sorrows. They reached their climax when Jehovah bade His sword awake. It found its billet in the bosom of Christ. The darkness descended, and the orphan cry of Jehovah's Fellow was heard, "My God, My God, why hast Thou forsaken Me? "

Now Jehovah's Fellow comes to reign over the world. But He still bears in His body the marks of Calvary's conflict.

Why must Jehovah take a dealing with His Fellow in this way?

December 15

'Therefore the Jews sought the more to kill Him, because He not only had broken the Sabbath, but said also that God was His Father, making Himself equal with God.'
(Jn. 5. 18.).

Our Lord Jesus had healed a man: He had been an invalid for 38 years. He was lying on his mat by the pool of Bethesda in Jerusalem. The Saviour told him to arise, take up his mat, and walk: This he did; it was a Sabbath day. According to the Jews, to carry something on the Sabbath was a sin. But the man was told to do these things by Jesus; therefore He was a Sabbath-breaker.

Then, in reply to the Jews, Jesus made the astounding claim that God was His own Father, making Himself equal with God. He said to them, "My Father is always at His work to this very day, and I, too, am working." Whether it be a Sabbath or not, both Father and Son were busy at work. They had a universe to maintain, and works of mercy to perform.

Jesus continued to point out to the Jews other spheres of activity which demonstrate the Son's equality with the Father:-

Just as the Father gives life, so the Son gives life to whom He will.

The Father has entrusted all judgment to the Son, because He is the Son of Man.

All should honour the Son, just as they honour the Father.

The work of raising the dead has been given by the Father to the Son.

Which of these works of the Son apply to you, and how do they apply?

December 16

'And I saw a great white throne, and Him that sat on it, from whose face the earth and the heaven fled away; and there was found no place for them.' *(Rev. 20. 11.).*

This scene is set at the end of Christ's millennial reign of peace and prosperity. The final rebellion has been put down. The devil has been cast into the lake of fire. Now is the time for the unbelieving dead to be judged. They are re-united with their bodies to stand before a great white throne.

The throne is great, because of its Occupant. There is none greater than God, the Son. There is none more majestic than He. It is great because of the vast number of persons standing before it, the unbelieving dead of all ages. It is great because of the severity of the sentence passed on those standing before it.

The throne is white, indicating the righteousness of the judgment, in keeping with the pure character of the Judge.

The One sitting on the throne is Jesus. The Father has committed all judgment to the Son, because He is the Son of Man. (Jn. 5. 22,27.). God has ordained Him to be the Judge of the living and the dead. (Acts 10. 42; 2 Tim. 4. 1.). Earth and heaven flee away from before His face.

The jury will consist of the following books; conscience (Rom. 2. 15.), men's words (Mat. 12. 36,37.), God's Word (Jn.12. 48.), secret works (Rom. 2. 16.), public works (Mat. 16. 27; 2 Cor. 11. 15.), God's book of life (Ex. 32. 32; Rev. 20. 15.), the Lamb's book of life. (Rev. 21. 27.). The sentence is eternal death in the lake of fire.

How can you avoid standing before the great white throne?

December 17
My beloved's voice

' "The voice of my beloved!   Behold, he comes, leaping upon the mountains, skipping upon the hills.   My beloved is like a gazelle or a young stag.   Behold, he stands behind our wall, he looks in through the windows, showing himself through the lattice. My beloved spoke and said to me, "Rise up, my love, my fair one, and come away." ' (S. of S. 2. 8-10.).

The chief characters in this love-song are king Solomon and the Shulamite (6.13.), who ultimately becomes his bride.   The song consists of a number of stanzas, each depicting a different scene.   Here, the Shulamite is describing how her beloved came suddenly, and called her to himself.   She recognised his voice.

One greater than Solomon is coming suddenly and soon, to claim and call His bride, the Church, from the world.   The long winter of His absence is past, and the springtime of His presence is coming.   One day soon, we shall hear the voice of our Beloved commanding us to rise up and come away.   We shall meet Him in the air, and shall be forever with Him. (1 Thes. 4. 16,17.).

Meanwhile, we hear our Beloved's voice assuring us of our security in Him, the Rock of our salvation. (S. of S. 2. 14.).   His voice of entreaty is then heard, as He longs for communion with us.   Also, he has a word of reproof for us to deal with the little sins which spoil the fruit of the Holy Spirit (v.15.).

If the Lord Jesus is your Beloved, how can you make sure of hearing His voice?

December 18

'In the same manner the chief priests, along with the scribes and elders, were mocking Him, and saying, "He saved others: Himself He cannot save. He is the King of Israel; let Him now come down from the cross, and we will believe in Him." '
(Mat. 27. 41,42.).

The passers-by had mocked the Cross-bound Christ, challenging him to free Himself from His iron bonds, and come down. Now the leaders of the people, members of the Jewish Sanhedrin, added their mockery.

"He saved others," they said; it was a fact beyond dispute. Many, in and around Jerusalem, could bear witness to the physical salvation wrought in their lives by the power of the Nazarene. But what of spiritual salvation? This was an impossibility, without the shedding of the blood of a perfect Sacrifice, the Lamb of God.

"He is King of Israel," they said, and rightly so. Pilate's placard above His head proclaimed the silent Sufferer to be King of the Jews, the descendants of Judah. But Israel included all twelve tribes.

In the past, the entire nation of Israel had only three kings, namely, Saul, David and Solomon. After the death of Solomon, the nation was divided. Now, its rightful King was on a Roman cross. At the outset of His public ministry, He was acknowledged by Nathanael, as the Son of God, the King of Israel. (Jn. 1. 49.). At the culmination of His ministry, our Lord was called King of Israel in mockery. But it is true.

Why did those Jewish leaders refer to Jesus as the King of Israel, and not as the King of the Jews?

December 19
A great worker

'Sanballat and Geshem sent to me, saying, "come let us meet together in one of the villages in the plain of Ono."   But they thought to do me mischief.   And I sent messengers to them, saying, " I am doing a great work, so that I cannot come down; why should the work cease, whilst I leave it and come down to you?" '   (Neh. 6. 2,3.).

The wall of Jerusalem lay in ruins.   The work of the Babylonian army was thorough. The wastage of the years had completed the destruction.   But God had appointed a man to rebuild the wall.   His name was Nehemiah (meaning 'Comforter of Jah, the Eternal.').   He was cupbearer to the king of Persia.

Armed with the king's authority, Nehemiah and his retinue journeyed from Susa to Jerusalem.

He enlisted the help of the exiles who had returned: They began to build the wall. Then opposition reared its ugly head.   The enemies of God's people threatened to kill the builders.   Then they sought by subterfuge to kill the leader.

Glimpses of Christ can be seen in Nehemiah, in his prayerfulness, faithfulness to God, courage, and resoluteness, in the face of great opposition.   He reflects the glory of the One who truly is 'the Eternal's comforter'.   The words of Nehemiah to his enemies ("I am doing a great work, so that I cannot come down.") were left unsaid by the Saviour on the Cross, when faced with the same challenge.   But His work was surely infinitely greater than that of Nehemiah.   He was building for eternity.   Salvation's wall is impregnable.

Although the great work of redemption was completed at the Cross, other walls must be built.   What part do you have in the work of building a protective wall for God's people?

December20
A great high priest

'Having therefore a Great High Priest who has passed through the heavens, Jesus, the Son of God, let us hold fast our confession.' (Heb. 4. 14.).

In Israel, three kinds of officials were anointed in preparation for service.   These were prophets, priests, and kings.

Melchisedec was a king-priest;   Moses was a prophet-priest;   David was a king-prophet. But only our Lord Jesus combines all three offices in Himself;   He alone is Prophet, Priest and King.

While here, in the body, on earth, our Lord exercised the office of Prophet.   When He returns to earth with His saints, He will exercise the office of King.   But, meantime, at the Father's right hand in heaven, he exercises the office of Priest.

Why is Jesus our Great High Priest?
Because of His incarnation.   He was made like His brothers (2.17.):   Because He was called by God, (5. 6,10.) who confirmed it by an oath (7. 21.):   Because of His human experience, of temptation (4. 15;   2. 18.),   of dependence upon and obedience to God (5. 7,8.), and of perfect suffering (v.9.):   Because he offered Himself, as a perfect Sacrifice to God (8. 3;   9. 14.):   Because of His present position, exalted above the heavens. (4. 14;   7. 26.).

What is the present work of Jesus, our Great High Priest?
He encourages us to hold fast to the faith we possess (4. 14.):   He sympathises with our weaknesses (v.15.):
He encourages us to approach the throne of grace with confidence (v.16.).

What other work does our Great High Priest undertake for us presently?
See chapters 7. v 25;   8. 6;   9. 24.

December 21

'Behold the day of Jehovah comes, and thy spoil shall be divided in the midst of thee. For I will gather all nations against Jerusalem in battle; and the city shall be taken, and the houses rifled, and the women ravished; and half of the city shall go forth into captivity, and the rest of the people shall not be cut off from the city. Then shall Jehovah go forth, and fight against those nations, as when He fights in the day of battle.' (Zech. 14. 1-3.).

The day of Jehovah is that great and terrible day at the end of the three and a half years of the great tribulation. (Joel 2. 31.). On that day, Jehovah-Jesus will return to earth, in fulfilment of the angelic promise given to the apostles. (Acts 1. 11.). His feet shall stand on the mount of Olives. (Zech. 14. 4.).

He will return with His saints (v.5.) at least seven years prior to this event, the Lord had come to the air, to summon to Himself the 'church' saints. (1 Thes. 4. 16,17.). They shall be with Him, at His return to earth.

Jehovah-Jesus, the Warrior has returned to rescue the remnant of His ancient people, Israel. All nations are gathered together in and around Jerusalem. The number of persons will be in excess of three hundred million. The battle-field 'will extend from Megiddo (Rev. 16. 16.) to Edom (Isa. 34. 5,6; 63. 1.), a distance of 1,600 stadia, which is approximately 200 miles. (Rev. 14. 20.).

The Warrior's weapon will be the word of His mouth. (Rev. 19. 15.). The power of the nations is completely crushed, and their armies are totally destroyed.

How can we, in a spiritual sense, emulate Jehovah-Jesus, the Warrior, in order to defeat the foe? See Ephesians 6. 17.

'And Jesus said to them, "I am the Bread of Life; he who comes to Me shall never hunger; and he who believes on Me shall never ever thirst." ' (Jn. 6. 35.).

Here is the first of seven self-descriptions given by our Lord in the Gospel of John. Our Saviour claims to be 'the Bread of Life', the source of spiritual satisfaction and nourishment.   On four occasions, in this narrative, Jesus of Nazareth makes this claim (vs. 35, 41, 48, 51.).   He is claiming to be God, when He says, "I am........" (Exod. 3. 14.).

Where does this Bread come from?   It comes down from God, the Father, in heaven, via the incarnation of God, the Son, who thus became the Son of Man. (vs. 27, 32, 33.).

What is this Bread?   It is essential Food for spiritual life and for living (spiritually).   It is our Lord Jesus, Whose flesh was broken and Whose blood was outpoured on the Cross.   Just as bread is baked in the fiery heat of the oven, so our Lord, the Living Bread, endured the awful fire of God's wrath against sin, at Golgotha.

What is the purpose of this Bread?   It gives eternal life; there is more than enough for the whole world (v.33.).   It completely satisfies spiritual hunger, and even thirst! (v.35.) It prevents death (v.50), and produces union with Christ (v.56.).

How may I obtain this Bread?   I receive it as a Gift, by faith in the Risen Lord Jesus; by coming to Him and believing on Him; by eating His flesh and drinking His blood; by appropriating Him spiritually.

What else should we do with Jesus, the Bread of Life, apart from receiving Him?

December 23

' "And behold, I come quickly, and My reward is with Me, to render to each as his work shall be. I am the Alpha and the Omega, the Beginning and End, the First and the Last." ' (Rev. 22. 12, 13.).

This descriptive title is found on four occasions in the Book of the Revelation (in the King James translation). (1. 8, 11; 21, 6; 22. 13.). The Speaker on the first occasion is the Lord God Almighty (1. 8.). The Speaker on the last occasion is the One Who is coming quickly, that is, our Lord Jesus (22. 12,13.). Therefore Jesus is the Lord God Almighty, thus giving us another proof (if needed) of the Deity of Christ.

Our Lord describes Himself as the Alpha and the Omega. These are the first and last letters of the Greek alphabet. The first and last letters in the Hebrew alphabet are 'Aleph' and 'Tau'. When Hebrew scholars wished to describe completeness, they used the expression, "from Aleph to Tau". Thus, as the Alpha and the Omega, our Lord Jesus is the complete revelation of God to man. He manifests all God's attributes permanently and indelibly, including His righteousness and holiness, His loving-kindness and goodness, and much more. He is the beginning and the ending of the ways, the works, and the words of God.

Moreover, each letter in the Hebrew alphabet has a meaning. The first letter 'Aleph', from which the Greek letter 'Alpha' is derived, means 'Ox'. The last letter 'Tau', corresponding in its position to the last letter 'Omega' in the Greek alphabet, means 'Cross'. The ox is a reminder of our Lord's patient service, while the cross is a reminder of His supreme sacrifice.

How does this description of our Lord Jesus, as the Alpha and the Omega, have bearing on your daily life?

December 24
Altogether lovely

' "My Beloved is white and ruddy, the chiefest among ten thousand." '
' "His mouth is most sweet; yea, He is altogether lovely. This is my beloved, and this is my friend, O daughter of Jerusalem." ' (Song of Sol. 5. 10,16.)

Here, the Shulamite is challenged by the daughters of Jerusalem. They ask her to say why her beloved, Solomon, is different from any other: She answers readily. The allegorical word-picture which she paints may be applied spiritually to One greater than Solomon by His bride, the church.

The dazzling splendour of our Lord's deity is combined with the perfect health of His humanity (v.10.).
He is our Standard-bearer, the Captain of our Salvation (v.10.).
He is King of kings, the Resurrection and the Life (v.11.).
He regards His bride, the church, with a pure and steadfast love (v.12.).
That which identifies Him as unique (namely, His face and His voice) brings fragrance to His bride (v.13.).
He is God's Artisan and Apostle (v.14.).
He is the bride's Sure Foundation and her Strong Tower (v.15.).
The words which He received from His Father were faithfully transmitted to His bride (v.16.). He is her glorious Mediator.
This One Who is altogether lovely to His bride is also her close Companion (v.16.). He has promised never to leave her, nor forsake her.

Which feature of the description of the altogether lovely One is most precious to you? Give the reason for your answer.

December 25
The son of the highest

'And the angel said unto her, "Fear not, Mary, for thou hast found favour with God; and, behold, thou shalt conceive in thy womb, and bring forth a Son, and shalt call His name Jesus. He shall be great, and shall be called the Son of the Highest; and the Lord God shall give unto Him the throne of His father David: And He shall reign over the house of Jacob for ever; and of His kingdom there shall be no end." '
(Lk. 1. 30-33.)

This was no ordinary angel whom God had sent to Mary. His name was Gabriel, meaning 'Mighty Man of God'. The message which he brought to Mary was extraordinary, too. It concerned a child whom, according the angel, she would conceive and bring forth; and this without human insemination. So this Babe would be truly the Seed of the woman, the Son of Mary, thus fulfilling the ancient prophecy. (Gen. 3. 15.).

After instructing her to name the Child Jesus, the angel said, "He shall be great, and shall be called the Son of the Highest." It seemed far from reality when Mary stood, some thirty-four years later, on the hill of Calvary, gazing up at her crucified Son on the centre cross.

The name 'Highest' or 'Most High' is a description of God, used, for example, in Deuteronomy 32. 8. in the context of giving the nations and Israel their allotted places. Nebuchadnezzar, king Babylon, had to learn that "the most High rules over the kingdom of men, and gives it to whomsoever He will". The Highest has given it to His Son, Who will be called in that day, the Son of the Highest. His is the highest place on earth and in heaven by right and by blood.

Is it possible for us to be sons of the Highest? How can we receive such a great reward? Read Luke 6. 35.

December 26

'Then Haman took the robe and the horse, and arrayed Mordecai, and led him through the city square, and proclaimed before him, "Thus shall it be done to the man whom the king delights to honour." (Esther 6. 11.).

In the providence of God, Mordecai the Jew was in the right place at the right time. He discovered that two of the palace guards were plotting to kill their master, Xerxes, the king of Persia.   He reported the matter to Esther, his uncle's daughter.   When her parents died, he took care of her.   Now, she was Xerxes' queen, again in the providence of God.

When Esther relayed Mordecai's report to the king, he found that it was true, and the plotters were hanged.   The incident was recorded in the book of the annuls, giving credit to Mordecai (whose name means, among other things, 'Bitter Bruising'.):   Stark reminder of our Lord Jesus, the Righteous Prince, Who was bruised for our iniquities.

Some years later, all the Jews were under sentence of death.   Their enemy had done this.   He was Haman the Agagite, who had become the king's favourite.

Again, in the providence of God, the king discovered from the annuls that Mordecai had never been rewarded for saving his life.   The king immediately ordered Haman to honour Mordecai.

God, the eternal King, delights to honour the Man, Christ Jesus.   He is seated at God's right hand: Upon His head are many diadems: When He returns to destroy His foes, he shall ride upon a white horse.

In what ways can you give honour to the Man Whom God the King delights to honour?

December 27

'Although He was Son, He learned obedience from the things which He suffered; and having been perfected, He became the Author of eternal salvation to all who obey Him.' (Heb. 5. 8,9.).

The Christ was the Son of God from eternity.   When He became a Man, God saluted Him as Son at His baptism in the river Jordan, and at His transfiguration on the holy mount.   It was heaven's testimony to the authenticity of Jesus, the Nazarene.

Yet the Son must suffer, and this He did.   On the Cross, He suffered the abandonment of God, and the agony of death as the Sin-bearer.   His cup of suffering was filled to overflowing.   "It is finished," He said, and having bowed His head, He delivered up His spirit.

But God raised Him from the dead, and received Him into heaven with this salutation, "Thou art My Son; today have I begotten Thee".   Thus was the Lord Jesus perfected in his experience of Manhood, so that He would become the Author or personal mediating Cause of eternal salvation.   It is eternal because He is eternal.   Its scope is also eternal, since it affects irreversibly the whole man, in his spirit, soul and body.

But note the pre-requisite for obtaining this eternal salvation.   Our Lord becomes the Author of it to all who obey Him.   It is the response of individuals to the Gospel, resulting in their obedience of faith in Christ. (Rom. 1. 5;   16. 26.).   For example, in the early days of the church, a large number of priests became obedient to the faith. (Acts 6. 7.).

What else happens to us, when we are obedient to the truth?   See 1 Peter 1. 22, 23.

December 28

'But for you who revere my name, the Sun of Righteousness shall arise with healing in His wings; and you will go out and leap like calves released from the stall.'
(Mal. 4. 2.)

The special Name of God is Jehovah. He revealed it to Moses in Horeb, the mountain of God: He is the eternal One, Who keeps covenant with Israel. In a coming day, the day of Jehovah, there will be a remnant of Israel who will revere His Name. They are His peculiar treasure. They will be preserved during the terrible day of Jehovah, right to the end of the great tribulation, spoken of by our Lord Jesus. (Mat. 24. 21.).

Then shall the Sun of Righteousness arise, to dispel the darkness of the world. This Sun is the Son of Man. The splendour of His coming will destroy all the arrogant evil-doers, including that lawless one, the son of perdition. (2 Thes. 2. 3,8.). Because our Lord is the Sun of Righteousness, all that is unrighteous must be banished from His Presence and kingdom.

He shall also arise with healing in His wings. Just as the rising sun brings light, life and comfort to the world, so the rising of the Sun of Righteousness will bring healing. The backsliding and wounds of Israel will be healed (Jer. 3. 22; 30. 17.), when they turn to Jehovah in that day. (Hos. 6. 1.). The remnant of the nation will acknowledge that the source of their healing was the suffering and stripes of Jehovah's Servant, the Sun of Righteousness. All of nature will be healed, and the nations will enjoy a millennium of peace and plenty.

How can you obtain the healing you require from the Sun of Righteousness?

December 29
A good man

'Then the Jews sought Him at the feast, and said, "Where is He?" And there was much murmuring among the people concerning Him; for some said, "He is a Good man"; others said, "No, but He deceives the people." ' (Jn.7. 11, 12.)

The Lord Jesus Himself had said that "a good man out of the good treasure of his heart brings forth that which is good." (Lk. 6. 45.).

In the house of a centurion named Cornelius, the apostle Peter described "how God anointed Jesus of Nazareth with the Holy Spirit and with power; Who went about doing good, and healing all who were oppressed by the devil, for God was with Him." (Acts 10. 38.).

The Gospel record abounds with examples of the 'well-doing' of Jehovah's righteous Servant. (Mk. 7. 37.). There are at least thirty-five miracles described in some detail. Ill people were restored; the lame were made to walk, the blind to see, the deaf to hear. Demoniacs were liberated, and the dead were raised. Moreover, He stilled the storm, fed the hungry, and sent the fish into the disciples' net.

These were the works of a Good Man. But our Lord was more than that; He was a Holy Man, perfect in His righteousness. On one occasion, He said to the Jews, "Can any of you prove Me guilty of sin? " (Jn. 8. 46.). There was no reply from them.

But the greatest good of this Good Man was accomplished on the Cross, when He took upon Himself the iniquity of us all.

Can you enumerate some of the good things which this Good Man has done for you?

December30

' "I, Jesus, have sent My angel to give you this testimony for the churches.   I am the Root and Offspring of David, and the Bright and Morning Star." ' (Rev. 22. 16.).

The Lord uses His human Name, Jesus -- precious to every believing heart.   He is the Source of the witness to the assemblies.   He is also, through king David, the source and Spring of blessing for Israel.   In his final prophetic words, David saw the vision clearly.   'He shall be as the light of the morning, like the rising of the sun, a morning without clouds;   when from the sunshine after rain, the green grass springs from the earth.'   (2 Sam. 23. 4.).

Satan aspired to be Lucifer (meaning 'Bright Star of the Morning').   He fell into darkness because of his pride. (Isa. 14;   Ezek. 28.).   Our Lord Jesus alone is worthy of such a title, and self-description.   He, alone is the Bright and Morning Star.

One day soon, our Lord will come for His bride, the church, as the Bright and Morning Star.   It will be before the dawn of a new era for Israel and the other nations.   He will summon His own into the loving light of His Presence, to be forever with Him. Here is the great gift promised by our Lord to the overcomer, that is, the true believer in our Lord Jesus Christ. (Rev. 2. 28;   1 Jn. 5. 5.).

The apostle Peter exhorts his readers to heed the prophetic word.   'It shines like a lamp in a dark place until the day dawns and the Morning Star arises in your hearts.' (2 Peter 1. 19.).

What should be a suitable response, on our part, to our Lord's assertion that He is the Bright and Morning Star?

December 31

' *"Set me as a seal upon thine heart, as a seal upon thine arm; for love is strong as death; jealousy is cruel as Sheol. Its flashes are flashes of fire, the flames of Jah. Many waters cannot quench love, neither can the floods drown it. Even if a man gave all the substance of his house for love, it would be utterly despised." '*
(Song of Songs 8. 6,7.)

At the end of another year, it is fitting to call to mind the infinite and eternal quality of our Saviour's love for us. This is the theme which runs like a golden thread through the Song of Songs.

The Shulamite invites her beloved Solomon, the Shepherd-king, to prove his love for her. It must be from the heart, as symbolised in a necklace, with a pendant resting on his breast. It must also be displayed publicly, as symbolised in a bracelet round his wrist.

On that momentous day, when our Lord rose from the dead, He came and stood among His disciples. After His salutation of peace, He showed them his pierced hands and riven side. If any proof of His love was required, here it was - the seals of love.

Next, the Shulamite reminds Solomon of the almighty power of divine love. It broke the bands of death, and overcame the flames of Sheol. It survived the waves and billows of God's wrath against sin, which enveloped our Saviour's holy soul, at Golgotha.

Lastly, the price of such love cannot be assessed by human means; but it will be evident for all eternity. The slain yet living Lamb in heaven bears in His own body the seals of undying, unspeakable love.

In the final moments of another year, shall we give back some of that love to the One Who bears the seals?